PRAISE FOR *WHAT'S HAPPENING TO OUR GIRLS?*

'I found myself so engrossed that for two days running I nearly missed my tram stop ... A definite must-read for parents with daughters, for teachers and for other people dealing with girls. In fact, everyone should read this book.'
Books+Publishing

'A crucial tool for greater understanding.'
Sunday Mail

'*What's happening to our girls?* moves parenting into the 21st century by highlighting the power of outside forces in shaping the personalities, morality and ultimate wellbeing of our daughters. The idea of teaching girls as early as possible about the importance of appearance in order to mould their later consuming practices is frightening from a psychological perspective. Although directed at raising girls, the message is equally important for those parenting boys. This work is a must-read for both parents and young adults attempting to understand and bridge the generation gap.'
Bill O'Hehir, Senior Psychologist

'Having worked with men and boys for twenty years, I was amazed, fascinated and quite horrified to read such a succinct and well-documented account of all the issues facing girls today. The pressures created by society's expectations and the marketing evil that is being unleashed on our girls means that every parent should read this book as a way of understanding what is really going on, and what they can do.'
Dr Arne Rubinstein (MBBS, FRACGP) CEO, Pathways Foundation

'I found this book to be very interesting ... [it] helped me to understand why girls like myself are behaving the way they are. Sex, drugs and drinking are just a few of the things that are becoming increasingly popular in teen culture. This book is great; I would advise any parent or teenager interested in learning more about girls' behaviour to read this. Thank you.'
Amanda, teenager

'Just wanted to say thank you. Thank you for raising the awareness level of (in particular) parents and caregivers about what is going on in their children's world.'
Moira, mother of two teenage girls

'As a grandmother of two small girls, I have found your book on girls invaluable.'
Marianne, grandmother of two young girls

Affirm
press

Maggie Hamilton has written over a dozen books, which have been published in Australia, New Zealand, Holland, France, Portugal, Italy, the UK and US, the Arab States, South Korea, China, Lithuania and Brazil. Her social research books include *What Men Don't Talk About*, the lives of real men and boys behind the stereotypes, *What's Happening to Our Girls?* and *What's Happening to Our Boys?*, which are both about the 21st-century challenges our boys and girls face and solutions to these issues. Maggie also writes for magazines, hosts talks, workshops and lectures, and is a seasoned media performer with a keen interest in social trends. www.maggiehamilton.org

What happens to our kids when we fail to grow up?

MAGGIE HAMILTON

Affirm press

books that leave an impression

Published by Affirm Press in 2022
28 Thistlethwaite Street, South Melbourne,
Boonwurrung Country, VIC 3205
affirmpress.com.au
10 9 8 7 6 5 4 3 2 1

A catalogue record for this
book is available from the
NATIONAL
LIBRARY   National Library of Australia
OF AUSTRALIA

Title: What Happens to Our Kids When We Fail to Grow Up? / Maggie Hamilton, author.
ISBN: 9781922626936 (paperback)

Cover design by Trisha Garner
Author photo by Emilio Begali
Typeset in Minion Pro 11.25pt by J&M Typesetting
Proudly printed in Australia by Griffin Press

MIX
Paper from
responsible sources
FSC
www.fsc.org   FSC® C009448

*For those who dare to do difficult and dangerous things
for the wider good, making the hard decisions
so we can thrive.*

Contents

When I was a child, I spake as a child, I understood as a child, I thought as a child: but when I became a man, I put away childish things.

1 Corinthians 13:11

Introduction

What Happens to Our Kids When We Fail to Grow Up? is a response to a growing disquiet at the level of entitlement we're witnessing – the frequent use of the words 'special', 'deserving' and 'unfair'; an increase in self-focused behaviour and conversations; a rise in boredom, anxiety and depression; people laughing less, reaching out less and complaining more.

For almost two decades there's been a growing trend towards delayed maturity – adolescents behaving more like small children and those in their twenties acting like teenagers. These trends are intensifying, and don't always manifest when and where we expect them.

Whenever the question of immaturity arises, we're quick to rail against young people, blaming millennials and their indulgent parents. The current growth in immaturity doesn't begin and end with millennials; it is far more widespread.

We see this in the changes in our behaviour, in over-the-top, often immature responses to everyday annoyances along with an almost neurotic obsession with the minutiae of our lives. We're also witnessing an unhealthy level of competitiveness; a decline in commitment in the workplace, and towards family and friends; and a hardening of attitudes towards those less fortunate.

That's not to say adolescence doesn't have a lot going for it. The wide-eyed wonder and enthusiasm of adolescence is exhilarating but it has a shadow side in its determination always to be right and to be viewed as exceptional, whether or not it's been earned. Teenagers being easily swayed by their peers and other influencers is also of concern, as is their constant need for assurance. Added to this is an excessive tribalism and defensiveness among adolescents that doesn't serve anyone well.

Physical, mental and emotional growth is often painful, especially during our adolescent years. Highly sensitive to criticism, our immature selves make it hard for those best equipped to offer us better approaches or sage advice. Convinced we know best, we choose what's familiar and what's easy over opportunities for growth, and whenever life gets too hard, the adolescent in us looks to be rescued, to have others handle life's trickier moments, to make the important decisions for us.

Our new communication technologies 'endorse self-centredness and inflated exhibitionism', suggests sociologist Simon Gottschalk. 'They promote an orientation towards the present, rewarding impulsivity and celebrating constant and instant gratification. They flatter our needs for visibility, and provide us with 24/7 personalised attention, while eroding our ability to empathise with others.'[1]

For too long brokenness has become something to celebrate, rather than overcome, which keeps us in a state of adolescent helplessness. Imagine what life would be like if we were able to find solid pathways to transcendence and could access the many life-enhancing qualities that await us on the other side of our hurt and confusion.

What we all need to understand is that we're not powerless. As adults we have an important role in helping those who come after us. We all have something of worth to contribute but we can only achieve this if we ourselves have grown up.

The young have a great deal of energy and new ways of seeing that are of benefit to our rapidly changing world, but they rarely comprehend their *intrinsic* worth or the varying strengths and valuable insights apparent in each generation. We need to assist them to see that any contribution they make to the planet will be greatly enhanced when they have the wisdom and humility to build on what other generations have to offer.

We need to fully engage with not just our own lives but with humanity at large and the many intricate layers of ecology we're part of. If we have any hope of making our presence on the planet count, we can't allow others to do all the heavy lifting and decision-making. We can't leave others to build the much-needed bridges in our fractured communities and find meaningful ways through our current difficulties, while we simply concentrate on having a good time.

Chasing happiness, for some, has become a raison d'être. Neglecting opportunities for solitude and serious self-reflection, the child in us demands to be entertained 24/7. While the polar ice caps melt and freedom becomes ever more fragile, we prefer to spend our days lost in petty issues, blaming and complaining, feeling bored and out of sorts. It's little surprise, then, that we have come to value happiness over competence.

Understanding what we are capable of in our short lives takes time and patience. This can seem impossibly hard at times as it can be difficult to rise above our fearful times and growing isolation. Much of our news is little more than sensationalised infotainment focused almost exclusively on revenue and ratings, offering us inconsequential tidbits that do little more than incite and/or excite.

Our politicians treat us more like children needing to be indulged than adults fully able to comprehend the truth, however unpalatable it may be. Our unwillingness to grow up impacts how we behave in our homes, families and workplaces. It impacts our democracy too. Who is there to make wise, far-reaching decisions, if we're forever caught up in childish fantasies?

Who is there left to work on genuinely innovative ways to progress when politics is increasingly about popularity and the cult of celebrity rather than policies that can make a real difference? Our political leaders seek to please rather than lead, to obfuscate and blame instead of focusing on better ways to meet the challenges (and opportunities) before us. Our democracy is built on engagement, on the importance of our individual and collective choices. Without engagement, democracy becomes fragile and potentially disposable.

We need to revisit our attitude towards getting older, our morbid fear of ageing, where maturity is seen as boring, suspect, to be avoided at all costs. It's not surprising, then, that the care of our elderly has been so lacking of late. What happens to the lifetimes of wisdom, to our collective story, when we neglect the aged among us? If, as is frequently suggested, we peak during our twenties, what is left for us to strive for, to experience, to discover?

> **It's better to be knowing than unknowing. It's better to be experienced than inexperienced. It's better to be sophisticated than callow.**
> Steve Kux, explorer and social psychologist[2]

At every turn marketers and pop culture encourage us to remain forever young. It's not ageing we need fear but the swift march of time; the assumption we'll live forever, wasting our lives in fruitless pursuits. 'Maturity is ever cognizant that the clock is running. Life is finite and among the greatest mistakes is to believe otherwise,' essayist Joseph Epstein warns.[3]

It's not just individuals who think and act like teenagers. Societies and nations can also be driven by a misplaced sense of adolescent entitlement, grandiosity and/or rage. Often smugly unaware of historic and cultural nuances, and of their own shortcomings, they strut the world stage, congratulating themselves on their ill-informed decisions. Bullying some and invading others, and beating others to a pulp, they continue to exploit human and other resources with little thought for the consequences, then move on, leaving decimated, if not displaced, peoples and cultures in their wake.

Such thinking feeds into an unhelpful sense of the grandiose, as seen in the push to 'Make America Great Again'. Agnieszka Golec de Zavala, a psychologist specialising in intergroup conflict and collective narcissism, suggests that what differentiates such groups from other movements is that they don't just want equality, they seek 'special privilege'. 'What I think is happening to us now worldwide is that this collective narcissistic construction of national identity has become the norm,' she reflects, 'and if you look at our research on collective narcissism, that's a bad sign.'4

'Puberty,' states rock critic Michael Corcoran, 'is not about hair or pimples or cracking voices: it's a beast, a demon. It's a beautiful rage that wants to belong.'5 What sort of belonging do we offer our adolescents as they make their way towards adulthood? What do we teach them of the worth, of the challenges (and potential) of adult life, beyond an overwhelming focus on possessions and popularity? Why are we surprised at the growth in anxiety and depression among our young, when this is all they have to hold onto?

Does it matter if people want to linger in a child/adolescent space? It matters when we've been raised to be vulnerable; to be enslaved by the choices and opinions of others; when we're left with little appetite for real issues, for engaging with the real world. It matters when white-collar crime and cheating has become a way of getting what we want. It matters that in clinging to our immature ways, we're more likely to feel isolated and to carry significant, if not crushing, debt.

Ultimately, we're all a mix of infantile and mature traits. The difficulty comes when, as 'adults', we're more immature than grown up. Over the two years I've spent on this book, I've learned a lot about myself, my strengths and my shortcomings. Many moments of illumination have shown me how I operate in different settings – in those where I'm happy to step up and in others where I've tended to shy away, hoping someone else will sort things out.

As a result, I feel much clearer about who I am and where I need to be. I hope this book will enable you to take a similar journey, to help you identify those immature aspects of yourself that may be holding you back. The brief questions at the end of each chapter are designed to offer you new possibilities, new ways of thinking and being in the world. You may even like to use a journal or simply to contemplate these possibilities as you go about your day.

In my research I'm always keen to explore current thinking and behaviour, and to see how these trends assist us and where they bring us down. Often, it's in our personal experiences that the most profound insights are found. We must understand how our impulse towards our child/adolescent ways plays out and how this is impacting our young.

I draw on the observations of experts as well as everyday people, whose comments and opinions I found in numerous online forums such as *Quora*, *Reddit* and *AskMetaFilter*. I have changed individual names to preserve anonymity, and used first names only in their pseudonyms to give an immediacy to their insights. While a few of these quotes have been edited for clarity, or to correct typos and misspellings, every attempt has been made to be true to the original intentions.

1

In Need of More Grit?

Just before midnight on 16 April 1912, the impossible happened. Four days into her maiden voyage, RMS *Titanic*, the largest cruise ship ever, hit an iceberg, damaging this 'unsinkable' vessel irreparably. After the impact, the ship's eight-piece band hurried to the lounge to play for the passengers to help keep them calm. In spite of the bitter night, these young men then moved out onto the deck, where they played rousing tunes while passengers were loaded into lifeboats.

The band played on as long as they were able. Two and a half hours after the collision, the *Titanic* was swallowed up by the icy waters of the Atlantic, along with the band, the remaining passengers and crew. It's hard not to be awed by these young men, aged twenty-one to thirty-three, who put aside all thought of their own safety to help calm the terrible fear around them. How did they manage to keep on playing while facing certain death? What dreams big and small dissolved before them?

What Does It Take to Be Brave?

Could you or I be so courageous? It's probably best we don't wait until we're under such intense pressure to see if we make the grade. Preparation for life's difficulties is, in part, the gift of growing up.

Becoming a fully functioning adult helps ready us for whatever life throws at us. To stand strong we need sufficient life experience and skills to help ourselves and others. Hopefully, a willingness to mature as a person becomes a habit, so we continue to learn and grow.

If we fail to grow up, we remain vulnerable. Whenever bad things happen, we tend to regress into our childlike ways, hoping someone else will come along and rescue us. Maturity, by contrast, enables us to stand on our own feet whenever things get tough, to be an asset rather than a liability and to become someone others can rely on.

Growing up takes time, effort and patience to listen and learn, to discover more effective ways to be in the world. It's also about being useful. The payoff is that life delivers more certainty and less pain. What matters is that we remain open to new and better ways of doing what we do, so we can continue to acquire fresh skills.

Stepping Up

One day during my student years, I arrived home to find my father injured. I hated seeing him hurt and remember thinking, 'I'm not sure I can handle this.' There had always been competent adults around to deal with such moments but, as the only other person at home, it was up to me to get my father to hospital. I'd only just got my driving licence, which upped my panic levels. When we arrived at the hospital, I was so relieved to see the triage nurse, I praised her for being so brave. 'What makes you think I'm brave?' she said. 'I'm just doing what needs to be done.'

I have recalled that nurse's words numerous times over the years, generally in moments of crisis when I find myself wishing someone else would sort a situation. Few of us would choose to be in an emergency or experience a moment of crushing loss. Sooner or later such situations will come our way so we need to be prepared. We need to learn how to step up and find our *own* way to be strong and help show our kids the way.

We can help this maturing process along by looking to fully functioning adults to see how they operate, what they value. We need also to *engage* with life. We'll never become strong if we hide away or look for someone else to fix things. To be brave, we must be willing to see things as they are, not how we'd like them to be. This means becoming someone we and others, especially our kids, can rely on.

True grit is not about patting ourselves on the back for a job well done. It's about understanding we are part of something bigger and that we owe it to ourselves, and others, not to be a liability. It's also about realising there will be times when we need to take good care of those around us, without acknowledgement or reward.

Losing the Plot

Right now, it seems that many of us have lost our way. We've become fragile and inwardly focused, unsure of ourselves and those around us. Consider the responses of those young musicians on the *Titanic* and the stalwart triage nurse I met. How different to the frenetic pushing and shoving we see during department store sales; to the inexplicable run on toilet paper and other goods during the onset of COVID-19. And what about those who spend their days grumbling on social media and elsewhere about the restrictions during the pandemic? Never mind that countless health workers are putting their lives and health at risk to assist others during this massively challenging time.

How did we descend to such pettiness? Why are we so averse to discomfort? Everywhere we look we see examples of rampant self-interest in the many large and small incidents that play out daily, such as: out-of-control parents at their children's sports events; an unwillingness to stand up for those in greater need on public transport; and aggression on our streets and roads.

Unfortunately, affluence has made us soft and self-centred. 'We don't so much have the opportunity to fulfil our heart's desire, as to satisfy our every mood and whim,' Australian researcher Liz Dangar reflected a couple of decades back.[1] Many of us busily grab as much as we can, regardless of whether we need it, whether it's sustainable to take so much or whether others will have to make do with less as a result.

> **Never before has it been more difficult to obey the**
> **injunction to act one's age.**
> Joseph Epstein, essayist[2]

Slow to Mature

With increasing numbers of adults acting like teenagers, we're now seeing even more self-centred, impulsive and entitled behaviour. Like adolescents, we have become extremely sensitive to criticism. Even well-meaning attempts at constructive feedback tend to have little effect. If these and other signs of immaturity point to a solid trend, where is this taking us, and our kids, who tend to follow our behaviour?

It may be that the more sophisticated and affluent we've become, the more we expect to live in a world purely of our own making, devoid of pain, sacrifice or failure, and all the other awkward and exacting life moments that come our way. Is this why we've become intolerant of others' mistakes, however innocent; of those older or younger, or different from us? Even though we have so much, why are we intolerant of those less fortunate, judging them harshly for their inability to thrive? We seem to have become so wrapped up in our own lives that we don't want to inconvenience ourselves in any way, let alone offer a helping hand.

Professionals now talk of immature personalities as a disorder, seen in those unable to handle life's normal ups and downs.[3] Such people are held hostage by constant mood swings, choosing to surround themselves with those willing to bolster their shaky egos. Perpetually dissatisfied and always on the move, the immature are on the lookout for short cuts and quick fixes.

With scant regard for the past and little interest in laying down solid foundations for the future, they live for the moment, with little idea of how uncertain this approach to life can be. 'Adolescence has become, and this must not be missed, the *goal* of our culture,' suggests writer John Stonestreet. 'Somewhere along the way, we ceased to be a culture where kids aspire to be adults, and became a culture where adults aspire to be kids.'[4]

The Fabric of Life

In spite of our intelligence and the advances we've made, the world has become an increasingly fragile place, dogged by a complex array of local and global issues and dwindling resources. To combat this fragility, we need to draw on all the strength, foresight and courage we can muster to create a grounded vision for the way ahead – for us and our kids. Big times do stretch us and there's a lot to take in right now, given the speed, change and pace of life and technology, the 24/7 news cycle and the demands of social media, leaving us with precious little time for reflection.

> **Standing before the elephantine chaos of today's world, we all have a tendency to feel like children.**
> Andrew Calcutt, cultural critic[5]

Add to this the usual pressures of everyday life as we try to hang onto our jobs, keep up with our mortgage payments, feed the cat and the kids, clean the house, shop for groceries and pay the bills. Some days are a struggle but that's life. Every generation has the routine aspects of life, along with bigger life events, to deal with.

Can't Someone Else Sort Things Out?

In the West we grumble and are easily depressed when things go wrong. It doesn't take much for us to get stuck on blaming and complaining and telling ourselves, and anyone else who'll listen, that life's not fair. We can become so enmeshed in our own story we're no longer able to see beyond our own needs.

First and foremost, the child/adolescent in us is averse to tackling life's messier moments, much preferring to find someone else to make challenges magically disappear. The only way to cope in moments of difficulty is to give serious and sustained thought to our situation and sort out what's actually happening. We can then set a firm course and support our kids to face what they need to face with confidence.

> **A profound civilizational shift has taken place, but, shockingly, it [infantilisation] is one that few recognise.**
> Diana West, *The Death of the Grown-Up*[6]

I Can't Do This

We've also become unwilling to see the pain other people face. At the faintest whiff of something unpleasant, we rush to draw down the shutters, expecting others to make the hard decisions. Yet, like petulant children, whenever things go wrong we're quick to blame decision-makers who are trying to make a difference. We prefer to criticise them, rather than taking the time to reflect and to come up with workable solutions.

There have always been immature individuals, but what happens when this way of life becomes the norm? 'Being young today is no longer a transitory phase,' reflects Jacopo Bernardini, of Perugia University. He says that it's a life choice, marked by people always wanting to be free to have fun, creating 'a sort of thoughtful immaturity, a conscious escape' from responsibilities.[7]

Could our childlike need to be endlessly happy, to be seen as special and to want constant entertainment be having a negative impact on our lives? How is this impacting our kids? Our inability to admit we're wrong might be compromising our relationships at home and work. If perpetual adolescence is so prevalent, where are the adults to make the important decisions, while we hide away, doing everything possible to remain happy and, of course, young?

Kickstart Your Maturity

We often worry we're not able to deal with a difficult person or situation. We're afraid we might mess up, so we live small and hide away. We teach our kids to do likewise, and so nothing changes.

- What is it you most fear?
- What if you have all the life tools you need to make a difference, possibly a profound difference? What if you simply don't know how to use these tools yet?
- Is there someone wiser to help you deal with an issue and come up with a plan? There's a wealth of TED talks, blogs, podcasts and YouTube clips to help you begin to fill in the gaps.
- How will you deal with this current difficulty? Remember there is always a solution, even if it's simply to monitor the situation for now and see if it eases.
- Try to stay calm and focused. Be open to how the situation may unfold. Listen carefully to what's being said around the issue and be prepared to build a bridge, to better communicate with others caught up in the event.
- When you've tackled the situation, how did you go? What aspects of your approach need tweaking? Who can help you debrief? Even if the issue isn't fully solved, you've made a start, and that's important.

2

Forever Young

Let us look a little closer at our infantile ways. 'Adolescence – imagined as a pleasant mix of adult rights without adult responsibilities – begins before puberty and, for some, lasts forever,' notes *Newsweek*'s Robert J Samuelson. 'This drift into age denial is everywhere,' he adds.[1]

'The classic dilemma of today's adolescent is whether to become part of the adult world,' cultural critic Andrew Calcutt suggests. 'Pop culture describes this moment of indecision, cultivates it as a way of life, and invests the resultant juvenilia with a significance that is hard to justify.'[2]

It's easy to forget that the concept of adolescence is relatively new. For millennia people simply went from being children to adults. Then, just over a century ago, we settled on the idea of the 'teenage' years – that ten to twelve-year transition from childhood to our adult selves marked by hormonal fluctuations, risky behaviour, frequent mood changes and squabbles with parents and authority figures.[3]

Stuck in Transition

Being an adolescent wasn't necessarily expected to be a comfortable experience. The whole point of this transitional, often uneasy in-between phase is that, having waded through our teen years, we get to emerge more complete. We expect to be more independent and responsible for ourselves, with the tools required to make our own way in the world, and to then teach our kids these essential life skills.

That's the theory. In recent decades, many of us have chosen to cling to our adolescent ways, to remain in this place that was only ever meant to be one of transition. As a result, we continue to experience all the vulnerabilities of adolescence as we struggle with everything from ageing and unfulfilled expectations to what we're meant to be doing with our lives.

Sociologist Jacopo Bernardini suggests that we've become part of a 'collective regression'.[4] More and more of us find ourselves drawn into a frenetic loop of trying to remain forever young and happy, bright-eyed and beautiful, only to 'play without spontaneity, buy without a purpose, and live without responsibility, wisdom or humility'.[5] Adolescence, with all its energy and chutzpah, has much to recommend it. There are times when its youthful exuberance takes our breath away. While we don't wish to rid ourselves of this effervescence, American cultural critic Micki McGee reminds us, when we come to see continued adolescence as 'normal', then we're forced to excuse all the 'poor behaviour' that comes with it.[6]

So Many Young People

How did this focus on, if not adoration of, youth come about? After the ravages of World War II – in which some 56 million people were killed, 28 million died from the fallout of war and resulting famine, and 60 million Europeans alone were left homeless – there was a massive spike in births as peace returned. Remarkably, by 1950, a third of the world's population were fourteen years or under. After so much pain and loss, suddenly life seemed full of potential as the heady joie de vivre of youth spiced the air. With rationing finally coming to an end from the mid-

1950s, the road ahead promised good things.

Even during these heady times, American critic John W Aldridge had reservations. He was concerned by what he saw as a 'fetishizing of youth', not because the energy and potential of youth doesn't have a lot to offer but as this narrowing life focus to purely adolescent concerns comes at the expense of many wider possibilities that remain unrealised. This encourages what Aldridge saw as 'a lifelong excuse for immaturity and childishness'.[7]

> **You can only be young once, but you can be immature forever.**
> John Landis, director of *Animal House*[8]

As a child of these buoyant times, it's no surprise that British actor Michael Caine stated, in the recent David Batty documentary *My Generation*, 'Youth is not a time of life, it's a state of mind.' The promise of limitless youth is extremely seductive. Just consider the countless millions who embrace surgery and other revitalising therapies in an attempt to hold onto their fleeting youth. The simple truth is that none of us can remain a child/adolescent forever – or can we?

Mustn't Age

This massive growth in cosmetic surgery is the result of our fear of ageing. Increasing numbers of us are going to great lengths to conceal our age – cajoling, if not forcing, our bodies to appear forever young. One long-term forecast suggests the industry is set to achieve a turnover nearing $51 billion by 2028, with women accounting for 85 per cent of cosmetic procedures worldwide.[9]

Studies also show a clear correlation between plastic surgery and psychiatric issues, particularly depression and anxiety, which often manifest as 'relationship issues' and 'unrealistic expectations'. Even though they had undergone successful surgery, just over four out of ten cosmetic surgery patients continued to battle 'poor self-image, relationships and general quality of life'.[10]

Terrified that one day those we love will leave us, we do all we can to outrun the inevitability of ageing and death. This leaves less time and energy to acquire strong life skills. Wisdom, laced with a little stoicism, is needed if we want to become fully formed adults able to help our kids become courageous.

Austrian neurologist and Holocaust survivor Viktor Frankl suggested that to thrive we need not so much a life without tension but 'a goal worthy of us'.[11] Forever distracted, needing to be happy 24/7 and drowning in too much choice, we frequently struggle to come up with a solid life goal.

Neverland

Should we fail to make the transition to adulthood, we find ourselves vulnerable and with an alarmingly fragile sense of self. 'When people experience the world in child mode, they feel powerless and at the mercy of others, as well as overpowered by their own feeling reactions,' psychologist Robert Firestone explains, reminding us that in a child's world 'the child is helpless and totally dependent'.[12]

What happens to households and communities when we become lost in self-interest and dependency? Body maintenance for many becomes their supreme goal, which leaves little time to nurture deep friendships, to follow our unique passions and take on a world of possibilities. Valuable time is lost that could have been spent discovering what lies beneath the visible layers of everyday life.

With many of us determined to remain forever young, we only ever have our partially formed selves to fall back on. Childishness becomes our default mode. Nowhere was this more evident, or poignant, than in Michael Jackson's tragically complex life. 'Eventually,' his biographer Randall Sullivan told an interviewer, '[Jackson] gave himself the nose of the boy, the young actor Bobby Driscoll, who was the model for Peter Pan in Walt Disney's movie.'[13]

Beyond Vulnerability

Our journey to adulthood is rarely linear. Most of us are grown up in some areas but infants in others. The infantile parts of us are easy to spot. Quick to take offence, whether or not others mean to offend, we tend to be highly emotional and to demand our own way, often creating hurt and resentment around us.

Here's how to start to make the transition:

- Develop friendships across the generations and differing cultures, to widen and enrich your life experience.
- What areas are you most sensitive about? Is it your looks and possessions, or perhaps your standing in the community or at work? Or are you investing your energy in impressing your parents, your friends? Whatever your sensitivities around how others view you, know that this can make you extremely vulnerable.
- Who, then, can you trust to offer wise advice? Look for people of substance. Which of their qualities would you like to emulate?
- Look further afield. Read the biographies of those who made a positive difference. Note their struggles and sometimes crushing disappointments, as well as their success. What can you learn from this?
- Where can you make a difference? Think practical and manageable, and see where this takes you.

3

Peter Pan and His Lost Boys

While being forever young and carefree may seem an attractive life goal, it prevents us from reaching our potential and can unfairly place the burden of our care and wellbeing on others. In the early 1980s, psychologist Dan Kiley came up with the term 'Peter Pan syndrome' to describe those unwilling or unable to take any real responsibility for themselves, and/or to commit meaningfully to others and thus grow up.

In the original JM Barrie story, Peter Pan escapes back to Neverland after a short stint in the real world, terrified that people might attempt to make a man of him. The Peter Pans of this world are also averse to growing up and have a distinct disdain towards those who are grown-ups. Their self-centredness is matched only by their (often carefully) concealed lack of confidence.

Behind every adult Peter Pan, suggests Kiley, is a Wendy Darling – that tireless someone who spends all their time and energy mothering and sorting out the Peter Pans in their lives. Often Wendy ends up taking care of all the Lost Boys (and Girls) that Peter hangs out with.

When We Become the Caretakers

Whenever Peter Pans are in a mess, Wendy comes to the rescue. A lesser-known aspect of Barrie's story is that when Wendy is too old and weary to help Peter Pan out, her daughter, Jane, agrees to be Peter's 'mother'. Later, when Jane too is worn out, Wendy's granddaughter, Margaret, takes on this thankless task.[1]

Adolescent individuals of any age take a lot of looking after. The Peter Pans we meet in life are often so much fun that it can take some time, if ever, before we tumble to how draining and selfish they are. While Peter Pan and his friends are busy enjoying themselves, life isn't nearly as fulfilling for Peter's back-up team, as there's little, if any, reciprocity.

Right now, many of us seem unable or unwilling to make the transition to adulthood, let alone admit to how breathtakingly short and precious life is. We prefer to live in a fantasy world of our own making. With 'forever young' stamped on our calling cards, we fight hard to stay youthful, spending a fortune on rejuvenating potions, lotions and diets and on an ever-changing wardrobe.

Forever Vulnerable

When we're young, we're dependent. Continuing with this dependency is a perilous course. Previous generations placed great emphasis on taking care of yourself, so as not to burden others, on putting your 'nose to the grindstone' and 'shoulder to the wheel'. The less privileged left home early, often as young as fourteen or fifteen, simply to be one less mouth to feed. Some in straightened circumstances even pretended they'd reached the age for recruitment, volunteering for war, purely to support their families, their country.

My Scottish dad was one of these characters. In later life he admitted how lonely and scary it was to be thrown completely on his own resources so young but he found the courage to make the leap anyway. He was also at pains to emphasise the joy and satisfaction that came with daring to commit to something greater than himself. It was this same impulse, I think, that compelled the musicians on the *Titanic* to be so brave.

Stepping Up

This sentiment is captured powerfully in John F Kennedy's 1961 presidential inauguration speech, in which he encouraged his fellow Americans: 'Ask not what your country can do for you, but what you can do for your country.' Now too many of us spend our days, and money, in search of constant reassurance, buoying ourselves with our new purchases and partners, with a surfeit of streaming services, and with one getaway holiday, if not more, in the wings. With all these distractions, we have little willingness to broaden our lens, to see what else might be needed of us.

'To make it [today] you really have to plunge into much more superficial social relations,' London School of Economics professor Richard Sennett reflects, referring to a life in which what you are wearing, or your charisma, is of more interest than the substance, or lack of substance, that your possessions and persona might conceal.[2] Right now, can we afford to be forever chasing distractions and quick fixes, rather than actively helping solve the big issues of our day? We let other people do the hard thinking and future planning for us when we'd be better served to find a more meaningful way to progress for ourselves and future generations.

Lost in Adolescence

It helps when we can see what this dependency looks and feels like close up for our young. 'I am so hell-bent on finding someone to "rescue" me, to give me the safety and reassurance I never had growing up, to teach me how to be a person, to walk this path with me … that I just seem to be completely stuck and unable to move forward on my own,' admits Sean in an online forum on those trapped by their need to be rescued. 'It feels like the only solution is to connect with other people – but when I try to, I just ruin friendships by burning people out, always needing too much.'[3]

Steph, in the same forum, agrees: 'I definitely have the fantasy of being rescued! I just want an "angel" to swoop down, heal me and save me without any more struggle. Especially with relationships. I am tired of being hurt and hurting people.'[4]

A society that is suffocating on its own sense of entitlement is unlikely to remain productive.
Sabine Wolff, formerly of
Australia's Institute of Public Affairs[5]

'The problem is that once we're in adulthood, that entitlement [to be rescued] is no longer granted,' Brad adds. 'We are adults, and no one will take responsibility for us except ourselves, which personally makes me feel very pissed off.'[6]

Caught in a Self-defeating Loop

There's an important, albeit subtle, difference between choosing to stick with our adolescent ways and keeping a fresh outlook on life. Yet this distinction can so easily become blurred. Where, then, is all this exhaustive attention to the infinitesimal details of our lives taking us – all the entertainment and shopping and travel? Does it deliver the satisfaction, the insight, the calm we yearn for, or do we find ourselves forever stuck in an exhausting loop that leaves us always needing more?

As writer and philosopher Benjamin Cain points out, 'Children don't understand rules and responsibilities ... their primary occupation is just to play, to go where their imagination takes them.' But with this approach, we end up 'rudderless'.[7] Instead of getting on with life, we become lost in our needs, which, if looked at a little closer, may just reveal they were never our dreams in the first place.

Little Personal Growth Here

Aching for adventure, our immature selves are easily bored and while we yearn to be fully independent, we're also hungry for validation, needing to be judged as 'special' and 'deserving'. We still want to have someone else deal with life's messy bits. Hating any form of self-reflection or constructive advice, we make it hard for those who are knowledgeable to offer valuable guidance. As life coach John Kim warns us, 'Children can believe their own lies; they live in fantasy. But if you keep lying to yourself, you will always be a stunted child.'[8]

According to psychologist Carl Pickhardt, if we fail to grow up, we also miss out on experiences that allow for a level of personal growth and independence that's genuinely liberating. Without this level of maturity, we're unlikely to develop empathy or create healthy long-term relationships and pursuits, ending up disappointed with everyone and everything.[9] Our unwillingness to mature also affects those close to us, who support us physically and emotionally, if not financially. Our angst and confusion can so easily make us part of the problem, rather than the solution.

> **The world has become adolescent. Chaotic 'teenage' intensity, dark-tinged extreme experience, is business as usual, the stuff of everyday life.**
> Michael Ventura, US essayist and film critic[10]

Vulnerable Equals Suggestible

Trying to be forever young leads to uncertainty. The resulting lack of self-esteem makes us an easy target in our relationship and life choices, and in our spending patterns and resulting indebtedness. Canny marketers play on these anxieties, promising us the world so we continue to spend, to buy the lie that we're exceptional, forever deserving, the coolest of the cool, and need never age.

Those who actively encourage us to stay young profit handsomely as we rush off to buy young people's clothes and accessories to maintain a carefree life, devoid of 'grown-up' challenges and responsibility. Staying young requires our sustained effort and attention. As American political theorist Benjamin B Barber suggests, offering a much 'flatter' range of youth-centred products for a much wider age group mightn't ultimately serve us, but it works nicely for manufacturers.[11]

Spectacular Growth in Young Adult Books

Our determination to chase youth is seen in the growing numbers of adults gravitating to YA (young adult) books, with over half the audience now eighteen or older and the largest proportion of YA readers aged thirty to forty-four.[12] What sets YA books apart, notes journalist Ruth Graham, is that they present a teen world view that lacks 'the emotional and moral ambiguity of adult fiction'.[13]

We see a similar trend in the rise of comic book sales. 'Twenty years or so ago, something happened – adults decided they didn't have to give up kid stuff. And so they pretended comic books were actually sophisticated literature,' reflects comedian Bill Maher. 'Now when adults are forced to do grown-up things like buy auto insurance, they call it "adulting", and act like it's some giant struggle … The problem is we're using our smarts on stupid stuff.'[14]

The same applies to TV and movies. Over the last fifteen years, notes *New York Times* film critic AO Scott, there's been huge investment in films that 'advance an essentially juvenile vision of the world'. These include 'comic-book movies, family-friendly animated adventures, tales of adolescent heroism and comedies of arrested development'.[15]

This shift, suggests Scottish novelist and film critic Gilbert Adair, began with the first Disney theme park, which was built on the outskirts of Los Angeles in the mid-50s. In his article 'The Mouse that Ate Western Civilisation', Adair observed that 'watching a movie is [now] closer to the experience of being whizzed round a theme-park ride, than to reading a novel or watching a play or listening to an opera. How did it happen that the cinema, the century's quintessential art form, has been permitted to degenerate into candy, and not just candy, but candy floss, forgotten as soon as consumed, disintegrating into sugary nothingness even as one consumes it?'[16]

Needing to Belong

What, then, can we offer the vulnerable child/adolescents who are reluctant to grow up? In need of a place to belong as a teenager, Dave Smith ended up in a gang, a scene he describes as 'racist and violent … attractive and revolting at the same time'. Now an Anglican priest, Father Dave has made it part of his life's work to harness at-risk boys' potential so they get to feel 'fully alive'.

Through his Old School Boxing Academy in Sydney's Inner West, Father Dave creatively channels the many drives adolescent boys have, by building a community around them that helps them use their drives positively. 'They need to be part of a community that cares, that gives a damn,' Father Dave told me during the afternoon I spent with him.

'If a boy has issues, then he doesn't do well in the ring. Self-control is the key. I say to the guys, "If you can get to the stage where someone is trying to take your head off, and yet you can stay in control and focused, and can be proactive and make your own decisions, instead of just responding to the pressures, then you can do anything."' The Boxing Academy is 'about boys being able to make their own [good] decisions, while being put under an enormous amount of pressure'.

Imagine if we, and our kids, were to reach a more meaningful sense of belonging, to have the resources to withstand numerous challenges and make better decisions. A path that leads us and those who follow us to a tangible sense of community, to feeling fully alive. This is what genuine adulthood offers us.

If You're Caught in a Peter Pan Cycle ...

Sometimes our Peter Pan tendencies creep up on us, sometimes they're in plain sight. They are evident whenever we feel defensive, or hope to be rescued.

There's a time to be serious, and a time to play. Yet Peter Pan's default position is always play, creating major commitment issues.

- What situations provoke your Peter Pan behaviour? Where do you feel vulnerable, fearful or uncertain? If everything you do is focused on your own needs, you may just have a major dose of the Peter Pans.
- If someone offers constructive criticism, be open to their advice. Be clear about your flaws. Learn to say sorry and make amends with grace. Be a better friend to yourself, so you're less needy around others. Dare to believe in a stronger, more consistent you, who can step up and follow through.

If You're Always Playing Wendy ...

- Who are your Peter Pans, your Lost Boys (and Girls)? (Hint: there's a reason why these children are *Lost* Boys (and Girls).)
- How much physical and emotional time do these people demand of you? How much do they give back? Is this a fruitful path, or does it leave you angry, resentful and drained?
- How might you progress?
- Practise putting yourself first and be clear about the time you can give to such relationships. Set clear boundaries and don't rush in the moment something goes wrong. Ask supportive questions instead. Resist taking on other people's emotions and issues. Learn to say no. Enjoy how much more time and energy you now have.

4

We Don't Know What We Don't Know

When we're immature, we tend to operate with a false, perhaps inflated, sense of our abilities. We allow for this lack of judgement in children and teenagers but it becomes problematic when adults behave in this way.

With more people thinking and acting like adolescents, there's a growth in naivety, buoyed up by inflated egos and not much else. As American cultural critic Micki McGee notes, 'Ours is a culture largely ignorant of economic theory, political distinctions, or the rules of logic, but one that is fully up to speed on the latest from *American Idol*.'[1]

Community and connection, strong families and friendships, healthy workplaces and the very foundations of democracy are built on *engagement*. We need always to find new and better ways to enhance the way our society functions, from our medical and education systems, our transport needs, food delivery and care of the aged to the nurture of the young, the disabled and the disadvantaged, and more. Yet many of us seem to be drifting away from the chance to participate actively and positively in our future. The adolescent in us much prefers to play, especially when times get tough.

To suggest that a growing number of us still need to mature is likely to result in a storm of defensive comments. Yet without thoughtful reflection and a finely honed self-awareness, our adolescent self remains curiously inflexible and often dismissive of others.

Our immature selves much prefer to go their own way, creating the kind of dynamic where, as writer and philosopher Benjamin Cain states, 'the wise are shunned, because their kind of knowledge threatens the childish social order. In the same way, children eventually view adults as impediments to their playtime.' And 'the horror [of our current situation]', he warns, 'is that we have no parents to correct our waywardness.'[2]

> **It is a kind of moral death in a culture that claims youthful**
> **self-invention as the greatest value.**
> AO Scott, chief film critic at *The New York Times*[3]

A Liability to Others

Adolescent naivety can imperil us and others. When we're stuck in our adolescent ways, our decision-making is narrow at best. We chase goals because we can, not because they're the best or most ethical option, with no thought to their impact on other people or the environment. 'We [our infantile selves] understand how the world works and can exploit that knowledge, redesigning nature to suit our interests,' reflects Benjamin Cain. 'We're masters at figuring out how technically to achieve our goals, but that's a far cry from knowing which goals we should achieve.'[4]

Even on the good days, the adolescent mind can struggle to think things through. When a teenager veers off track, there is likely to be some pain. More so when we have 'kidults' running corporations and other big institutions, or heading up political parties, even nations, and making decisions based purely on self-interest, on grandiose visions, and/or need to win regardless of the cost.

Disruption and Chaos

Our adolescent selves take a perverse delight in disruption. Reconfiguring the world has become our most cherished pursuit. Fuelled by our uncertainties and teen rage, we love to play with the building blocks of our communities, workplaces and nations, creating a rate of change that's exhilarating, yet often exhausting and unrelenting. Pull too much apart and our lives lose familiarity and coherence, becoming isolating and chaotic instead.

With the carelessness and overconfidence of youth, we revel in rebelling against the institutions we benefit from, while doing little to help nurture or reform them. 'We all regress – become delightfully cheeky and playful, have tantrums, or are irresponsible and do naughty things,' admits writer Ruth Ostrow, who then asked a key question: 'So when does [our regression] become pathological?' It is, she suggests, 'in the degree.'[5]

'The great challenge of our moment is the crisis of isolation and fragmentation,' suggests David Brooks of *The New York Times,* as this creates 'the need to rebuild the fabric of society that has been torn by selfishness, cynicism, distrust and autonomy.'[6]

Back to Me

Just how pervasive the growing child/adolescent mindset has become isn't always immediately apparent. 'I've noticed that there has been a gradual social change, since I entered the workforce 25 years ago,' observes Trevor Warden, an expert in corporate rewards and remuneration. 'Back then, if you spoke to people about fairness, they would talk about treating everyone the same. Today if you ask the same question, you will hear them talking about wanting their rewards to reflect their individual efforts, and not that of their colleagues or team.'[7]

I'm often impressed at how much more cohesive families and communities are in poorer parts of the world, and how mindful people are of the impact their actions have on others. Here the social fabric is tended with greater care. In the West we know little of placing others' needs alongside, if not ahead of, our own – and, by and large, we much prefer it this way.

> **Pop culture has disengaged our brains and arrested our development.**
> Michael Hogan, entertainment writer[8]

What Does Affluence Have to Do with It?

Studies suggest that teens are more likely to become genuine adults if they come from big families or low-income homes. Basically, children from more challenging backgrounds grow up quicker than those from more privileged settings.[9] We don't want to make childhood overly challenging. However, some teens from affluent backgrounds are now seen as being at heightened risk. This is evident in their escalating out-of-control behaviour, and in their anxiety and depression.[10]

This trend was starkly evident in one 2020 end-of-year muck-up day checklist put together by pupils from some of Sydney's most prestigious schools. Over 150 challenges were dreamed up to mark their final days at school. These ranged from getting arrested and taking illegal drugs, to 'sack-whacking' (bashing someone in the testicles).[11] Additional challenges encouraged pupils to spit on a homeless man, 'shit' on a train or 'get an Asian chick',[12] or take part in sexual assault.[13] Here we see a group of adolescents adrift from their homes and communities. How these vulnerable individuals will fare in the workplace, in their relationships and in parenting, only time will tell, but they've hardly made a promising start.

Affluence and Depression

Too much ease, it seems, is detrimental to our mental health and wellbeing. In just a decade from 2007, teenage depression in America alone rose by 59 per cent. In 2017, over one in ten US teens admitted to experiencing a major depressive incident in the previous twelve months. This represents two million more teenagers suffering depression than just a decade earlier. In 2017, 20 per cent of girls admitted to experiencing a significant depressive episode over the previous year.[14] This concerning growth in teen depression is apparent in other studies across the globe.

When we raise the question of immaturity, it's fashionable to dump on millennials, laying the blame for all the infantile behaviour we witness at their door. Millennials aren't the only ones wrestling with immaturity. What is clear is that, by failing to nudge our young people out of the family cocoon, we're failing to prepare them for adult life in all its complexities. And in so doing, we fail ourselves too.

Not Ready for Adult Life

Robert Epstein, former editor-in-chief of *Psychology Today*, suggests that prolonging our kids' childhoods means they end up suffering arrested development, leaving them less able to navigate the adult world.[15] This is evident in the number of Gen Z young adults now entering the workplace and university who struggle in unstructured learning and work environments.

Many students are baffling and frustrating their uni teachers, who are now providing far more pastoral care than in previous eras. 'Around 2014, we started getting students protesting, because a speaker would be "dangerous", or a book would be "dangerous", says New York University social psychologist Jonathan Haidt. 'And so they [students] would request a trigger warning. So, there was this new idea that students are fragile, and that adults need to protect students from books, words, ideas, and speakers. And this completely confounded most of us. What are they talking about? Like violence, how is reading a book violence?'

Haidt sees there's 'a kind of a moral incoherence on campus now', where 'we think what we're doing is pursuing truth and transmitting it'. Yet today's students view such initiatives as threatening, if not personally harmful.[16] Alongside this, notes Haidt, is a demonstrable rise in depression and anxiety, to the extent that today's students are in need of 'anti-fragility' training, and would, for example, benefit from less oversight from their parents.[17]

How did our kids get to be so lacking in resilience? What is clear is that we can't help current generations be fully formed adults, if we're not. Right now, society is struggling to furnish young people with a persuasive account of what it means to be an adult, suggests sociology professor Frank Furedi.[18] Sociologist Richard Sennett agrees. 'Masses of people are concerned with their single life histories and particular emotion as never before,' which has proved 'a trap rather than a liberation'.[19]

Harnessing Adolescent Rage

We need to ensure adolescence is only ever a passing phase, one that's useful to all concerned. 'Tribal adults didn't run from this [adolescent] moment in their children as we do,' insists Michael Ventura, pointing out that tribes celebrate the darkness and complexity of adolescence, giving its swirling emotions, potentials and uncertainties a voice to help it become something 'useful'.

'They [tribal adults] waited until their children reached the intensity of adolescence,' Ventura says, 'and then they used that very intensity's capacity for absorption [for new approaches], its hunger, its need to act out, its craving for dark things, dark knowledge, dark acts, all the qualities we fear most in our kids.' This approach ensures that 'through what the kids craved, they were given what they [most] needed'.[20]

A Better Way Ahead

There's little value for us or our kids in being their best friends but we are their best chance at becoming well-rounded adults. As Australian researcher Liz Dangar noted some time back, 'We've lost our touchstones', distracting ourselves 'with thrill-seeking and escapism' and retreating 'to look after ourselves and our own'. Yet 'we are searching for solace'.[21] These stretching times may prove to be an immense gift, helping us to grow ourselves and our kids up.

To achieve real solace, which is not the same as escape, we need to dig deep and come to terms with the less comfortable aspects of life to find a meaningful centredness. If we achieve this, our children also benefit. As identity researcher Karen Eddington says, 'Confidence is not about being self-centred, it is about being emotionally centred, so you can better see other people.'[22]

Growing Our Humanity

When we dare to expand our life experience and vision, we get the chance to become more human, to embrace life's joyous moments, along with those that fill us with dread. We have the confidence to meet life without the constant need for sugar-coating, the insight to discover the extraordinary concealed in those things we assumed were ordinary, of little worth.

'In a very real sense,' reflects psychologist Robert Firestone, 'we must feel our sadness and mourn our mortality, in order to fully accept and value our existence.'[23] Everything has something of value for us and for others. As one young adult wrote in a Reddit forum on teen years, 'I can feel myself getting better at being a member of society, and what I do is starting to matter in the world. I love it.'[24]

What We Don't Know That We Need to Know

Sometimes we slip into unconscious patterns, not realising how harmful they can be.

- Have you fallen into the trap of going after something simply because you can? Did it deliver all you hoped for? What are the lessons here?
- What darkness, what intensity in you, in your kids, needs positive expression? What moment of worth might it help you/them achieve?
- If being young and carefree were less important, what other passions might fill this space?
- What are your most significant goals right now? Will they help you/your kids embrace the highest form of yourselves, or will they sell you short?
- What might a more emotionally centred life look like? How might this new level of 'groundedness' feel? How can you imbue your kids with this gift?
- Who exemplifies the qualities you most want to cultivate? What can you learn from them?
- What is it that you do, or can do, that matters in the world?

5

Our Need to Be Noticed

At the heart of our child/adolescent angst is our hunger to be seen, an impulse that can demolish the many possibilities in our friendships and families, our workplace and beyond. Sometimes we go to extremes with risky behaviour to get others to take note, only to have them head for the hills.

On some level we've all felt this ache to be seen and heard. Whether this thirst to be noticed is detrimental depends on the degree. It can be hard to strike a balance when over 94 million photos and videos are shared on Instagram every single day. The most successful social media operators post between two and ten times daily, and we're led to believe it's our social media profile that counts.

> Not everything is about 'me'. There are sometimes bigger
> things that we should be concerned about.
> Dr Jennifer Crocker, psychologist[1]

Individuality on the Rise

One study across seventy-eight countries suggests that the growth of individualism is due to more people accessing higher education; smaller families meaning more attention for individual members; and more of us choosing to live in cities. Our increased wealth is also a key driver to our growing self-centred outlook and behaviour.

The better our qualifications, occupation and income, the more likely we are to focus on ourselves.[2] No longer so dependent on others, we value our independence and uniqueness above all else, and if we're not self-aware, we seek always to place ourselves front and centre.

Out of Control?

Our growing need to be seen can easily tip over into narcissism, a psychological condition inspired by Narcissus, the mythic handsome Laconian hunter figure who loved beauty in all its forms. Some of those who fell in love with his extreme good looks suicided to try to prove the depth of their love. Meanwhile, Narcissus was so mesmerised by his own reflection that there wasn't room in his life for anyone else. The toxic emotions underpinning narcissism have a way of leaking into our lives and poisoning all the good there, leaving us caught somewhere between self-doubt and self-loathing.

> **It is not love we should have painted as blind, but self-love.**
> Voltaire, author and philosopher

Former professor emeritus of world literature Mason Cooley notes that, in spite of everything Narcissus had, he spent much of his time weeping because his reflection failed to return his love. American actress Emily Levine, known for her deft musings, assumed narcissism was simply about self-love until someone pointed out that narcissism is *unrequited* self-love, a total inability to love ourselves. Clinical psychologist Leon F Seltzer sees narcissism as 'a spectacular triumph of self-deception'.[3] Imprisoned by self-love, Narcissus slowly faded away, then died – a salutary tale for all of us.

When Uncertainty Bites

Our need to be noticed is often a defensive mechanism, as we can see in small children. Whenever they're feeling uncertain or ignored, kids start badgering their parents and others for attention. When we lack strong life skills, we often resort to grabbing the limelight any way we can. Department stores and malls fill with shoppers determined to find that perfect something to help them stay ahead of the pack. Should these shoppers find their 'perfect' purchase, would it truly comfort them? Or would they, like Narcissus, be forever looking for love and nurture in all the wrong places, finding none?

Grabbing attention can become our default position to spice the moment or solve a tricky situation. A whisper at work that jobs are to be lost causes us to panic. Our immature self prompts us to rush out and get a bold, yet not too bold, haircut or new gear in the hope we'll 'look the part', to lose ourself in a variety of substances or perhaps to put in less effort and to complain constantly to friends.

By contrast, the fully formed adult first takes stock, deciding to upskill and/or network, to spend time with supportive friends and activities, to take time out in nature so they can recharge. By carefully preparing for what lies ahead, whether they lose their job or not, they're in a much better position to move forward. The mature adult is also better placed to guide their kids through their ups and downs.

Flawed Thinking

It's essential we realise that the child/adolescent's way of solving situations is often only partially thought through. When we've yet to mature, we tend to seize on the first thought that comes to mind, which is often laced with drama, or we try to bluff our way out of the situation. The childish self also prefers to paper over the cracks, rather than finding a more effective way through a difficulty.

Grown-up solutions tend to be more holistic, more consistent and considered, to help us prepare practically for what lies ahead. These more grounded approaches provide our kids with a more effective roadmap and less pain, when dealing with the dizziness and uncertainty of adolescence.

The Price of Self-esteem

To thrive we need positive self-regard, which takes love, patience, time and attention to build. The child/adolescent in us is always in a hurry. It much prefers to spend its days searching for a readymade identity, preferably one it can purchase. It's essential we realise that our self-esteem, our identity, is uniquely ours. Our self-esteem must be nourished and formed from within if we are to build a firm foundation for our lives.

It takes clarity and strength to hold our true self close, to dare to make decisions that feel intrinsically right for us. We need to be acutely aware of the people and situations that seek to change us into something glossier or easier to manage, into something we're not.

Staying true to ourselves isn't always easy. As American poet and essayist EE Cummings reminds us, 'To be nobody-but-yourself in a world which is doing its best night and day, to make you everybody else – means to fight the hardest battle any human can fight; and never stop fighting.'[4] To be one's true self is our greatest endeavour, says Cummings, and is far more important than praying to be 'great or good, or beautiful or wise or strong'.[5] Unless we nurture our authentic self, we'll never achieve the genuine wellbeing and peace of mind we yearn for, or get to share this wisdom with our kids.

Buying Love

The immature part of us will nearly always look for a fast track to love and attention and will happily buy its way to greater esteem. Having the right look, the right gear, is how the child/adolescent seeks to shield itself from an uncertain world, from the inevitable difficulties we encounter at work, in our wider relationships, and at home. This pattern of evasion starts young and can become a habit that too few understand. Rarely does evasion enrich our lives or offer much solace in the moments when we need it most.

One study of British teenagers found that peer pressure and the need to conform was high among adolescents. These teens told of how important it was to be seen by peers to be 'consuming the correct possessions, at the right time'. This was 'essential for social acceptance, gaining and maintaining friendships, and thus [for their] self-esteem'.[6] Basically, these kids went with the status quo, taking in each and every detail, however small, to ensure they belonged, because they felt they had few options.

Given we're tribal by nature, most of us can't bear the thought of being rejected by the pack. Blindly chasing the expectations of others rarely delivers the belonging, safety and happiness we hope for. That's when we become hyper-vigilant, constantly monitoring what everyone else is doing to ensure we remain ahead of the game. Unaware of this destructive pattern, we continue to wrestle with anxiety and a lack of self-esteem.

> **Fear is the greatest threat to discovering who we are, what**
> **we want, and figuring out how to get there. It can be subtle.**
> **It can be obvious. But if you are unhappy in any area of**
> **your life, I promise that fear is present.**
> Nulla, *Reddit* forum[7]

What Does Fear Have to Do with It?

The fear that lies at the heart of our ache for attention has become so intense in recent times that we've become like hungry ghosts – those sad, if not terrifying, wraiths (first spoken of in Hinduism, then Buddhism) who roam the Earth, starved of sensation. Sydney collector Linda Heaphy describes these ghoulish figures as 'remnants of the dead, afflicted by insatiable desires, condemned to inhabit shadowy and dismal places in the realms of the living'.[8] Profound emptiness and desperation plague the hungry ghost. Forever restless and constantly on the move, they seek out any comfort possible, finding none.

The hungry ghost is a powerful symbol for our times. Some are so in need of attention right now, relationship expert Craig Malkin suggests, that 'just like with any other drug, they'll do anything to get their "high" including lie, steal, cheat, betray, and even hurt those closest to them'.[9] There's a secretive element to this childish yearning to stand out. Slowly yet deliberately, we draw others into our circle, purely for our own benefit.

Define Special

'Why is it that some people believe that their *special circumstances* are more special than another person's special circumstances?' asks clinical psychologist Dr Edward Dreyfus. 'I don't believe these individuals are mean-spirited or selfish. I do not believe that they are trying to take advantage of me. In my experience, these folks are hurting, damaged individuals, who never really felt special to anyone.'[10]

If the child/adolescent in us doesn't feel seen or heard, we feel invisible, and the social fabric wears thin. With kindness and a willingness to reach out in short supply, we start to focus on our own needs, further compromising any, if not all, opportunities for growth, connection and meaning.

It's sometimes hard not to feel invisible, if not helpless, at times. This is all the more challenging when we approach life's inevitable challenges with a childish outlook, only to find we don't have the life experience, vision or tools to push through our feelings of inadequacy. If we don't have the tools, our kids are also unlikely to have them, leaving everyone floundering.

We all wrestle with inadequacy now and then – a sure sign of the child/adolescent in us seeking firmer ground. The secret is to shift our focus, to pay attention to our *own* dreams and aspirations so we don't get caught in the same old self-defeating loop of always looking to others for our cues. We start to think instead about how we can give our most cherished dreams a voice. Put simply, taking our aspirations seriously is our 'get out of jail card'. It helps the adolescent in us to grow.

To follow our path takes courage. It can be uncomfortable at times, but it's not as uncomfortable as living an inauthentic life. 'What's wrong with most people is that they have this block,' physicist David Bohm once reflected. 'They feel they could never make a difference, and therefore, they never face the possibility, because it is too disturbing, too frightening.'[11]

Economist and co-founder of *The Possibility Project,* Kim Pearce agrees. 'Too many of us are conditioned to believe that the causes and answers to our problems lie in the hands of others,' she states. Pearce and her partner support women living and working in India's Jaipur slums by selling garments the women make. 'My approach to greater social justice is not about changing people … It's wholeheartedly about changing people's impossible thinking [so they can see how much they are capable of].'[12]

Blinkered Thinking

By seeking to be constantly noticed, it is possible that, instead of learning and growing, we remain in an almost infantile state of helplessness and are dangerously self-absorbed. Dangerous, because we're wired to connect and disconnection is often a precursor to mental health and other crippling issues that prevent us from leading rich inner lives, and feeling genuinely fulfilled around others.

The dangers of blinkered thinking may seem overstated, but is it really? One of the characters in Robert Jordan's novel *New Spring* is described as 'swimming in a sea of other people's expectations', with the accompanying reflection, 'Men had drowned in seas like that.'

> **When you make your self-esteem contingent on something**
> **other than your basic value as a human being, it's not**
> **a good thing, even if the source of your self-esteem is**
> **something as praise-worthy as getting good grade.**
> Dr Jennifer Crocker, psychologist[13]

Weak Boundaries

When we're in continual need of attention, we have little sense of ourselves beyond the clicks and likes others bestow on us. 'Of course, you want those important people in your life to love you,' counsellor Bridget Webber affirms. 'But when your happiness depends on their love, you're vulnerable. Not in a healthy way, because you've given them the power to make or break your happiness.'[14] When the child in us becomes overly reliant on others to reassure us or bail us out, we become subject to other people's expectations, and unable to function without their ongoing attention and regard.

Too often we let go of our most valuable personal qualities in the hope we'll fit in. This is starkly apparent in Joseph Heller's novel *Something Happened*. Here Bob Slocum appears to have it all: a perfect wife, beautiful home and three lovely kids. Yet he is desolate, confessing to 'this subtle, sneaky, almost enslaving instinct to be like just about everyone else I find myself with ... It operates unconsciously.' Slocum reflects: 'Usually I do not realise I have slipped into someone else's personality until I am already there.'[15]

Better Choices

Who we hang out with matters, so we need to choose our friends with care. We need to seek out those who'll be honest with us, even willing to disagree with us on occasion. Social historian Christopher Lasch suggests that the 'best hope' for emotional maturity is found in 'a recognition of our need for and dependence on people, who nevertheless [must] remain separate from ourselves and refuse to submit to our whims'.[16]

> **My bottom line is that self-esteem isn't really worth the effort. Self-control is much more powerful.**
> Roy F Baumeister, social psychologist[17]

Psychologist Dr Jennifer Crocker at the University of Michigan's Institute for Social Research reminds us that there's a personal and social cost to our 'frantic pursuit of self-worth through external trappings'. Accolades and possessions deliver only fleeting benefits, while demanding a lot of us.

This doesn't mean letting go of our ambitions, but we don't need permission to feel good about ourselves or how we lead our lives. In Crocker's study of almost 650 students in their first year at university, those who pinned everything on attaining high marks experienced more stress and disagreements with their teachers than the rest of the sample. The first-year students who set great store by their looks found themselves in more 'aggressive and hostile' situations, used more drugs and alcohol, and were more vulnerable to eating issues such as bulimia.[18]

Thinking Like a Teenager

When we're driven by an adolescent need to always come out ahead of everyone else, we lose perspective. In extreme cases, we compete with those dearest to us and so begins our downward spiral. Half a century ago, groundbreaking psychoanalyst and philosopher Erich Fromm observed, 'We live in a historical period characterized by a sharp discrepancy between the intellectual development of man … and his mental-emotional development, which has left him still in a state of marked narcissism.'[19] As we look around us, these trends seem to have intensified.

The Comparison Trap

There's rarely an endpoint to our infantile need for attention unless we actively change our behaviour. To live by comparison is to die from comparison. We never reach that sweet spot where we can relax a little and enjoy our wins as there's always someone brighter, wittier, more attractive out there, to take the edge off our joy.

World Economic Forum Global Shaper Emerson Csorba knows this territory well. 'We [millennials] are a generation that is ruthlessly comparing ourselves with those around us and our role models at the same time,' he reflects. 'And if we are not doing something exceptional, or don't feel important and fulfilled for what we are doing, we have a hard time.'[20]

> When we are not chosen, we feel bad. When we are
> chosen – even by idiots – we feel good.
> James Altucher, venture capitalist[21]

How do we escape this self-defeating loop that can only ever lead us down more rabbit holes? 'We need to unlearn this imprisonment,' James

Altucher insists. 'Not dissect and analyze it. Just completely unlearn it.'[22] We need to operate in ways more congruent with our dreams and values and let go of unhelpful comparisons, the need to be noticed and mindless consumption and grow up.

A Different Path

Perpetual adolescence keeps us needy, ever restless, always on the lookout for that magical someone to come along to meet our every need. 'Most of us have never truly grown up or feel in our heart of hearts "adult",' reflects Michael Ventura, 'and are left instead hoping to be somehow initiated by chance somewhere along the way.'[23]

Self-esteem is ours alone to nurture. To experience true freedom, we need to be more proactive, to reflect on how we're currently operating and to learn from those who display true strength and insight. We need also to be crystal clear about the values we embrace, while being flexible and wise enough to understand there are always new and better approaches out there. Only then can we become empowered adults, well able to help empower our kids.

Growing up is a complex business and not a linear process. Some parts of us may be remarkably mature, while other parts remain stuck in childhood or adolescence. To create a meaningful life and make full use of our talents, we need to reclaim those parts of us that are languishing in immaturity. As the Indian philosopher Krishnamurti once cautioned, 'It's no measure of health to be well adjusted to a profoundly sick society.'[24] In daring to grow up, we get to see what we're truly capable of and to assist upcoming generations to make this powerful journey.

Finding a Space to Thrive

Each of us needs to settle on our own way to be in the world. How can we do this?

- Is there anything in the Narcissus story that resonates with your life experience?
- When do you most feel in need of love and attention? Which people and situations spark this longing? What might you change?
- Where do you tend to seek out comfort?
- Does this path fulfil you, or leave you empty and out of sorts?
- What aspects of your life need of greater kindness?
- Where could you be more honest with yourself? How might this liberate the parts of you that are struggling?
- What grown-up approaches might serve you well? How best can you pass these insights on to your children?

6

What Happened to Childhood?

Like teenagers, many of us are confused about what we're meant to be doing with our lives. Where do we, and our kids, acquire the solid life skills, strength and resilience to create a grounded sense of belonging?

Often, we hate how up in the air our lives feel so we retreat to shopping and entertainment, into over-scheduled lives, further feeding our fears and vulnerabilities. When this self-obsessed way of life isn't working for us, still we encourage our kids down this same sad route because we haven't found anything more satisfying.

Missing Out

Increasing numbers of us are products of hijacked childhoods. Without a firm foundation, we become ever more preoccupied with ourselves, which is often starkly evident in how we feel when someone else has a win; in how we regale others constantly with our woes, leaving precious little room for anyone else to be seen or heard. These and other unhelpful habits don't deliver a clear vision, the chance to evolve.

The Seeds of Self-hate

Being constantly videoed and photographed, our children and teenagers are drawn into our relentless performance culture at an early age and struggle with the resulting weight of expectation. Forever vigilant, our kids try desperately not to fall out of step with their peers and can easily become prey to anxiety, depression or worse.

Who'd have thought that kids as young as three now wrestle with body issues?[1] That some small children worry about time spent around their peers, fearing they'll be criticised or taken down?[2] Or that they're persuaded to pay constant attention to their looks and possessions to belong?

Hijacked Childhoods

Instead of a childhood filled with flights of imagination, time in nature and spontaneous play, our little ones now fret over their looks and weight, falling into fashion long before they can read or write or have the skills to form their own independent opinions.

> **At the beginning of the year we had a little celebration for
> the class. All the girls couldn't stop talking about what they
> were going to wear, and how they would look at the party.
> It was all they could talk about. I couldn't believe it.**
> **They weren't quite 4.**
> Jeanne, pre-school teacher[3]

Around the age of two, children start to recognise themselves in the mirror and soon check in on how they look at every opportunity. This growing obsession with their appearance can only ever deliver a shallow sense of 'self', as who they are becomes all about their hair and clothes, their body weight and shape, their accessories. So begins the hijacking of our children's lives and potential, crushing their ability to push past their limitations and become empowered adults, to grow up.

Empty Promises

Fixated on their appearance and what they own, our kids become anxious and plagued by self-doubt. 'Advertising at its best is making people feel that without their product you're a loser,' Nancy Shalek, former president of Grey Advertising, suggests. 'Kids are very sensitive to that.'[4] They persevere with shopping, checking on their appearance and comparing themselves with their peers, because they're desperate to find a place that's safe and nurturing where they can thrive.

As our kids grow, they try ever harder to fulfil the fake dreams they're offered by the glamorous, deliberately seductive images of men and women seen on social media, TV, billboards, in ads and film. They look at themselves and their world with an ever more critical eye. So begins, for girls at least, what Harvard psychologist Nancy Etcoff calls 'the survival of the prettiest'.[5]

The Questionable Value of Cool

Our young quickly become addicted to the lives of celebrities and the brands they promote. 'Stuff' becomes their go-to solution to the issues they face. Instead of learning the value of boredom, or the powerful insights that can come from learning to pick themselves up, our kids are now more likely to throw a tantrum, demanding yet more possessions to prop up their fragile sense of self.

'Materialism is a way to compensate for impaired implicit self-esteem,' notes Jiang Jiang, the lead author of the study 'Can't Buy Me Friendship?'.[6] No amount of stuff can dissolve the aching inadequacy, confusion and sadness that an anxious or bewildered child/adolescent feels.

With nothing solid to hang on to, our kids try to find new ways to be noticed, to compete with and/or shock friends. Even negative attention is seen as better than no attention at all. Relating to peers becomes about competition, making sure they surpass their friends wherever possible.

They miss out on all the benefits of supportive friendships; on sharing experiences worth savouring; on laughter and on sympathetic support. Lacking a growing positive sense of themselves, they start to judge everyone as either a winner or loser – a trait of those in survival mode. This suggests that many of our kids are barely surviving this hothouse culture they're currently raised in.

> **Kids like the idea of 'belonging to' … For the marketer, well, it can be the beginning of a lifelong relationship. What a deal!**
>
> James McNeal, former professor of marketing at Texas A&M[7]

Our 'always on' pop culture intensifies the pressure, with its 24/7 offerings promoting messages about the looks, leisure activities and products kids need to belong. How can our kids develop an intimate understanding of themselves when they're forever doing all they can to prove they're the coolest and, not infrequently, the riskiest?

In survival mode, there's no time to take stock. We fall back on snap decisions, default to what we know, so there's little, if any, growth here. Essential parts of us are effectively silenced or shut down, if not shamed, making it even harder for us to push beyond our limitations and mature.

What About Our Wellbeing?

The wider environment kids grow up in also encourages them down less than helpful routes. For the last two and a half decades, US studies indicated that the more materialistic we are, the less happy, satisfied and vibrant we end up, and the more likely we are to suffer from anxiety, depression or other mental health issues.

A recent review of these studies, which took in kids as young as ten to those in their eighties, as well as people living in Europe, the Middle

East and Asia, confirmed these earlier findings. It also highlighted the inconsistent attitudes and behaviour that tend to come with an over-reliance on materialism, creating a range of issues, from out-of-control spending to higher levels of self-doubt.[8]

Drowning in Stuff

Is this need for 'stuff' purely indulgence, or is there something more insidious at work here? 'At first glance, a society based on mass consumption appears to encourage self-indulgence in its most blatant forms,' reflects historian and social critic Christopher Lasch. 'Strictly considered, however, modern advertising seeks to promote not so much self-indulgence as self-doubt. It seeks to create needs, not to fulfil them; to generate new anxieties instead of allaying old ones.'[9] In our eagerness to make money out of our young people, we're effectively transforming them into the hungry ghosts discussed previously.

This obsession with self and addiction to stuff intensifies as kids grow. Many adolescents now mix almost exclusively with their peers so, surrounded by equally insecure, inward-focused teens, kids share the same aspirations and anxieties. 'To develop intellectually,' English professor Mark Bauerlein reminds us, 'you've got to relate to older people, older things: 17-year-olds never grow up if they're just hanging around other 17-year-olds.'[10]

Good Parenting Matters

Older, wiser cultures are well aware that a parent's job, and that of the community, is to give children as many life skills as possible so they can be self-reliant and able to weather the worst of life's storms. Raised with such maxims as 'after seven good years, seven lean years follow', kids learn the importance of putting aside money and resources for a 'rainy day'. Instead of looking to be noticed or rescued, they focus on how best to stand on their own feet, and find their own path through life's inevitable difficulties, while supporting others along the way. This is what a cohesive society, populated by genuine adults, offers.

Part of maturing is about taking good care of our resources. The cultures that live close to Earth have always understood this principle. Handling their resources with immense care, they put aside as much as possible to see them through the darkest winters. Extravagance and self-focus have no place because that makes individuals and their communities vulnerable. Nothing is wasted and all the joy is funnelled into family and community, with people looking forward to feast days to *share* food, laughter and dance.

Those travelling in less privileged countries get to see how alive and engaged many of their young people are, how much they know about their land and crops, the flora and fauna and medicinal herbs. Sadly, we have neglected our families and communities in favour of our own agendas and know little about how to grow engaged, vibrant 'villages', or how to nurture and enhance them.

We have also come to distrust restraint, not realising that we sabotage our children's ability to thrive when nothing is denied them. This brutal flattening of our children's experience offers few life tools. And with a teen's immaturity repeatedly affirmed by their peers, their ache to stand out flourishes, until it becomes all-consuming, leaving them lost in self-absorption and self-doubt.

A Lack of Substance and Strength

It's time for some serious recalibration, and not just in our vulnerable young. We need to redefine what adulthood entails and also expose the glittering lies fed to us by marketers.

As we've offered our young a sugar-coated existence for so long, we may fear they don't have any appetite for the truth, for reality, but we underestimate this emerging generation. Sharing his thoughts in an online forum, Adam says that seventh grade was his best year at school. 'I was real high and mighty,' he admits, 'until the best teacher I've ever had checked my attitude. No participation medals in his class.'[11]

Might your bitter pain not be the voice of destiny, might
that voice not become sweet once you understand it?
Hermann Hesse, *If the War Goes On ...*[12]

Time for the Truth

Our kids need us to be kindly and wise truth-tellers. Inter-generational sniping gets us nowhere, nor does the suggestion that those who are older have emerged from a golden age. Some days life is patchy; some days it's a complete disaster. Hopefully there are many transcendent days in between. Let's be honest about life – the good, bad and indifferent bits. A decade ago, English teacher David McCullough gave a short end-of-year address, 'You Are Not Special', to Wellesley High School in Massachusetts. The talk was so powerful it went viral, and it's not hard to see why.

Truth Is Liberating

McCullough urged these young graduates to worry less about impressing people, to approach study with a desire to learn, to genuinely enjoy their journey of discovery and to follow their own path. 'Climb the mountain not to plant your flag,' he offered, 'but to embrace the challenge, enjoy the air and behold the view. Climb it so you can see the world, not so the world can see you.'[13] That this message has been viewed by just under three million YouTube viewers suggests what our young most need from us.

In my work with adolescents, I've found that beneath the attitude and false confidence, our teens yearn for the truth and to be shown a more empowered way of being in the world. Emerging adulthood is an infinitely precious and vulnerable time when we begin to explore all we're capable of. Needing constantly to feel special, and to grab at anything and everything we're drawn to, robs us of this journey of discovery.

Right now, we do have some hefty challenges (and opportunities) but we are equal to the task, as long as we're prepared to make the leap. We can begin by replacing the myth that we're 'special' and 'deserving' with more inclusive and grounded ways of taking our place in the world. It helps if we can recognise whenever the child/adolescent in us comes out to play, when we can catch ourselves slipping into less helpful attitudes and behaviour.

'Special' Can't Deliver

'The true marker of an infantilised people is not being able to accept responsibility for themselves,' reflects Irish writer Fionn Rogan. 'While certainly my generation has inherited a broken system, where it has become increasingly difficult to realise the adult independence afforded to previous generations, it is our responsibility now to ensure that we don't become mere pawns, or victims, of this broken system … the onus is on us to reject our infantilisation and realise our potential. We are not useless. We are not incapable. We are the best chance this country has for the future. There is simply too much at stake for us to lie down and continue to permit ourselves to be infantilised by a broken system.'[14]

This powerful reflection takes us to the heart of why we need to strike back against influences that keep our emerging generations (and many 'mature' people) helpless and hopeless. Unless we assist young people to live and thrive in the real world, we condemn them to half-lives at best.

Time to Push Back

We need also to get rid of all the unhelpful influences that seek to bend us to their will. Those influences use and abuse us and leave us anxious and dependent, addicted to stuff and the opinions of others. 'The greatest need of our time,' 20th-century mystic Thomas Merton suggests, 'is to clean out the enormous mass of mental and emotional rubbish that clutters our mind.'[15]

It's time to discover more effective and powerful ways to deal with life's complexities. What's currently on offer isn't delivering what our kids or the child/adolescent in us need to flourish. This takes us back to the importance of truth-telling, helping our children develop a healthy appetite for seeing things as they are, and not some Disney-fied version of how we or they would like them to be.

Recalibrating

'After growing up to praise that I'd find success so easily and thrive, not knowing what I wanted to do or pursue left me feeling like a waste or a disappointment,' Isla confesses in one online thread. Listening to Bon Iver's 'Holocene' was a profound wake-up call for Isla. Realising she was not always amazing provided her with a 'catharsis for relief and sadness'. This powerful song brings her 'tears of joy or sadness depending on when I hear it', she says.[16] Assisting our kids to embrace the real world helps take the pressure off, as they learn to deal with *real* people.

Exposure to a range of viewpoints, generations and ways of doing things, and being prepared to be proved wrong, helps us form a more considered view of life in all its complexity. As the esteemed Vietnamese Buddhist monk Thich Nhat Hanh reflects, 'For things to reveal themselves to us, we need to be ready to abandon our views about them.'[17]

We need also to encourage our kids to get to know themselves, their strengths and shortcomings and passions. We must help grow their empathy by encouraging them to appreciate how life is for others and find a richly layered life, beyond the need for constant approval.

Why Helping and Gratitude Matter

A study that followed a group of teenagers over ten days noted a lift in their mood whenever they helped others out, even when they weren't feeling great themselves. The impact of reaching out was most dramatic among those struggling with depression. Helping behaviour, the study concluded, 'is most rewarding for people experiencing social anxiety, neuroticism and body dissatisfaction'.[18]

Gratitude also offers a way out of our longing for meaning. Studies involving over 900 teenagers showed that those who used a gratitude journal gave 60 per cent more of their money to charity than teenagers who had no outlet to think about and express gratitude.[19] Activist and high-performance endurance athlete Christopher Bergland admits to working constantly on fine-tuning his 'gratitude radar'. Arming himself with such sayings as 'expect nothing' and 'I do not want what I haven't got' helps him stay on track.[20]

It's high time to reclaim childhood and adolescence, to give our young people and the child/adolescent parts of ourselves all the hope and life skills possible. By so doing, we craft a future with far more promise, creating stronger, more cohesive home environments, workplaces and communities.

Reclaim the Child/Adolescent Within

Vulnerable is not an ideal space to be.

- Where are you most vulnerable to the approval of others?
- If you were to put this vulnerability aside, just for today, how might you react? How does this approach feel?
- 'Wobbly' moments help us recognise when we're feeling vulnerable. What if you were to push through your unsettling feelings? How might it feel on the other side?
- Pay attention to what your inner critic is saying. Where did these unhelpful thoughts/messages come from?
- If your negative self-talk or lack of confidence is deep-seated, talk this through with a trusted friend or family member, or get professional help. Working towards greater awareness with skilled assistance helps lift us out of this crushing loop.

7

Special Snowflakes

With all this focus on ourselves comes an unhealthy sense of entitlement. Is that why so many of us now aspire to be treated like royalty? This may feed our child/adolescent fantasies but we need to realise how ludicrous such thoughts are. No one stands out in every aspect of their life. The more we focus on our needs and goals, the more isolated we feel, as there's little time for valuable self-reflection, or to give to those around us the time and input they deserve. When we can admit to being less than perfect, we take the pressure off and start to progress.

Really, I Am Brilliant

Over three decades from 1976, a large study compared the attitudes of more than three hundred and fifty thousand seventeen- and eighteen-year-olds. Apart from a growing tendency to accumulate possessions, the study authors, Jean Twenge and Tim Kasser, saw a widening gap between what young people wanted and what they were willing to work for.[1]

While it's comfortable to assume it's only our young who've been bitten by the entitlement bug, the truth is less convenient. After a decade examining entitlement and how it manifests in the workplace, psychology professor Janet Mantler concluded that entitlement in the

West is rising across *all* ages. We don't know the full extent of this trend, as almost all research is focused on young people.[2]

Aching to be seen as special leaves us constantly needing to 'perform'. We worry if what we wear, where we go and who we mix with have the desired impact. This effort demands a lot of time and planning. Life also becomes fairly exacting for those we mix with as they are, no doubt, aware of our hunger for attention and endless praise.

Drowning in Debt

Where is this adolescent ache to be special taking us? Sophisticated advertising campaigns and a culture addicted to 'stuff' mean many of us are no longer saving and sometimes spending way more than we earn.

Money expert Martin Lewis blames the 'binge culture' of the West on previous generations. 'We have educated our youth into debt,' he states, 'We got rid of the stigma of borrowing … That has been a terrible thing for society … Nobody took custodial care.'[3] There's also little respect for caretakers and boundary-setters in a culture fuelled by adolescent needs.

The child/adolescent is quick to dismiss those who are mature as dull and boring, and never wants to think too hard or put too much work in. Australian young people in financial straits 'have accrued $2.55 of debt for every dollar earned'.[4] This has created levels of debt among our young, reflects Paul Drum, head of policy at CPA, Australia's peak accounting body, 'that once would have been unthinkable'.[5] In one estimate, 29 per cent of all Australian households were carrying debt 'three or more times their annual disposable income', according to Derek Parker, former editor of *In the Black,* Australia's widest-circulating business magazine.[6]

No Easy Way Out

Where does this indebtedness leave our young?

'I've made quite a few bad decisions in the last few years, before I got this [stable] job, that have hindered my ability to save money or make any sort of dent in my debts [of $30,000],' says Nathan, twenty-five, in one online forum. 'I hate living pay check to pay check, and not being able to make all my payments, when I make good money. I feel like I shouldn't be having such a hard time with this.'[7]

Dan, thirty-one, in this same thread, adds, 'I've spent money willy-nilly for almost eight years straight, [accruing $45,454 debt]. Now that I want to plan for my future, I'm absolutely freaking out internally (as I should be) because of how supremely I've fucked myself over. I've botched it as supremely as Da Vinci drew Mona Lisa. I have a sense of humour about these things … Unfortunately, comedy isn't the trade I ply, so it won't feed me or pay my bills. This is my roundabout plea for help.'[8]

The child/adolescent in us needs constant reassurance. With little life experience or emotional intelligence to call on, we attempt to spend and entertain our way to social success, only to discover that our indebtedness leaves us feeling anything but worthwhile or loved.

'I am $7,000 in credit card debt. I feel sick. I can't focus at work. My spouse is rightfully angry with me. I'm ashamed. I let automatic payments and using my credit card as my debit card backfire on me,' admits Shelley in an online forum on credit card debt. 'I can't eat. I feel horrible and anxious. I've cried over this many times. I work a full-time job. I make sure all my bills are paid – student loans, car, mortgage, etc. But now I have this looming dark cloud.'[9] This isn't what empowerment looks like. The time and effort needed to discharge such levels of debt can prove crushing.

Short on Empathy

When we're so focused on our own needs, we're unlikely to give much thought to others, especially those who rely on our help and compassion. One London School of Economics study of eighteen- to forty-nine-year-olds split participants into two groups. One looked at ads for high-end goods, tabloid photos of celebrities and their luxurious lives, as well as rags-to-riches features, while the control group were shown a series of nondescript ads, newspaper headlines and photos.

All it took was a sixty-second immersion in 'materialistic media' to create a 'significant' rise in anti-welfare attitudes towards those less well-off, which helps explain why there's less interest now in helping those living in poverty or the unemployed. This comes at a time of a swiftly widening divide between those who are well-off and those struggling with rising living costs. In these less certain times many are facing tenuous employment – that is when they are employed at all.[10]

> The most critical time in any battle is not when I'm
> fatigued, it's when I no longer care.[11]
> Craig D Lounsbrough, counsellor

When Well-off Isn't a Great Look

In our child/adolescent rush to acquire as much as we can, rarely do we feel we have enough. American psychologist Paul Piff conducted a series of studies that looked at the attitudes and behaviour of those who are well-off. Entitlement, it seems, is entrenched in *some* of those who have plenty, creating what Piff labelled 'the asshole effect'.

In one experiment, researchers were stationed at crossroads to see if the type of car a person drove affected driver behaviour. Those driving luxury vehicles were four times more likely to cut other drivers off, and three times less likely to stop for someone at a pedestrian crossing.

In a second laboratory experiment, well-off students were more prone to 'stealing or benefitting from things' that weren't theirs than less-privileged students. Those students, when encouraged to *imagine* themselves as wealthier than others, were more likely to help themselves to the sweets set aside for kids in an adjoining lab than the remaining study participants. What emerged from this research was that the less well-off are more generous, even though they have fewer resources.[12]

Harming Others

The child/adolescent in us much prefers to live in its own bubble with little interest in how life is for others. This lack of awareness, often seen in teenagers, is an unhelpful trait in adults. When we cease to take interest in our communities, people start to fall through the cracks. With less empathy, there's a growing assumption that everyone who's fallen on hard times has been negligent or is not deserving of help.

Food security is of rising concern in a number of Western cities, with workers in many city restaurants unable to afford the meals they serve. It's not that these people are hungry per se, but they do struggle to feed themselves and their families. In New York City alone, those workers who receive tips are 30 per cent more likely to be 'food insecure' than those who do not receive tips.[13]

Just as concerning, one in six American children, around 12.5 million in all, are thought to be food insecure. Around 750,000 of these children live in New York City and Los Angeles alone, and these are pre-pandemic figures.[14] While in the UK a staggering one-third of all children, some 4.1 million kids, live in poverty, according to Iain Wilkinson, sociology professor at the University of Kent. Two and a half million of these kids live in homes where the family can't always afford enough food to keep them healthy.[15]

Worse still, 10 per cent of these children now face such severe food shortages that health professionals are seeing the highest figures in half a century for rickets, the bone disorder caused by severe malnutrition.[16] Another study recently found that children living in low-income parts of the UK were around a centimetre shorter by the time they were ten, compared to kids in well-off areas.[17] If we were genuinely connected to the lives and needs of those around us, this wouldn't happen, but with increasing numbers of us busily indulging our every child/adolescent whim, we've become dangerously self-absorbed.

Where Entitlement Leads Us

However superior the entitled may appear, there's a 'flawed self' at work, according to clinical psychologist Leon F Seltzer: 'Hidden beneath their outward bravado' this flawed self 'has been locked up and placed in permanent exile' but sooner or later 'this walled-off self' will 'become all too painfully obvious to those around them'. When the mask slips, the 'many unappealing characteristics' of this individual are evident.[18]

It's shocking to witness an entitled person unmasked. It can also be exceedingly painful to wake up to how detrimental our entitled behaviour has been, but we make progress by daring to let go of painful patterns. When we're caught in a childish loop, we cut ourselves off from the love and nourishment of those closest to us and don't tend to make good decisions. First, though, we must recognise the truth of a situation.

'My father passed ten years ago,' Slater says in an online thread he initiated. 'I remember getting calls from mom, telling me he was getting sicker and sicker. I was getting busier and busier, on the verge of a big promotion. I kept putting my visit off, hoping in my mind he would hold on. He died, and I got my promotion ... WHAT WAS I THINKING? ... and now I am dead inside.'[19] These are deeply painful realisations, but they can also be liberating. When we're nudged out of our infantile self-absorption, we're free to grow, to flourish and to better assist our kids.

Letting Go of Entitlement

I have this sense that we all 'land' in life with a piece of the cosmic jigsaw puzzle – some with a dramatic jigsaw piece, others with a quieter, less obvious piece. We can't all be glorious painters or dancers, great sportsmen or women, but individually and collectively we have the capacity to make a serious contribution to the planet.

> There is a vitality, a life force, a quickening that is translated through you into action, and there is only one of you in all time. This expression is unique, and if you block it, it will never exist through any other medium; and be lost. The world will not have it. It is not your business to determine how good it is, nor how it compares with other expressions. It is your business to keep it yours clearly and directly, to keep the channel open.
> Martha Graham, dancer and choreographer[20]

Our journey towards adulthood takes time, and it demands that we pay attention. Genuine empowerment doesn't happen by allowing the child/adolescent in us to grab the spotlight, by seeking to suck all the air out of a room, or by needing to take all the resources before us. The best way is informed by taking small, considered decisions that lead to larger, more solid decisions that positively impact ourselves and others. As the ancient Chinese philosopher Lao Tzu once suggested, 'Do the difficult things while they are easy, and do the great things while they are small.'

Beyond Special

Our ache to be special can prove crippling. It's important we get to know where we're most vulnerable so we can catch any unhelpful thinking and behaviour before it colours how we see ourselves and how we meet the world.

- What situations or beliefs plunge you back into child/adolescent thinking?
- Where are you most vulnerable to the views of others? How do you respond in these situations? Where do such scenarios leave you?
- How much does all this angst cost you – in both time and energy? Where does this leave your life passions, your relationships and friendships?
- What if you were to shut off your comparison filter for a few days? What would you have room for? What would you be able to let go of?
- How does this possibility make you feel?

Take a moment to read Martha Graham's quote on the previous page once a day, if not more often, to help light your way.

8

The Child/Adolescent Up Close

What is it that keeps us, and our kids, infantilised? How do we push past our immaturity to discover which gifts and passions we might bring to the world, to create a useful life?

In these affluent times, we've developed a complicated relationship between our sense of self and that of our kids. We often fall back on buying 'things' for our children to plug any gaps in our parenting. We forget that the patterns we lay down as parents our kids tend to seize on and take to a new level. They come to place an even greater value on possessions, turning to constant spending to give themselves a lift.

> **In a material world, we're the sum total of our possessions –**
> **they are an intrinsic part of who we are, so we fall into the**
> **habit of buying belonging, if not prestige.**
> Russell W Belk, distinguised research professor[1]

We also tell our kids that they're special and deserving, rather than letting them earn this place, so they soon start to operate from this flawed assumption. Like many experts, Carol Dweck of Columbia University suggests it's far better to praise our children for the *work* they put in, so our kids develop a more grounded, practical sense of their worth.[2]

Allowing younger generations to feel special for no reason reinforces their immature ways. Without the skills to be truly effective in real life situations, too many are ill prepared for personal let-downs, let alone global downturns. The widening gap between their expectations and what life can realistically deliver can set them up for a painful landing in a world now deeply impacted by the pandemic.

Why All This Indulgence?

While it's convenient to blame emerging generations for their immaturity, the dynamic isn't that simple. The boomers have allowed young people to think they're special, to a level that doesn't serve anyone well. They grew up with relatively little, frequently subject to draconian parenting. Being regularly caned or 'belted' and told good children were seen and not heard, they wanted their kids to have easier lives. With the global prosperity that followed, boomer parents showered their kids with all the things they never had, so their children would know they were special. When these kids venture outside the family bubble, reality for some has proved impossibly hard.

Child Predators

Today's young also grow up in a predatory environment, where 'adults' wantonly cultivate them to become serial shoppers. In the US alone, studies suggest they view around 40,000 TV ads a year,[3] with teens averaging around 145 discussions about brands a week.[4] These stark statistics shouldn't surprise us. Marketers have little interest in our children beyond what they can contribute to their bottom line, and countless billions have been made from our kids as a result.

Massive amounts of time and energy are lost to our young as they shell out what money they have, hoping to buy their way to acceptance and love. Sadly, when a child's sense of self is based on their possessions and the opinions of others, their ability to bring new ideas and approaches to the world is compromised and we all miss out. One major study also indicated that those affluent countries that place great store in money and possessions scored lower on UNICEF's child wellbeing index.[5]

> **Put the television in the closet. Cancel your subscription to**
> **glamour and gossip magazines. Stop wandering in the mall**
> **or shopping on the Internet.**
> Tim Kasser, *The High Price of Materialism*[6]

Parents Are Vulnerable Too

Busy parents have also fallen prey to sophisticated marketing as they eagerly embrace the packaged images of what 'cool parenting' is supposed to look like. They work long and hard to buy the much sought-after items their kids crave as a way of proving their love. Grandparents also fuel this trend, with US grandparents spending an average US$179 billion annually on their grandchildren.[7] What essential life skills are learned with all this money and effort?

Purchasing Popularity

It's hard to be a working parent with enough available time, emotional energy and money to give to your kids, while keeping everyone afloat. Receiving lots of possessions growing up, we're likely to continue this pattern of constantly treating ourselves as adults, as we associate 'stuff' with the warm fuzzies we felt when our parents showered us with things.[8]

Adolescence is marked by insecurity, by wondering who we are as individuals. It's not hard to see how appealing it is to simply buy the right gear as a way of creating an acceptable identity, but there is rarely an endpoint to our need for more stuff. Studies suggest that this leads to a tendency to carry more debt,[9] struggle with your finances[10] and experience less 'marital' joy.[11]

> **If any of us were overindulged as children, we were not responsible for that. It is not our fault. However, it is our responsibility as adults to fill any holes left in our skill set or self-awareness from that experience.**
> Jean Illsley Clarke, Connie Dawson, David J Bredehoft,
> *How Much Is Too Much?*[12]

Back to Me

Overindulged kids, studies suggest, turn into self-indulgent adults. As psychologist Dr David J Bredehoft says, far from thriving, these individuals are at risk of 'painful lives' as they struggle with poor boundaries, clinging to their fading dreams of fame, wealth and good looks to get by. They also tend to overeat and overspend, and with little interest in personal growth, meaningful relationships or helping others out, they are woefully ill-equipped for life.[13] With the stark reality of a world gripped by a host of challenges, we've unwittingly set up whole generations to experience far greater mental anguish than need be.

Beyond Spending

Given many of us suffer from the 'affluenza' – from over-spending and the constant, almost mindless need to acquire – what can we do about this? Where do your child/adolescent vulnerabilities kick in? What do your spending patterns look like? Why buy the items you do? Do these objects deliver more peace, joy and contentment?

- When you're feeling fragile, take a moment to step back. Are you really fragile, or simply tired or a little overwhelmed right now? If you're feeling a bit fearful, what are you fearful of?
- Where are your favourite places in your town or city, beyond shopping? When did you last spend time there?
- Is it time for a coffee catch-up with someone whose company you genuinely enjoy? Would you benefit from a trip to a local park, or somewhere else in nature close by?
- Why not put aside your heavy feelings until you've had one or more of these outings, then check in to see how you're tracking?
- Who are the people whose presence feeds you most? Is it time to see more of them?
- What new habits can you cultivate to nurture a genuine sense of self?

9

Living in La La Land

If we grow up with the expectation that we'll constantly be happy and that we're special, we look forward to plenty of excitement, adulation and easily won success at work, in personal relationships and in basically anything we turn our hand to. Rarely do we question whether these goals are realistic or sustainable. Following our lead, many of our children and adolescents end up living in a fantasy world.

Lost in Make-believe

As children we all indulge in a level of make-believe but part of maturing is the ability to see things as they are. In *Ages & Stages: How Children Use Magical Thinking*, Susan A Miller, Professor Emerita of Early Childhood Education at Kutztown University of Pennsylvania, explains that when we're little, we're drawn to fantastical views and explanations. In our early years we tend to interpret the world through our infantile desires by constantly reshaping reality to 'fit' our worldview.

'For example,' Miller explains, 'four-year-old Lily tells her teacher every day that she really wants a pony. One day, Lily decides if she collects a big pile of grass and leaves it on the playground, it will tempt her desired pony to come and eat. Imagine Lily's excitement the next day when the pile of grass is all gone. Lily is convinced that the pony she wants so badly visited overnight. Her plan worked! It does not matter that it was very windy, and the pile of grass really blew away.'[1] Fantasy may have its place in a child's world but our eagerness to cling to fantastical thinking doesn't serve us well as we grow.

Getting Real

If we don't learn to navigate reality, we can end up basking in our own version of reality. Even fairytales offer copious warnings about getting caught out by things that aren't as they seem, urging us to look deep into the heart of a matter and to never take people and situations at face value. Right now, though, it seems that our passion for make-believe is possibly greater than it's ever been.

Early into this new millennium, teachers, counsellors and mental health professionals working with children and teens began to see increasing number of kids saying they wanted to be famous when they grew up. 'Famous for what?' they were asked. Some had a sense of where they might shine bright, many did not. They simply wanted to be famous to access the wealth and adulation that would surely follow.

History is littered with kids who grew up to be exceptional individuals, but growing numbers of celebrities are famous for simply being more 'out there' than the rest of us. The often garish, if not downright bizarre, over-the-top lives of celebrities can make our own lives seem pale by comparison. This trend is having a powerful, increasingly detrimental impact on our young, who are terrified of leading what they may judge as ordinary lives.

Bedazzled

We also started to really focus on children as consumers in the 1990s, which led to a massive increase in movies and sitcoms for small kids.

An explosion in licensed products followed, including branded DVDs, which swiftly found their way into the home, where they were played over and over.

Children's bedrooms became replete with themed toys, books and clothing of their favourite characters. Instead of playing and learning how to connect with other kids and with nature, kids began to stay home, immersing themselves in passive entertainment and branded toys.

The Birth of the Tween

During the 1990s, marketers invented another market segment that they labelled as 'tweens' – those aged eight to twelve, no longer small children and not yet adolescents. They longed to be teenagers, to wear teen clothing and accessories and do the things teens do. Marketers set to work to create yet another lucrative market, exploiting tween aspirations and anxieties.

Already good little consumers, tweens were soon consuming the lives and spin-off products of icons such as Justin Bieber and Miley Cyrus (then the star of *Hannah Montana*). This was further entrenched by the arrival of social media, which served up a daily diet of tween celebrity gossip and regular behind-the-scenes glimpses into the privileged lives of tween stars. According to clinical psychologist Joanna Lipari, suddenly tweens, who had no power or money of their own, came to see being famous as the road to a better life.[2] Almost overnight, there was a growing ache to be famous.

In Search for Fame and Fortune

Looking at TV shows over a fifty-year period, the *Rise of Fame* study noted that when tweens aged nine to eleven were asked what mattered, 'community values' were a seen as essential until 2007, when a 'fairly dramatic change' took place in their aspirations. Qualities such as kindness were swiftly displaced by a desire for wealth and fame.[3]

'When being famous and rich is much more important than being kind to others, what will happen to kids as they form their values and their identities?' asks Yalda Uhls, a UCLA doctoral student in developmental psychology and lead author of the *Rise of Fame* study. Co-author Dr Patricia Greenfield, from UCLA department of psychology, also raises concerns about how unrealistic these tween aspirations are, given tweens have little, if any, idea of what is needed to be famous.

This switch to seeking celebrity was also noted by the UK's Learning and Skills Council from around 2006. Heavily influenced by such shows as *Big Brother* and *The X Factor*, 16 per cent of British teenagers aged sixteen to nineteen believed they were on track to becoming famous. Eleven per cent of this sample told of how they were prepared to ditch their studies to make this happen.[4]

Spending our formative years stargazing doesn't stand us in great stead for the rest of our lives. With little time to gain key life skills such as resilience, tenacity, emotional intelligence, critical thinking, focus and self-control, our lives drift past, lost in vague longings. We spend most, if not all, we earn trying to satisfy our yearning for more glamour, more things, more attention, while struggling with the realities of grown-up life.

Some of us spend an inordinate amount of time trying to make real life fit our fantasies. Some end up feeling hopeless while others are plain angry or sad. The vulnerable child/adolescent is left feeling lost when faced with the everyday issues and things needing to be done. Unable to make the leap, our childish self looks for someone to rescue us, to deliver on our dream.

Reality Needn't Bite

When we raise kids ready to be adults knowing wishes aren't enough to get by, we give them a great start. They're well aware of the need to work hard, to plan and strategise, to follow through if they want their goals to eventuate. They also know they are not cowed by failure.

'Shallow men believe in luck or in circumstance. Strong men believe in cause or effect,' US essayist and poet Ralph Waldo Emerson reminds us. We grow up to become less vulnerable, more resilient, more grounded, more able to meet the many wonderful, and sometimes complex situations, the future presents. Failing to do so leaves us forever on the back foot. 'Armed with endless expectations, this new generation of "emerging adults" now in their twenties is being set up for disappointment,' psychologist Jeffrey Arnett warns. 'The dreary, dead-end jobs, the bitter divorces, the disappointing and disrespectful children … none of them imagine that this is what the future holds.'[5]

Celebrity Worship

Psychologist James Houran has come up with what he calls 'celebrity worship syndrome'. In one study, 20 per cent of participants casually checked out the lives of stars for 'entertainment/social' reasons. A further 10 per cent had an 'intense' connection with a celebrity, to a level that was becoming addictive. One per cent of the sample had an extreme connection to certain celebrities, bordering on the pathological, resulting in stalking and self-harm. Celebrity fans were 'significantly' more likely to experience anxiety and depression, as well as difficulty in relating to others. This study also noted that if celebrity worship is left unchecked, it's likely to become more intense over time. A passing interest in a star can become all-consuming and have very real negative consequences for fans.[6]

With ready access to celebrity lifestyles and gossip on social media and in the wider media, it's not hard for the child/adolescent in us to get our celebrity fix. American psychologist Philip Cushman suggests we focus on celebrities as a way of soothing our 'empty self'.[7] Yet our over-identification with celebrities and their larger-than-life lifestyles can also contribute to our feeling inadequate. If we're caught in this loop, we need to move on. How many of us have no real idea who we are, beyond the constant tinsel and titillation marketers and celebrities and social media platforms offer us?

When Life Takes a Different Turn

Any desire we may have to live in our own version of Hollywood heaven is little more than pure escapism that leaves us unprepared for real life. This is evident in the pain people are now experiencing, with reduced job markets and reduced disposable income. The gap between the expectations we've been encouraged to hold and our current situation is, in some cases, impacting on our mental, physical and emotional wellbeing.

This pain is felt most keenly among our young, as they've been primed to expect an abundance of choices and to be successful in all they undertake. In one pre-COVID-19 study, participants of this emerging generation were asked if they agree with the statement 'I am very sure that someday I will get to where I want to be in life'. Alarmingly, 96 per cent of this sample felt *all* their goals were within reach.[8]

> **Wasn't until recently that I realized I accomplish the same things everyone does day to day, and my life isn't the glamorous adventure I believed it would be.**
> Glen, *Reddit* forum[9]

What about our duty of care towards our young? Have we unwittingly misled them, causing them unnecessary pain? Renowned sociologist Richard Sennett believes this is so. After interviewing a range of twenty-somethings working in financial services, new media and IT, Sennett observed, 'Everyone thinks they are going to be the next Martha Lane Fox, but they are learning very quickly that all these fantasy worlds just aren't going to happen.'[10]

Having It All

Has our determination to 'have it all' ended up selling us and our kids short? Luck and looks come and go, as do job opportunities, romance, friendships and more. In the West, we expect to be the ones who always come out on top but we rarely admit to how delicate our life chances and choices can be, or how ephemeral any success we may have. Sadly, too many of this generation will end up disappointed in themselves and their lives and, through no fault of their own, they lack the life skills needed to steer a steady course through the many challenges of our hugely complex world.

A Wiser Outlook

The ancients were acutely conscious of the changeable nature of life and valued stoicism, the ability to stand firm through thick and thin. They spoke openly about how every person was subject to the wheel of fortune and were aware that at times they would experience abundance and success, but sadness and/or misfortune could follow.

They didn't waste time and energy complaining or hiding under the duvet, hoping life's messier moments would magically disappear. They focused on finding the best way through with the resources they had. It's not that the ancients never aspired to do wonderful things – they did, and achieved a great deal. They also knew it wasn't wise to live purely for peak moments, as these don't represent the sum total of a life.

Daily, we're encouraged to indulge our every whim, which leaves us with an overarching need to be viewed as noteworthy at every turn, only to become victim to our expectations and suffer more than we need to.

Staying Stuck

It helps to get a sense of how this pain of disappointment feels up close, especially for our young. Suzi talks in an online thread about her need to be seen as 'special', and how often it undermines her sense of achievement: 'I get into a depression when a new kid does things better than me, started younger than me, or [is] making better progress than me. I then feel really down about it and can get into a depression, when I just want to do nothing anymore.'[11]

When we lack a mature perspective, we judge everything that happens to us as a personal win or disappointment. But life is far more intricate, and such a stark outlook doesn't allow us to credit others for their wins or to take genuine pleasure in life working out for them. As our ability to connect meaningfully and joyfully with others drops away, so too does all the support, nourishment and inspiration such moments of connection offer. Imprisoned by a cloying sense of entitlement, we come adrift from those around us, only to rail against the resulting isolation. But it doesn't have to be this way for you, or your children.

Getting Real

Whenever you get lost in an ache for instant fame and/or fortune, it's a sign your child/adolescent self is feeling fragile. Why not use these reflections to help you find your way forward?

- Where might you have fallen victim to the lure of fame?
- What is driving your need to excel? Is it a deep-seated passion, or a need to be noticed, to have others adore you, to see you as some kind of star?
- If you're heading towards an unhealthy reliance on how others see you and on wealth and fame, take a step back. What other possibilities await you in the wings?
- What's the worst thing that could happen, should you take the road less travelled? What gifts might be there for you?
- Which of your inner resources need more work?
- How can you better flex your resilience muscle?
- Who can you rely on to be truthful and supportive? What can you learn from these individuals? Do you need to spend more time in their company?

10

Great Expectations

Primed to see the world as endlessly bountiful, our childish self is always searching for the many must-have items we're convinced we need, not realising our very restlessness undermines us. 'Don't commit, don't be dependent, stay loose. Loyalty is very low on this list [right now],' sociologist Richard Sennett reflects. 'But if you think dependence is bad, what you produce is a damaged human being.'[1]

Genuine flexibility is only possible when built on solid foundations. 'In a liquid modern life there are no permanent bonds,' esteemed sociologist Zygmunt Bauman reminds us, 'and any that we take up for a time must be tied loosely so that they can be untied again, as quickly and as effortlessly as possible, when circumstances change.'[2] This level of fluidity may seem fun, but ultimately it leaves us hopelessly adrift.

> **Everlasting pain is often caused by the**
> **pursuit of fleeting pleasure.**[3]
> Mokokoma Mokhonoana, satirist and philosopher

Maturity requires having the patience to spend the time needed to gather a whole range of useful skills. In these more affluent times, we're all used to having our needs swiftly taken care of, failing to realise that a world of such bounty is unsustainable, both environmentally and socially.

Easy Solutions Rarely Deliver

Our immature selves have become accustomed to taking the 'easy' route, rather than thinking situations through, thus compounding our unhappiness with our incomplete approach. 'When the adolescent allows unhappy feelings to "think" for him or her,' psychologist Carl E Pickhardt warns, 'what "feels" best to make things better is often exactly what will make things worse.'[4]

Easy solutions rarely take into account the complexities of a situation. We learn little from our life experiences and we don't get to mature. Easy routes certainly don't help us problem-solve.

Difficult Can Deliver

When we think back to how unstable and confusing our teen years were, we're reminded of just how uncomfortable adolescence can be. Yet this very discomfort has real value if we allow it to help us push past our challenges, so we can learn and grow. As poet and visionary Khalil Gibran puts it, 'Your pain is the breaking of the shell that encloses understanding.'[5]

Too often our child/adolescent selves prefer to distract ourselves from the difficulties ahead. When we fail to tackle what needs tackling, we fail to grow, and our life becomes one of avoidance, rather than transcendence.

I'm Bored

Contrary to how we may feel when bored, boredom can also be immensely useful. Studies suggest that boredom helps us be more imaginative and productive and can also give our overstimulated brains a much-needed break.

Our children and adolescents don't tend to get these essential nuances, so they can't benefit from them unless we help them out by modelling grown-up behaviour and by keeping things real. 'That's right,' Bernadette tells her daughter Bee in the novel *Where'd You Go, Bernadette*. 'You are bored. And I'm going to let you in on a little secret about life. You think it's boring now? Well, it only gets more boring. The sooner you learn it's on you to make life interesting, the better off you'll be.'[6]

Instead of helping our kids resolve issues, we distract them, yet they'd be far better served if we were to coach them through a difficulty. As Scottish psychiatrist and expert in psychosis RD Laing reminds us, 'Pain in this life is unavoidable, but the pain we create by avoiding pain is avoidable.'

Impatience Isn't the Answer

We must be cautious about instant and easy, as instant can and does bring us undone. Mid-March 2020, the Australian government allowed people to access their superannuation (pension) accounts before the mandated retirement age to help out those in financial difficulty due to COVID-19. This enabled them to withdraw up to $10,000 in one fiscal year. A staggering $1.3 billion was withdrawn from personal pension funds over the first eight weeks alone. A follow-up survey indicated that those withdrawing money spent an average of $3000 more than usual in just a couple of weeks after accessing their funds.[7]

A closer examination of this data revealed that 40 per cent of those withdrawing funds had experienced no drop in their income, so they weren't experiencing any kind of hardship. What did they spend their superannuation payout on? In spite of being told that if this $10,000 were left in their pension fund, it would be worth $40,000 to $50,000 in coming years, four out of ten people used this money on gambling and alcohol or to buy furniture. Only 22 per cent of people used their money to buy groceries and essentials, while 14 per cent used it to repay personal debt.[8]

There's a natural impatience in children and teenagers, a quality that some marketers cleverly exploit. Why grow up when you can linger forever in a carefree space where all your needs can be swiftly met? Why fend for yourself? Such messages appeal to our immature self, which wants what it wants *now*. Yet the child/adolescent in us is just as swiftly 'over' a must-have item, rapidly moving on to the next object of our desire, and the next. This may at first seem fun but sooner or later we have to deal with the fallout. Our impatience robs us of numerous chances to reflect, strategise and come up with a workable plan.

Looking to the Future

When we're addicted to instant, we diminish our capacity to think things through or to consider the long term. Without the stabilising influence of proper planning, we're more likely to feel anxious about our future as we lack the life skills to steer a consistent course.[9]

To get over our many expectations, we need to push past the constant, often needling demands of our child/adolescent self and learn to appreciate the power of patience, of *slowly* building towards a goal. As counsellor Craig D Lounsbrough, who has worked in psychiatric hospitals and related settings, notes, 'It is the restraint of patience that yields the magnificent in life.'

Being Grounded Matters

Those who understand there will always be mean and lean times are far better placed to bounce back from disappointment. Instead of wasting time and energy in complaining and blaming, they're not afraid to work hard on finding an effective way through difficult situations.

The grown-up knows we can't always be happy, that we won't always succeed and that whole aspects of life are mundane: someone has to clean the house, grocery shop and mow the lawn. It's often our daily routine that helps see us through our worst chapters. Having to make the effort to get out of bed and walk the dog or feed the children helps keep us going on the days we'd rather hide away. As the great Zen saying reminds us, 'Before enlightenment; chop wood, carry water. After enlightenment: chop wood, carry water.'

When we make the effort to attend to our daily routine, we start to discern the extraordinary in those things we deemed ordinary. Writer Willa Cather describes this subtle process as where our perceptions are 'made finer, so that, for a moment, our eyes can see and our ears can hear [the subtleties of] what is there around us'.[10]

It's Good to Be Curious

Curiosity is another key to a more profound way of seeing. American–Irish novelist Tana French captures the essence of this in *Broken Harbour*: 'I have always been caught by the pull of the unremarkable, by the easily missed, infinitely nourishing beauty of the mundane.'

Stuck in an immature mindset, the child/adolescent in us hasn't yet learned to seek out the nuance in everything we do. By simply remaining vulnerable and confused, we end up suffering unnecessarily. 'I was a talented musician and my teachers constantly told me how I was made for greatness and that one day I'd be famous,' admits Jack in a chat room discussion on discovering you're not special. 'I really tried, but also was a realist, and got a normal career. Now, I struggle with anxiety over the monotony and basic-ness of life. When I have a full day of working, climbing, house stuff and relaxy time, I feel absolutely worthless that I didn't accomplish Oprah type shit [set the world alight] that day.'[11] Our inflated expectations undermine us, robbing us of the joy in each moment. Programmed to perform, we may well find ourselves playing the chameleon, the entertainer, the fool.

Working with Vulnerability

We need to stay grounded or we can end up dangerously exposed. Early in World War II, the Royal Navy was at a loss to explain why, when a boat went down in the freezing waters of the North Sea, a disproportionate number of older sailors in their forties survived while many younger sailors did not. The Navy asked the distinguished educator and founder of Gordonstoun School in Scotland, Kurt Hahn, to take a closer look at the situation.

Hahn discovered that older sailors had already been through a series of difficult life situations, which had honed their ability to survive the huge challenge of staying alive in icy-cold water. These seasoned sailors had a much greater *inner* capacity to help them handle truly stretching situations than did the younger sailors.

> **The more risks you allow children to take, the better they learn to take care of themselves.[12]**
> Roald Dahl, author and screenwriter

Hahn put together a successful program to assist younger sailors to develop a greater range of solid life skills. Countless younger men went on to survive sinkings in the same numbers as their older counterparts. This was the start of the internationally acclaimed Outward Bound program.[13]

Seeking Fulfilment

A more grounded approach to life helps us see more clearly how others move through difficulties, and to learn from them and become stronger. However, when life gets tough, the child/adolescent in us wants to push back, to sit down and sulk, to complain about how unfair life is, thus signalling we've just slipped into victim mode. Like little kids, we look for someone or something to rescue us, instead of moving carefully and purposefully through a disappointment. Following our lead, our kids fall into this same destructive loop, which frequently tips into loneliness and depression.[14]

Growing Our Emotional Responses

We also need to grow our emotional intelligence. 'It is through dealing with ... emotional upheavals,' sociologist Frank Furedi reminds us, 'that young people learn how to manage risks and gain an understanding of their strengths and weaknesses.' However, he observes, 'many youngsters are subject to influences [including over-protective parenting] that promote childish behaviour', leaving emerging adults reliant on 'levels of support and supervision that are more suitable for much younger children'.[15] Whenever life fails to meet our expectations as adults, we perpetuate our infantile behaviour when we immediately reach for something to make us feel better – be it sex, shopping, alcohol or other substances.

Don't Drag Others Down

Sociologist Richard Sennett also cautions us against burdening others with oneself, falling into confessional mode and forcing them to wade through our every up and down. We've all had friends who complain endlessly about every little thing. When this happens, our infantile self is indulging in far too much airplay and wasting the precious time we have with those we care about.

Sometimes we simply need to go it alone for a while. If we can easily sort a slight or mishap, why waste so much energy in complaining? Why squander precious time boring those we care about with the endless dramas and minutiae of our lives, when there are so many more uplifting subjects to discuss?

Wired to Connect

To build a fulfilling life, we need to find more meaningful ways to connect. From earliest times, despite mammoths, plagues, pestilence and war, we have relied on each other to survive and thrive. Over millennia we've come to value inclusion and cooperation and the forging of strong connections. That's why it's so painful when we're cast out of our family or friendship group, or dismissed from our workplace, as we no longer have access to this wider support.

Belonging is fundamental to who we are. Recent research underlines this, finding the greatest stressors we face as humans are threats to our 'social acceptance, esteem and status'.[16] What has this to do with our expectations? 'Without a stable sense of value,' reflects Tony Schwartz, CEO of The Energy Project, 'we don't know who we are and we don't feel safe in the world.'[17]

Drifting Apart

With great expectations comes a willingness to take short cuts and to use them to get where we want to be. Put simply, our neediness messes with the social fabric.[18] It fractures relationships, leaving everyone disappointed. 'I always want to be the best at everything or feel special,' Shivra admits in an online chat about the ups and downs of needing to be special. 'For example, I become jealous when there are people in my class with the same hobbies. It makes me somehow inferior.'[19]

To move beyond this self-defeating loop, we need to know how we react in moments of insecurity. 'All the things you thought defined your being are actually shared among millions,' reflects Noah in an online discussion around moving on from 'special'. 'It's a bittersweet realization on one hand. You can feel comfort in being able to relate to other people on the other hand.'[20]

When we recognise our defensive patterns, we can work on them and find healthier ways to move on, to grow ourselves up. There is room for each of us to shine, but we need to choose our goals advisedly. Or, as Lucas puts it in yet another thread on the subject, 'You are special … The only problems come when we begin to feel like we are more special than those around us. We don't get to be more special … So yeah, feel special. Encourage others to feel that way too.'[21]

Growing Up

Maturing is also about developing a wider perspective and being willing to go the distance with others, learning to support and encourage them. 'When I was young, I used to think, "I am the most intelligent, and exceptional person." This feeling stemmed from the constant appreciation of my parents,' Adan reflects in one online discussion about the journey from special to realistic. 'And from this appreciation I interpreted that as what you called [being the] "chosen one".

'Then something unexpected happened. I grew up. I started receiving criticism. No matter what I did and how good I did it, I always received criticism from someone. Eventually, I started believing I am not exceptional after all.'[22] As an avid reader and now a civil engineer, Adan has learned that life has its share of 'suffering', and that we're all good at some things and hopeless at others, and he's comfortable with this.

It's unsettling to realise we're not as special as we thought. For Eli, sharing his thoughts in a different thread, this came 'when I realised that people telling me I'm one in a million, meant that there's actually loads of me out there in the world'.[23] Striving always to be 'special' soaks up a lot of time and energy, feeding unhelpful expectations. Once we let go of this impulse, we often experience a tangible sense of relief. 'Eventually I realised that the key to being unique and special wasn't doing it on purpose,' admits Olivia in the same forum, 'but just being yourself.'[24] When you reach this level of acceptance, you liberate yourself from expectations that often weren't yours and are free to lead a more grounded, satisfying life, while still pursuing new and, at times, seriously ambitious goals.

> **Never understood why parents tried to push the idea that their kids were all special snowflakes. They've lived long enough to think otherwise.**
>
> Matt, *Reddit* forum[25]

If we're smart, we'll find something more sustainable than overblown expectations to see us through. To thrive, we also need the support of good friends; the energy and will to explore new passions; to remain interested in other people and places, and benefit from the joy and insights they bring; to contribute to and draw on the resources in our community; and to be sufficiently engaged in life to be open to learning new things.

These many rich textures and more are available to us when we trade our off-the-chart expectations for more authentic goals. As the wise 13th-century mystic and poet Rumi advised, 'Let yourself be silently drawn by the strange pull of what you really love ... This is a subtle truth. Whatever you love you are.'

Getting Real

Put a little time aside to study the 'must-have' items on your to-do list.

- If you had to cut this list in half, what could you let go of? How does that feel?
- If there were a fire or emergency, which of these items would you leave behind? Contemplating this, is there anything else on the list that could go?
- What else might you do with this freed-up time and money?

11

When Work Isn't Working

Our intense longing to be seen as special is spilling over into our workplaces, placing additional pressure on our managers and co-workers as they wrestle with how much personal attention is, in fact, enough. Business trainer Jennie Roberson sees an 'epidemic' of indulgence in organisations – employees who are constantly catered to. While it's convenient to call out millennials here, Roberson is quick to point out that this draining level of indulgence 'isn't confined to one generation'.[1]

> **Dignity does not consist in possessing honours,**
> **but in deserving them.**
> Aristotle, philosopher and polymath

Just because we've been in a workplace for a while doesn't give us the right to let the attention-grabbing child/adolescent within steal the show. Online forums on working life woes are full of nightmarish stories of entitled co-workers of all ages who delight in discord and in working to suit themselves.

The Entitlement Factor

The president of Pinnacle Leadership Solutions, Amy Shannon, suggests entitlement flourishes when employee expectations are met without those individuals being made fully accountable for their work, and/or when managers fail to properly supervise staff.[2] How can a person or team improve when they're not aware of what's required, or what the consequences are if they fall short?

We've all encountered brattish, deliberately destructive behaviour in the workplace – people withholding information, ignoring deadlines, creating toxic fiefdoms and bending the rules. Entitled individuals at work waste precious time, shatter trust and cooperation, and undermine an organisation's ability to build momentum.

Often, disruptive individuals are tolerated, as managers don't have the time, energy or experience to deal with the constant dramas, so all the good work others do is continually sabotaged. Hoping these characters will come right doesn't get us anywhere, as entitled individuals have little or no interest in changing or improving, or toeing the line.[3]

Entitlement also manifests in unrealistic expectations – demanding a severance package even though you've just been fired, or pressing for a bonus even though you've failed to meet your target.[4] Entitled individuals don't hesitate to burn through all the goodwill on offer. What they're focused on is how far they can push things. Immature individuals want what *they* want, whether or not it's possible, practical or they have earned it.

Calling Entitlement Out

Entitled behaviour is best nipped in the bud but managers are often reluctant to deal with conflict, as child/adolescents are well practised at spectacular tantrums and/or malicious gossip to seize attention and undermine. And they're not hard to spot. Self-obsessed individuals are not 'part of a secret underground club', leadership consultant Cindy

Wahler reminds us. 'They are noisy, obvious and stand out. They display a righteous sense of injustice.'[5] There is no reason for any manager worth their salt to retreat. Let a child/adolescent off the hook and everyone is negatively impacted; emboldened, these characters press on, until their bad behaviour is firmly entrenched.

Healthy workplaces actively encourage people to look beyond their personal agendas and work for the wider good. The workers get to see the value in *everyone* being accountable for their actions, and there's a tangible ease when everyone can do what they do best and *enjoy* the process. There has to be a willingness to get clear about where your work culture is right now and to start afresh, if need be, by laying down new ground rules. Healthy work cultures ensure everyone is crystal clear about what's expected, and only those who work *with* the organisation are rewarded.

Appearance Over Substance

Our over-the-top performance culture promotes values that lead to immature, often toxic, behaviour. In studies of a number of corporations, social critic Christopher Lasch noted a distinct change in what organisations had come to value. 'Professional advancement', he stated, has become less about one's abilities or loyalty to the company, than about 'visibility, momentum, personal charm, and impression management'. This 'dense interpersonal environment' encourages and advances those who are self-focused and who exhibit 'an anxious concern with the impression one makes on others'.[6]

Another intriguing study of MBA graduates found those lacking high marks or multiple job offers were more likely to wear expensive clothes and accessories to give them the *appearance* of unquestionable success.[7] This trend was evident in a study of first-year uni students, who were more likely to wear 'university-branded' clothing and accessories than fourth-year students.[8]

Such superficial gestures may buy us short-term attention, but the price and quality of our top-of-the-range suit and accessories can't possibly deliver long-term satisfaction and career success. These are the solutions our immature selves seek in a desperate bid to compensate for our lack of professional experience and/or life skills.

If we genuinely hope to make progress, we need to let go of easy solutions and behaviour, create more productive outcomes at work, think harder and more thoughtfully about what we do so we can be more strategic and more creative in our approach to work. And managers need to refocus staff to be solution-oriented, to make it clear tantrums and high drama won't work.

Absenteeism

Entitlement also manifests in the soaring rates of absenteeism, which costs Australia alone over $32.5 billion annually.[9] One survey of some 100 organisations found Monday was the most likely day employees called in sick, almost twice that of any other working day.[10] Increasingly, the provision of ten days' annual sick leave, designed as a safety net for employees who are unwell, is now seen by many as their rightful leave, with some staff now taking the full ten days every year, regardless of whether they're ill or not.[11]

Part of growing up is understanding the importance of fair play: that when we fail to do our work, we let ourselves and others down and create an even greater workload for our co-workers. Fully fledged adults are more sensitive to the needs of those around them, of their responsibilities and the importance of being reliable and doing their bit so as not to place undue pressure on others.

Fair Play Works Both Ways

Employers also need to be fair about their expectations, to be loyal and trustworthy and to provide strong leadership. Studies show the workplaces that actively encourage their staff are more successful than unsupportive cultures. Good leadership at work is currently in short supply, generating more fear and tension than necessary. Unhealthy work cultures make it harder for people to do a good job, let alone enjoy what they do.

The American Psychological Association estimates that workplace stress costs the country US$500 billion annually, with around 550 million days lost to on-the-job stress. Somewhere between 60 and 80 per cent of US workplace accidents are caused by stress, with 80 per cent of workers needing to visit a doctor due to their stress levels.[12]

Good leaders are well-rounded grown-ups, not overconfident individuals in shiny suits with poor people skills. Immature leaders don't serve themselves or others well. Their lack of wisdom and experience is seen in the way they reach for swift, often poorly thought-out solutions, or when they pitch for popularity rather than steering a more considered course. They tend to be more interested in their careers than in getting the job done, and are more likely to set targets related to what *they* want to achieve, rather than the realities of the marketplace.

Mature leaders understand their job is to build firm foundations, to be clear about expectations, and to help their team produce a solid, sustainable effort. Should they operate in a stagnant market, instead of setting impossible targets, they have the good sense to work with their team to cut costs and streamline products, while planning a revitalised set of offerings for when the market improves. Not everyone has the strength or experience to achieve this.

Unrealistic Expectations

Inflated employee expectations also don't help a workplace culture. How much encouragement can we reasonably expect from our employers and when do we just need to knuckle down? Prior to millennials entering the workplace, mentoring and coaching was thin on the ground, if it was available at all. Now, with millennials accounting for 50 per cent of the workplace (and set to reach 75 per cent of workers within a handful of years), we have a substantial presence at work, eager for group activities and plenty of dialogue.

This approach can be time-consuming and isn't always productive, given the many pressures on managers and the time available in a working day. Whatever support we offer in the workplace must be sustainable. We need to be clear about how much one-on-one engagement managers and team leaders can realistically provide.

What is often missing from this equation is the question of whether employers' effort will encourage more loyalty and longevity, or will current trends continue, where, according to America's PGI Data, six out of ten millennials will leave their workplace within three years?[13]

This same study noted that 71 per cent of millennials want their co-workers to be their 'second family', with 75 per cent expecting mentors to help ensure they're successful in whatever they undertake at work.[14] Millennials want to feel their job is helping them improve in some way.[15] Few would disagree with the value of mentoring and support, but we also need to be mindful of not slipping into the child/adolescent mindset of looking only to what's in work for us. The fully formed adult understands the importance of reciprocity and what our employer might reasonably expect in return.

Stepping Up

There are also times when we need to turn up to work regardless, as seen with our brave health workers from across the generations during the pandemic. Even when they were tired, terrified for their own safety and worried about their ability to cope, our health professionals did what was needed for the greater good. They displayed true selflessness and courage.

We all need to take a closer look at our workplace expectations and practices to identify those that are undermining our capacity to see a bigger, more nuanced picture. Perhaps we would be better served to consider what we can actively contribute to the social fabric at work, be it setting up a lunchtime yoga class or office bake-off, a pets' day at work, an evening ten pin bowling, or engaging with a local charity out of hours. How can we mentor someone in a more junior role, rather than focusing simply on what work can deliver us?

Need to Move On

One of the many hallmarks of adolescence is its restlessness and the determination to head off the moment things get bumpy. Moving on at work is a fact of life. Increasingly, it's a spur-of-the-moment decision, which often confounds managers and co-workers, as there's frequently no apparent reason for this decision, other than the 'need of a change'. Sociologist Richard Sennett tells of one foreman in a high-tech Boston bakery, Rodney Everts, who was perplexed at the behaviour of some of his staff. 'When somebody tells me there's no future here,' Everts reflected, 'I ask what they want. They don't know; they tell me you shouldn't be stuck in one place.'[16]

Can we afford this level of restlessness, and what is the impact of this 'churn' on work cultures? Millennials alone are now changing their jobs in the decade after graduating from college, twice as often as Generation X. This is significant, given that the cost of employee replacement is possibly as high as six to nine months of that employee's salary.[17] Added to which, every departure leaves a tear in the work fabric.

This is not about forcing people to stay on at work so much as being aware of the impact our presence or absence has on those we work with, and on our organisation's work culture, and being respectful of this. If we were more invested in our workplaces, what depth of knowledge might we acquire to be truly excellent at what we do? As Everts pointed out, 'There is something puzzling about the sheer impulse to get out.'[18]

The decision to leave may at first feel exhilarating but our constant restlessness can also create a lot of stress and uncertainty. Living life on the run and struggling with the insecurity from constantly moving from job to job can make us forget that we take ourselves (and our baggage) with us wherever we go.

First Things First

As we seek to progress it's essential we don't fall back on childlike fantasies of needing to be pampered and/or rescued at work, and instead focus on staying grounded and appreciating how much a more consistent approach to our job can deliver. 'The buzz about company culture continues to get louder,' reflects Mark McClain, CEO of SailPoint, which employs over 700 workers. 'Whether it's nap pods, private chefs, indoor tree houses or over-the-top parties, tech companies are pulling out all of the stops in hopes of creating the coolest corporate culture around. But flashy perks don't equal a good corporate culture ... Ultimately, it is the beliefs and behaviours that permeate your organization that are the essence of culture. Before you start picking out the perfect spot for your espresso and craft beer bar, it's important to recognise that culture begins – and can also end – with your values.'[19]

Masking Competence

When the child/adolescent is running the show, we tend to live in a bubble, largely unaware of our shortcomings. This 'illusory superiority' can leave us with a tenuous grasp on reality. Cornell psychologist David

Dunning and graduate student Justin Kruger first examined the 'illusion of confidence' in a number of settings, from undergraduate performance to how hobbyists fare at the gun range. They found those with the least knowledge tended to be the most overconfident, as they only had a superficial grasp of what was needed.[20]

Being unaware of the gaps in our knowledge or experience can leave us looking foolish. At worst, we can harm ourselves and others. The discrepancy between confidence and competence has real impacts. During the lead-up to the global financial crisis, those questioning the prevailing belief that the markets were self-correcting and thus safe were frequently shouted down. The global financial crisis hit, sparked by the subprime mortgage racket, causing a write-down of billions of dollars and leaving an estimated thirty million people unemployed worldwide, with countless others losing their life savings.[21]

How could so many experts have got this so wrong? Hubris is a core characteristic of the child/adolescent, who is unable or unwilling to accept wider or differing points of view. We see this in top leadership positions, including those of our politicians, who are quick to quash salary increases for others, while being very careful never to leave an increase in their remuneration to chance. Securing unwarranted massive salaries and bonuses, frequently at the expense of those down the line, is just what every child/adolescent hopes for.

Where are the adults when these kinds of decisions are being made, and how can we sustain a strong work culture in such conditions? Business trainer Jennie Roberson suggests we need a culture where the consequences of inappropriate behaviour and goals are clearly spelt out.[22]

We also need to be wary of the child/adolescent's love of short cuts: they're always looking for the easiest solution, as seen in the current trend towards asset stripping and quick profits over solid, sustainable business growth. The best way to succeed is to work hard, to gain appropriate qualifications, to be willing to fill the gaps in our knowledge, and to be open to new approaches – in other words, to grow up.

A More Grounded Approach

In a world struggling to move beyond the pandemic, there's an urgent need for each of us to get back to basics at work and to be more aware of those situations where the child/adolescent in us is aching to be rescued, to be singled out.

Perhaps the best question we can ask is, what's most needed at work right now, and how can we help bring this about? Some work cultures are pushing back against entitlement and moving in a more equitable direction. 'The compensation packages offered by many companies are changing,' Amy Shannon tells us, where 'employees are paid for contribution, not status'.[23]

The way out of our need to seize the limelight at work is to be a *genuine* asset to our organisation. This means being a good team player, working comfortably alongside others, getting clear about our strengths and weaknesses, and actively improving our skills. As always, we need fully fledged adults to lead the way, to stand firm and remain grounded in difficult times, and to make the right calls, even when under pressure.

First, we need to address, if not weed out, self-serving individuals, and to choose grown-ups as leaders who are able to call out bad behaviour, to model the desired skills and attitudes, and to mentor and serve others. We can then begin to create what Jonathan Haidt of New York University's Stern School of Business calls 'elevation' – the active generation of positive emotions, such as 'awe, gratitude and admiration'. By deliberately nurturing a tangible warmth and openness, we help motivate others to be more outward-looking, more willing to do the right thing.

In his studies, Haidt found that the leaders who were genuinely self-sacrificing captured the hearts of those who worked with them, inspiring them to great loyalty and commitment. A further study by Daan van Knippenberg at Rotterdam School of Management indicates that such leaders are also more productive, because their staff trust them implicitly. People are inspired by these leaders because they're also good at what they do.[24]

Make More Progress at Work

If you're feeling vulnerable at work right now, take some time to consider your weak spots – and your stock responses in tricky situations.

- Where does your child/adolescent come out to play at work?
- How well do its responses serve you?
- What people and situations fuel your uncertainty?
- What personal or professional skills of yours need fine-tuning?
- How can you achieve this?
- What can you give back?

Or perhaps you're dealing with entitled staff, feeling intimidated or overwhelmed.

- Nip each and every issue kindly, but firmly, in the bud.
- Be clear about your expectations and follow through on maintaining the standards and output you require.
- Problematic individuals at work need encouragement as well as constructive criticism. Help them progress by catching them doing things right.

12

Grandiose Plans

A couple of years back, while holidaying in Alaska, one of my girlfriends got talking to an American couple. When they discovered my friend was from Australia, the wife smiled brightly, saying, 'Well, of course, we're very lucky. We've really no need to travel anywhere as we have everything in America.' My normally articulate friend was speechless. What do you say to someone who thinks they 'have it all'? Of course, it's not just some Americans who hold this view. Countless immature people have a similar outlook towards their country, their suburb, their life choices.

I suspect most of us feel uncomfortable, if not bemused, whenever someone states that their child, neighbourhood or nation is the best ever, because no one has a franchise on brilliance or stupidity. There's little opportunity for growth here, for embracing new ways of thinking and behaving, so we become stale.

My World Is Best

As children, we tend to have a skewed view of ourselves and our abilities, as we have very little to compare ourselves with. It's comforting for the immature part of us to assume we're sensational and, because we're still to work on our social filters, we're not afraid to tell family and friends, and anyone else who will listen, just how clever we are. When we mature, it's often a relief to replace our complacency with curiosity, with a growing willingness to learn, to push out from our comfort zone and be more adventurous, to appreciate others and give credit where credit is due.

With increasing numbers of us stuck in our childish ways, we much prefer to immerse ourselves in larger-than-life fantasies. We bag the leading role or cling to those who shine brightest, living vicariously through their achievements, to give our days some sort of meaning, steadfastly ignoring life's big questions. 'Being alive is scary,' admits Shane in a thread on Kardashian mania, 'so, we buy into these prefabricated "meanings of life" [the Kardashians offer us] that simplify the dread of existence.'[1] When we take this route we never move beyond our flaws and limitations, choosing instead to bury our heads in the sand.

Dazzled by Excess

Who better to distract our child/adolescent selves from our shortcomings, than our current batch of celebrities, most notably the Kardashians, whose carefully stage-managed lives eclipse our own? Following hard on the appearance of Kim Kardashian's sex tape, these minor celebrities leapt into the spotlight with their debut TV show, *Keeping Up with the Kardashians*, which fast-tracked them to stardom and megawealth.

> As people, we can identify, or we want to identify with
> people who are totally obsessed with themselves.
> And they [the Kardashians] represent that in a major way.
> They're our guilty pleasure.'
> Rachel Adler, *Stylecaster*[2]

Daily, the Kardashians invite the child/adolescent in us to revel in their over-the-top lives. Unlike previous celebrities, who only allowed occasional glimpses into their world, advances in technology now enable us get so close and personal to our stars that we can almost imagine ourselves sitting next to Kim on the sofa or lounging with Kylie on her bed, as we follow the family's dizzying fashion choices and foibles, their love lives and cat fights, their weight and medical issues, their pregnancies and post-baby bodies, and more.

Bigger Is Better

The Kardashians offer the child in us 'an escape hatch into a world of glossy, empty glamour', suggests Irish music and arts journalist Jennifer Gannon, 'the home of big salads, private jets, chinchilla fur throws, and exotic holidays coupled with the relatable mundanity of sisterhood and family life.'[3] When the candy-floss moment wears off, our glimpses of grandeur can prove a double-edged sword. 'When I do watch [the Kardashians], I like the satisfying feeling of knowing that I'm not as vapid as any of them,' Nika says in a thread where she attempts to unpack their appeal, adding, 'and then I get sad, because I don't have money.'[4]

Why Do We All Look the Same?

The grandiose like to grab all the attention, to acquire as much as they can. This high-wire act comes with constant demands, where fans are there simply to adore us, to buy our products, to grow our bank account.

The grandiose also have a way of swallowing up those in their wake, leaving their followers mesmerised, compliant, starstruck. Child/adolescents love glitter and glam, and any chance to keep their most cherished fantasies alive. Countless women have adopted the same contoured Kardashian look, ditching their personal dreams and way of expressing themselves in the process.

Idolising celebrities can only ever deliver a superficial sense of belonging. Sometimes the price of that belonging can be inordinately high, costing us time and money, and the chance to create, explore and celebrate our own unique take on the world. Kate captures this dynamic well when talking of her social anxiety in a *Good Weekend* piece: 'An incredible amount of effort goes into trying to make sure I'm coming across okay.'[5]

> **Don't be into trends. Don't make fashion own you, but you decide what you are, what you express by the way you dress and the way you live.**
> Gianni Versace, fashion designer[6]

Wedding Extravaganza

Those dazzled by grandiosity often lose all touch with reality along the way – for instance, in the bridal stakes. A recent Goldman Sachs summer wedding study over five years revealed that while three-quarters of Americans had decided on how much they would outlay for their wedding, six out of ten ended up blowing their budget.

According to the Knot Real Weddings survey, the average cost for a wedding is now just over US$33,000.[7] Wedded Wonderland puts the average cost considerably higher, at just over US$51,000. According to Wedded Wonderland founder Wendy El-Khoury, 'Brides and Grooms today are using their wedding as a platform to express their relationship personality; wanting to impress, indulge, and create unforgettable memories.'[8]

'My belief is that the more we convince women that a wedding is the greatest day of her life,' states Amy, a New Yorker in the wedding business, 'the more money the industry makes.' Amy also sees a greater cost associated with all the messaging around what is now expected of couples, creating a 'lack of perspective' and 'wastefulness', not to mention the disempowering message to women that their wedding day will be their best day ever.[9]

How widespread, then, is excessive wedding spending? Many couples face pressure at their wedding. 'I work in the wedding industry,' Veronique says in a thread on out-of-control weddings. 'Popular venues and vendors make a killing. We do everything possible to encourage people to spend upwards of US$30k on one day.' TV shows such as *Bridezillas* pander to our childlike fantasies of being the prince or princess, the centre of attention who is loved and adored.

When the Dream Dissolves

In Australia, a recent ME Bank survey revealed that just over half of wedded couples regretted the amount of money they'd outlaid on their wedding day, given how much longer it took them to save for a house deposit. Just over a quarter told of how their emotions got the better of their wedding budget.[10] This puts additional psychological and financial pressure on newlywed couples.

'I've been having a mini heart attack today over the cost of our wedding,' Scarlett says in an online forum sharing wedding overspending regrets. 'We picked a BEAUTIFUL venue with horses in wine country and supposedly everything was included except for cake, flowers, music, and photographer, but after signing the contract last night, and giving our non-refundable deposit, the B&B sent us an invoice, which includes costs I didn't realise we had to pay for.' Without the kind of job to match these expenses and student loans, Scarlett describes herself as 'freaked out by spending so much money'.[11]

Scarlett is not alone. 'My cousin and his now-wife spent a good

$60,000 on their wedding seven years ago,' Hanna says in another online chat on the same subject. 'They've both realised what a huge mistake it was, as they don't even really remember the reception between talking with everyone, barely getting to eat, and taking photos. It put them in insane debt, and they struggled for a few years to get back to the financial position they were in before the wedding.'[12]

Meeting Expectations

It's not just the bride and groom who feel under pressure to deliver on 'the day'. Bridesmaids and groomsmen also admit to feeling obliged to spend up big, to be seen to fully support their friends' extravagant vision. One survey revealed that as many as 60 per cent of bridesmaids, along with 43 per cent of groomsmen, experienced this pressure. Many confessed that the expected level of spending soured their friendship, and a third regretted the amount of money they'd outlaid, with 43 per cent of maids of honour admitting to going into debt to meet expectations. The same was true of 38 per cent of best men, 35 per cent of the bridesmaids, and 30 per cent of groomsmen surveyed.[13]

Grounding Our Dream

There's nothing wrong with daydreams and the odd fantasy, which can help lift us out of ourselves, helping us create a more enriching, nuanced life. First, though, we must learn to take a more objective view to see clearly where these dreams might take us, so we don't lose our grip on reality.

When our child self is in charge, we lose all proportion. We damage, if not destroy, all the momentum we've built up. Many of us have dreamed of living life on a ridiculously grand scale and, of course, some achieve this. If we want our lives to sing, we need to be clear if what we're pitching for is worth the effort, or whether we're likely to find ourselves captive to our childish fancies.

It can be extremely painful when we finally emerge from our delusions. 'I have had the same [grandiose] thoughts most of my life,' admits Turner in an online thread around grandiose fantasies, '... that I'm special, deserving of special treatment, smarter, more "worthy" than other people, and that magically everything will turn out great for me. Now that I am in my 50's I have started to see myself more objectively. It's a big emotional drop to go from decades of thinking I'm the GOAT [greatest of all time] to thinking that actually I'm a fucked-up middle-age guy, who struggles to get through the week, and do normal shit, and not cause any damage to himself and others.'[14]

When We're Vulnerable

A lack of groundedness catches out the child/adolescent in us in numerous ways. The trick is to recognise this pattern and dare to push past those dreams that threaten to derail us. Just over a decade ago, my husband and I decided on a tree change. I'd had a few health issues and had been watching a lot of *Escape to the Country* and reading country lifestyle magazines. Finding a lovely house in the country with masses of space seemed like a dream come true, so we let go of our jobs, our home, and our friends, and relocated.

Where we lived was beautiful – everything anyone could hope for. We made a raft of new and supportive friends but in no time, our home was filled with a constant stream of city friends. We'd wave off another houseful of guests on Sunday evening, almost cross-eyed with fatigue. After a couple of years, we realised we were living someone else's dream. That rustic idyll turned out to be very hard work. So we sold up and moved back to the city, where life's more fulfilling, as we're city people.

I can see now that I was fragile at the time. None of the usual things I loved in life were bringing much joy, so my child/adolescent self seized on dreams of escape. All we really needed was a decent break, to slow down and just breathe. Instead, ironically, we ramped up the pressure with constant entertaining and taking care of our five and a half acres. We're immensely grateful for many happy episodes during our time in the country but ultimately it wasn't where we were meant to be.

Bring in the Cavalry

During COVID-19 we saw different fantasies emerge, with individuals turning up to anti-lockdown protests dressed as their favourite Rambo-style hero. One concerned US citizen told of witnessing 'an abundance of Nazi symbols and Confederate flags'. At another protest, a man turned up with a crossbow and arrows, explaining he was 'trying to protect them [the police] with what weapons I had', adding, 'and I backed up the law enforcement, you know.'[15]

Spurred on by our most cherished kiddy fantasies, we don the equivalent of a Batman or Ninja Turtle suit and rush off to a rally, fuelled by our vision of personally saving the world, not realising we're simply a public nuisance. I understand and respect the need for protest, but if these people had 'grown up', imagine where their powerful urge to serve others might have taken them.

When Grandiose Takes a Dark Turn

We saw this tendency towards the grandiose in Nazi Germany, and we're seeing it now in a number of countries that are embracing questionable definitions of greatness. The same compulsion, in part, drove the British and other Europeans to colonise huge chunks of the planet, accumulating immeasurable wealth and power in the process.

When I was around seven or eight, a teacher in my northern English primary school told us how lucky the Commonwealth countries were to be part of the British Empire. My young heart swelled to think of how Britain had 'civilised' the many pink territories on the world map and how these audacious moves had created common good (if not common wealth), bringing the English language, trains, trade and bureaucracy to the 'natives' of these lands.

I was so taken with this idea that I felt sad for the countries that had missed out on 'civilisation'. I was shocked years later to witness the grinding poverty and ongoing conflict in these far-flung places, sparked in part by the actions of my colonising forebears. Even to mention such subjects in certain quarters raises great ire. The immature among us much prefer to bathe in the reflected glory of our colonising ancestors. However, part of growing up is daring to stare the facts in the face – not just for our own sake, but for those on the other end of these far-reaching actions.

The Truth of the Matter

What is the cost of the bravery and boldness needed to conquer distant peoples and nations? While wandering through one of Sintra's enchanting palaces in Portugal, taking in its many wonders, I came across a large still life painting, filled with flowing silks, silver and gold *objets*, along with exotic fruits and birds.

I'd seen a number of such paintings in other palaces in Britain and Europe, but it wasn't until this moment that I truly understood what I was seeing. Not an item in that painting had come from Portugal but from its colonies, and I wondered how these objects had been acquired. For centuries, neighbouring Spain had been awash with unlimited wealth from the Americas. Yet few tell of how this colonising presence cost some eight million lives.

Eventually, the truth emerges and it is less than pretty. 'It feels as though the bubble of American exceptionalism is bursting and we're looking around, dazed, covered in its sticky residue,' reflected Washington-based Amelia Lester, in her piece 'Exceptional No Longer', during the final months of Trump's presidency, adding, 'For so long, the country has coasted along on its charisma, and now there's a dawning realization that charisma is no longer enough.'[16]

Counting the Cost

The adult in us must fully understand and face up to the damage, alongside the achievements, colonialism has created. New research by renowned economist Utsa Patnaik puts paid to the narratives many of us grew up with around the British occupation of India. From almost two centuries of tax and trade records, Patnaik estimates that Britain took some US$45 trillion out of India over almost three hundred years. This massive amount of money represents seventeen times the total annual gross domestic product of the United Kingdom today. How was this even possible?

Once established, the East India Company began taxing the Indian people, then used some of this income to purchase goods, so the British were effectively getting all their merchandise for free.[17] By 1922 the British Empire accounted for one-fifth of the world's population, spread over a quarter of the world's landmass – an impressive record that proved unsustainable. Too few British know the real story of their country's colonising ways. A recent YouGov poll in the UK found that 44 per cent of British people are proud of their once-great Empire. Twenty-one per cent found Britain's colonial path regrettable, while 23 per cent didn't have an opinion either way.[18]

It's essential we're aware of the dark side of grandiosity as it has the capacity to harm individuals and even whole nations. We see this in

America's belief in its 'manifest destiny', entering other countries with the same gung-ho attitude seen in western movies. But such incursions were in real life, where a lot of people got hurt, losing their homes and livelihoods, and having their lives torn apart.

Winner Takes All

Grandiose gestures often come with an inherent meanness. Like small children, the grandiose can't seem to help stripping others of as much as they can get away with. One of the darkest chapters in the East India Company's history took place during the 1770 Bengal famine, which over three long years was responsible for the deaths of ten million people – more than the deaths caused by the Black Plague that ravaged Britain and Europe.

Crop failure was an ongoing issue in India, so the ruling Moghuls would stockpile rice, but this policy was abandoned under the East India Company and countless innocent people starved. Winston Churchill would later state, 'I hate Indians. They are a beastly people with a beastly religion. The famine was their own fault for breeding like rabbits.'[19]

> **You have never known what it is to live under colonialism.**
> **It's humiliating.**
> Guy Arnold, *Africa: A Modern History*[20]

'Why did Africa let Europe cart away millions of Africa's souls from the continent to the four corners of the wind?' asks exiled Kenyan poet and playwright Ngũgĩ wa Thiong'o in his acclaimed novel *Wizard of the Crow*. 'How could Europe lord it over a continent ten times its size?' he continues. 'Why does needy Africa continue to let its wealth meet the needs of those outside its borders, and then follow behind with hands outstretched for a loan of the very wealth it let go?'[21]

These big questions demand serious consideration by the grown-up in each of us. How do we find our way out from under such grandiose notions? How do we arrive at a more mature, a more equitable approach to our national dreams? First, we need to recognise and evaluate our infantile urges.

A More Holistic Way Forward

In *Psychoanalysis Enters the Political Fray*, Peter Wolson suggests it is time to move on from simply satisfying our own needs as nations and to create 'a more mature form of international collaboration, in which giving and taking among nations is on an egalitarian, mutually respectful basis.'[22] Psychoanalysis, it seems, helps point the way.

'The successfully treated grandiose patient finds meaning in life from the fulfilment of realistic ambitions, that substitute for the illusory grandiosity in realistic strengths and limitations,' states Dr Frank Summers, Diplomat in Clinical Psychology of the American Board of Professional Psychology.[23] 'Understanding without a relationship is empty, a relationship without understanding is blind.' This holds true for individuals, communities and nations, challenging us to deal more fairly and thoughtfully with those beyond our borders.

A Little Respect

It has also been convenient for the child/adolescent to view people in developing countries as savages and/or simpletons, to explain away the unconscionable behaviour of colonisers. I'm always awed at the ingenuity, warmth and kindness from the people I encounter when travelling off the beaten track – the depth and intricacy of their culture, history and connection to the land, which constantly puts paid to the foolish narratives I was fed as a child.

The Western paradigm, for all its accomplishments, is not 'the paragon of humanity's potential', anthropologist Wade Davis reminds us.[24] 'Indigenous peoples aren't failed attempts to be us', he insists. They show us 'other ways of being, other ways of thinking, other ways of orienting ourselves in social and spiritual and ecological space.' To make this shift in thinking, we need to take a mature view that is fully capable of realigning and fine-tuning our perceptions. 'Culture is only a manifestation of options', Davis reminds us. 'There is no ladder to success that conveniently places ourselves [in the West] at the top.'[25]

We're talking about the subtleties of existence here. Davis points to Matthieu Ricard, a former molecular biologist at the Pasteur Institute, now a noted Buddhist monk, as someone well equipped to advise us. Drawing on 2500 years of Buddhism's direct observation of the nature of mind, Ricard reflects, 'So much of Western science is a major response to minor needs. We spend all of our lifetimes trying to live till we're a hundred without losing our teeth, instead of understanding the nature of existence ... Your billboards in the West celebrate naked teenagers in underwear, our billboards are many walls of prayers for the well-being of all sentient creatures.'[26]

Exceptional Skills Almost Lost to Us

The grandiose impulses of our immature selves show little understanding of life's subtleties. It's these very nuances that we're most in need of if we are to meet our world in new and astonishing ways. Several years back Wade Davis went on a sail in the *Hokule'a*, a recreation of a Polynesian double-hulled voyaging canoe, once used by these peoples to navigate huge distances across the Pacific Ocean.

The Polynesians were astonishing seafarers who were able to name 250 stars in the night sky. '[They] can sense the presence of distant atolls of islands beyond the visible horizon, simply by watching and studying the reverberations of waves across the hull of the vessel, knowing full well that every island in the Pacific has its own refractive pattern that can be read with the same perspicacity that a forensic scientist can read a fingerprint,' Davis says. 'These were people without a written tradition. They navigated by dead reckoning – by only knowing where you've come from. You have to remember every change of course over a long voyage – up to 6,000 miles.'[27]

Another Way of Being

Our child/adolescent selves have become far too smug, firmly believing that we sit at the apex of human achievement. In the West, we have a real need to place our personal stamp on locations, evident in our renaming of Indigenous locations. First Nations peoples have a tangible partnership with nature, a willingness to embrace natural features and capture the *essence* of place.

In Australia the few Indigenous placenames that remain tell an intriguing story. For example, Wangaratta is 'the resting place of cormorants' and Moruya is the 'home of the black swan'. In the UK, the name of the Calder River comes from the ancient meaning of 'rough water' and the Derwent speaks of a 'river lined with oaks'. Imagine if we were to experience this level of intimacy and respect for a place, to know and nurture its essence in naming it and then to let this inform how we interact with this particular landscape.

Such insights point us towards far more powerful ways of being in a relationship with each other and the natural world. To benefit, we must abandon our childish sense of entitlement, of the grandiose, the need to always be right and to have the last word. A more profound legacy will be in how well or poorly we've been custodians of Earth and its diverse peoples.

'In a non-written tradition there's a relationship to the natural world that I've experienced with non-literate societies,' Davis says. '... It's like the flight of a bird and becomes like a cursive script of nature written on the wind.'[28] To rein in our immature impulses, we need to commit to growing our child/adolescent selves up, continue to ask far-reaching questions, live with less certainty and more inquiry, and show more respect for our *innate* potential and that of others.

Time to Turn Down the Volume?

So much of our entertainment has become little more than white noise, keeping us constantly distracted and making it hard to sort out what we want from our days, from our lives.

- How and where can you dial down the noise that feeds your appetite for the grandiose?
- As you contemplate your dreams, which part of you is in the driver's seat? Could your child/adolescent be running the show?
- Perhaps it's time to examine your dreams more closely. What sparked these aspirations in the first place, and what can they realistically deliver?
- Are there deeper voices within that remain unexpressed? Where might they take you?

Know that the passions deep inside you are best placed to deliver profound experiences, beyond fame and fortune, offering something more satisfying by far. So don't settle for less.

13

Win at All Costs

Many times each day we face moments of choice between our adolescent desire to win no matter what, and having the courage to take a higher path. Every decision we make impacts ourselves and others.

At a town hall meeting at Lakeville South High School in Minnesota, during the run-up to the 2008 US presidential elections, the Republican nominee, John McCain, invited comments from the audience. One woman admitted she couldn't possibly vote for Barack Obama, given he was an Arab. McCain chose the path of dignity and truth, responding with, 'No ma'am. He's a decent family man, a citizen that I just happen to have disagreements with on fundamental issues, and that's what this campaign is all about.'

Years later, with only a short time to live, McCain said, 'I hope we can rely on humility, on our need to cooperate, on our dependence on each other to learn how to trust each other again, and by so doing better serve the people who elected us. It is our responsibility to preserve that [commitment], even when it requires us to do something less satisfying than *winning*.'[1]

As a senator, McCain would have been acutely aware that winning regardless has become 'our thing'. Not that winning in itself is wrong but winning no matter what fractures relationships and goodwill. The drive to win encourages others to behave badly, until everyone is only looking out for themselves.

When Winning Is Everything

These are subtleties the child/adolescent fails to grasp. Feeling vulnerable, our immature self is in constant need of praise and reassurance. It also has an obsessive need to beat anyone and everyone, even those it 'cares' about, to prove it has the most to offer. This blunt approach turns every situation into a competition. Yet any wins achieved by our immature self, constantly changing the rules and stacking the odds against others, are questionable at best.

When fully formed grown-ups are asked to compete, they seek the deep satisfaction that comes from winning fairly and squarely, from cooperating, and from taking others with them. They also know how to be gracious when winning *and* in defeat, and understand the importance of not assuming they have all the answers.

Chaotic, competitive and self-obsessed, child/adolescents are stressful to be around. They are at their worst in international settings, where leaders behave like overindulged children, actively seeking to displace and disenfranchise those who don't 'fit' their narrow mould. Here winning means taking as much as you can, with no thought to what it might mean for the dignity of others or their ability to thrive, or for the environment.

Why Sharing Matters

Some of life's most profound moments are ours when we share, when we volunteer, when we perform an unexpected kindness or when we willingly give of our time, energy and resources. We also experience this depth of satisfaction when we come together to celebrate life's best moments or to remember those lost to us in death. Such moments take us to a place of a deeper connection with others.

Ultimately none of us achieves all we do alone. 'Many times a day, I realise how much my outer and inner life is built upon the labours of people, both living and dead,' the great physicist Albert Einstein once remarked.[2] In contemplating this, Einstein came to believe that he must strive always to give out as much as he received. Understanding the depth of this observation nudges us out of any sense of isolation. It feeds our humanity, our gratitude. It liberates something profound within us, sharpening our vision, our willingness to strive to be better, stronger, wiser.

When Sport Becomes a Commodity

Despite all the good sport can deliver, it seems to be losing its way. The win-at-all-costs ethos is alive and well with such unhelpful slogans as 'you don't win silver, you lose gold' and 'second place is the first loser'.

'Sport elevates our spirits, because what we see is people doing extraordinary, sometimes impossible things, for no reason other than the thrill of achievement,' reflects Sydney lawyer and columnist Michael Bradley. 'The purity of motivation and intent, coupled with the excitement of competition and buzz of winning or losing, gives us something we can't get any other way.' But Bradley is quick to add, 'We are not any more witnessing something pure. We are being sold a product.'[3]

Travis Tygart, CEO of the US Anti-Doping Agency, agrees. 'Across today's sporting landscape, you don't have to look too far to see that those values ... are being corrupted,' he notes. 'Local newspaper headlines are flush with stories of hazing, hyper-competitive parenting, performance-enhancing drugs, address and birth certificate manipulation, safety concerns, unethical recruiting practices and a whole host of other indiscretions.'[4]

When Parents Don't Help

Ethicist Albert Spencer states that, increasingly, sport is about 'egotism, cynicism, nihilism, an obsessive focus on money, and win-at-all-costs mentality that fosters disrespect for competitors and society'.[5] This toxic approach impacts local sporting bodies and the way young players and their parents behave. One UK report goes so far as to suggest that as well as exerting huge pressure on their kids to win, some parents have taken to organising their child's access to performance-enhancing drugs.[6]

This is what happens when sport is increasingly about 'obliterating' one's opponents, rather than winning 'cleanly'. There's often a brute force, an implied violence here, as part of this equation. 'What is valued is more of a military style victory than a mutual moral quest for fair play and respect for human relationships,' states Nick Watson, former associate professor of sport and theology at York St John University. What gets lost are all 'the playful and joyful elements' of taking part in sport.[7]

Similarly, our relationship with players is no longer simply about the game with a myriad of associated products for sale. How can we claw back the essentials of good sport when sporting bodies are tied to numerous licensing deals, generating significant amounts of money? The relationship with the fan-base is muddied by all the celebrity glitz now central to many codes.

The child/adolescent loves anything that sparkles. By 'wearing their [sporting great's] shoes, drinking their drink and eating their burger,' states theologian Michael Grimshaw, we are invited to buy into a closer relationship with our sporting stars. But the childish part of us fails to see that this illusory relationship can never be more than 'a pixilated image on a screen, a flat image on a poster'.[8]

Winning Doesn't Always Deliver

One San Diego State University study into win-at-all-costs individuals exposed how obsessively self-focused they are and how poorly they behave in one-on-one situations. They enjoy seeing others fail and, as classic rule-breakers, they are determined to reach their goals, regardless.[9] This is a far cry from the view of philosopher and historian Bertrand Russell, who, having lived through two world wars, the Great Depression, the Cuban missile and other crises, stated, 'The only thing that will redeem mankind is cooperation.'

Winning is important but not at the expense of our humanity. Unhelpful adolescent-style competition can so easily sour all we share with others, including our partners. Our immature self is drawn to score-keeping, always focusing on others' failures. Every time our child/ adolescent self belittles others, is jealous, or issues ultimatums without talking issues through, it erodes, if not destroys, relationships. This immaturity doesn't just shame others; at some level we end up shaming ourselves.

True success means being willing to take on board other people's ideas and approaches. It's about learning to be more comfortable with difference, to cut others some slack, thus creating a space where we can all thrive. As family therapist Lesli Doares points out, 'Knowing that your partner has your back, and that you have theirs, provides a safe and secure foundation that allows you both to manage life's ups and downs.'[10] The same holds true for wider friendships and relationships.

> **Coming together is a beginning, staying together is progress, and working together is success.**
> Henry Ford, founder of the Ford motor company

Instead of having to be the one who always wins, we can chart a more nuanced path to make room for a rich mix of aspirations and points of view alongside our own.

A Different Path to Success

Winning comes in many forms. It may well entail personal sacrifice and apparent loss.

- What are you prepared to refine or let go of to find your unique path to success?
- When you're tempted to compete in a way that's unhealthy, it's important to ask what you fear in that moment. What's the worst thing that could happen if you don't win?
- Perhaps you're facing a recent failure. Know there are gifts for you here. Take a fresh look at the lead-up to this situation. What went wrong? What can you do differently next time?
- What truly sustains you?
- What qualities can you fine-tune from here on?

14

Driven to Short Cuts

Winning at all costs is ever more pervasive in our universities, with greater opportunities now for students to cheat, to buy ready-made assignments online, or have someone put together their project for them. Along with flourishing 'essay mills', just over 15 per cent of students are now thought to be buying, selling or trading notes, sitting an exam for someone else, or resorting to plagiarism or other forms of exam assistance.[1]

Cheating Is Alive and Well

The findings of one pre-pandemic study applied to the total number of students globally suggest a staggering 31 million students may have engaged in cheating.[2] These are concerning figures and beg the question: 'Where does this cheating end?' If this propensity to cheat spills over into the workplace, what implications might this have? What happens when there's an emergency in critical areas such as engineering, aviation, medicine and other high-risk environments, when people find themselves working alongside someone who's failed to grasp the essentials of their area of expertise?

Male students, it seems, are more likely to cheat, as are students struggling with English as a second language, or those who are out of their depth. When cheats see their degree simply as a means to an end, paying for help to get past the line seems the logical next step. Others believe that, as cheating happens all the time, it's no big deal.[3] In one study, all the students surveyed agreed that passing off someone's work as your own was plagiarism but only seven out of ten regarded passing off a downloaded essay as their own as plagiarism.[4]

How Cheating Plays Out

There are many reasons why people cheat at university: the weight of expectations; their inability to accept failure or poor marks; or undue pressure to succeed. The difficulty with cheating is that there are hidden, often long-term consequences: the guilt rarely goes away and, having cheated, a person is then forced to keep covering their tracks.

Becoming an adult requires that we walk through life with our eyes open. If we flunk an exam, it's incumbent on us to admit to ourselves that we fell short and to have the courage to ask why. We may have failed because we didn't do enough study or perhaps we're just not cut out to be an engineer, hairdresser or brain surgeon. It's uncomfortable but there are clear benefits if we can push past our personal roadblocks. Life offers us the chance to gain more insight into ourselves, to find something we're good at and give it all the love and attention we can.

> **The thing is, failure is not bad. Not learning from failure is.**
> Sanjay Das, blogger[5]

When We Make Our Own Rules

The child/adolescent doesn't get that rules bring order and greater ease to our lives, helping to keep misunderstanding, hurt and confusion at bay. For instance, when traffic lights are out we see how easily life can slide into chaos. Unable or unwilling to take in such nuances, the child/adolescent often takes a perverse delight in breaking as many rules as it can. Our childish self loves to wreak havoc while happily accessing the benefits of a functioning society.

By resorting to the 'kids will be kids' line to explain away adolescent shortcomings, we fail to fully grasp what happens when we don't leave our teenage selves behind. Adolescence is exhilarating but it can also be destructive, if not dangerous. It's not easy to tussle with a recalcitrant child or teenager, but it is essential to set clear boundaries because when a child/adolescent fails to grow up, the results can be catastrophic.

Revisiting the Enron Debacle

Two decades ago, Enron was hailed as one of the world's best businesses but few were aware of the billions of dollars of debt the company had accumulated, which was skilfully concealed from the board and shareholders.[6] At one stage Enron was trading at fifty-five times its earnings, with individual shares worth just over US$90, but when the company collapsed, shares fell to less than a dollar, precipitating the largest corporate bankruptcy to that point.

Shareholders lost billions, while thousands of Enron workers were out of a job and lost their retirement nest eggs. Before the company's monumental fall from grace, its most senior executives – aware of the tenuous situation – swiftly sold their stocks, amassing millions. One cashed in a staggering US$33 million of Enron stocks.

The crash also brought down its prestigious global accountants Arthur Andersen, leaving that company's 28,000 employees out of work. It also sent massive shockwaves across wider America, with gas and electricity providers suddenly facing higher costs. 'The trouble with Enron,' one employee would later reflect, 'is that there weren't any grown-ups [running the show].'[7]

White-collar Crime

We continue to see the fallout from reckless individuals bent on following their own rules, behaving like children with poor impulse control, seeking to grab as much as they can. Far less publicised than other forms of crime, white-collar misdemeanours are alive and well. They impact countless individuals, institutions and even whole nations, as witnessed during the global economic crisis.

We see this criminality in car companies tampering with vehicle emissions tests, and banned ingredients being included in animal feed. In India's shocking Bhopal tragedy, a toxic gas leak from a Union Carbide pesticide plant killed 15,000 people, injuring a further half a million.[8] Many local people were blinded and there was a subsequent spike in birth deformities among an already vulnerable population.[9]

These spectacular miscarriages of justice and lack of fair play continue, where just a handful of out-of-control child/adolescents end up compromising a whole organisation and all the good work they do. In May 2020 Australia's Westpac bank admitted to being party to 23 million money-laundering breaches, with one of their significant customers convicted of 'child trafficking and child exploitation, involving live streaming of child sex shows and offering children for sex'.[10]

In late September 2020, JPMorgan admitted to illegally interfering with precious metals and Treasury markets. Rogue traders in their employ had been busy 'spoofing' – creating dummy orders to falsely stimulate increased demand in the markets. By manipulating the algorithms, these traders artificially pushed up market prices tens of thousands of times between 2008 and 2016. Prosecutors would later allege that one trader described this as simply 'a little razzle-dazzle to juke the algos'. This 'razzle-dazzle' cost JP Morgan US$920 million.[11]

Who Commits White-collar Crime?

White-collar criminals are manipulative, erratic and frequently lacking in empathy. Behaving like adolescents and driven by self-interest, they revel in making their own rules, fully expecting to get away with their criminal behaviour. In far too many instances, they succeed.

These dangerously immature characters can end up influencing the way whole businesses and institutions operate, by cleverly manipulating work cultures in highly questionable ways. One recent Norwegian study suggests that white-collar crime is more costly than much-publicised social security fraud, with three out of four white-collar criminals walking free.[12]

In the UK, violent crimes are estimated to cost the country around £124 billion annually, but global accounting firm Crowe calculates that white-collar fraud costs British taxpayers £190 billion a year.[13] Added to this, the global movement One, an organisation set up to end extreme poverty and preventable diseases, suggests that developing countries alone lose $1 trillion or more every year to fraud and money laundering – enough to save a staggering 3.6 million lives, were these funds available to the poor.[14]

Winning at All Costs Close Up

Such work practices can permeate otherwise worthwhile organisations. As research from the San Diego State University reveals, 'Clearly, when bottom-line outcomes are valued over everything else, employees may be encouraged to act in their own self-interest, even if it means engaging in unethical behaviors. If the examples set by Enron and the mortgage industry are considered, this behavior can have dire consequences in the long-term, if left unchecked.'[15]

Unhealthy Competition

In everyday work situations, the win-at-all-costs approach can destroy any willingness people have to work well together and to create an atmosphere of goodwill. 'I feel like I'm very hard working, but this co-worker of mine is ALWAYS working at all hours of the day … he will send emails to management at 2:00am with a status update … It's not for overly high priority items either, just regular, everyday stuff,' admits Chas in an online thread around overly competitive co-workers. 'I've started answering my email at all hours of the day now, just because he has set the bar so high, because if I don't, I look like a slacker now.'[16] Ned adds, 'I (to an extent) used to be "that guy". People hate me for it … I've stopped being that guy in emails and in whatnot. It's just not worth the energy.'[17]

What is the benefit in operating within an ethical framework? In late 2020, Deloitte Access Economics Australia published a report, *The Ethical Advantage*, which indicated that just a 10 per cent lift in the country's ethical standards would generate an additional A$45 billion for the nation annually. This would provide greater employment choices and improve mental and physical wellbeing. A drop of 10 per cent, it projected, would lead to an equal amount being stripped from the country's GDP.[18]

Charting a Different Course

Winning fairly and squarely is something we learn over time. It allows for a genuine willingness to grow and to make room for needs and agendas beyond our own. It's an inclusive world that ensures the very best is achieved within the rules and regulations. It takes a degree of maturity to be magnanimous enough to include others, but the payoff is not having to go it alone.

Former London broker Mark Wager admits that all that mattered was 'getting the deal at all costs'. He savoured 'the brutal raw competition', but on looking back, he realises 'if you win without honour you have already lost, you just don't realise it yet'. There are much better ways to operate in business, he suggests, pointing to Warren Buffett, one of the world's most successful investors – a man known for his decency, who often closes his deals 'with just a handshake'.[19] We need a high level of emotional maturity – an ability to interact with others beyond fear and rabid self-interest to take the higher, more satisfying path.

Find a group of people who challenge and inspire you,
spend a lot of time with them, and it will change your life.[20]
Amy Poehler, actor, director and comedian

Jane McCarroll of New Zealand's Institute of Management concurs. 'A healthy attitude to winning will also include losing,' she reminds us, telling of how, during a school cross-country race, her seven-year old daughter ran back to help a small boy with a learning disability who was struggling to stay on track. Taking the boy's hand, her daughter remained with the boy until the finish line. 'I have never been more proud,' admits McCarroll. 'I couldn't tell you if she came 8th or 80th – it doesn't matter. Her making sure that this little boy finished the race was all the winning I could wish for. Winning comes from bringing out the best in ourselves – which encourages those around us to follow suit.'[21]

An unhealthy need to get ahead regardless is often found in familiar situations where we place certain friends or siblings in our sights, determined to best them, if not take them out. This may manifest in overly competitive behaviour around achievements and possessions; an inability to accept a family member who is different; a need to prove who loves a parent or mutual friend more. It may take a more pathological turn, as when someone works actively to exclude their siblings from family gatherings – even from wills.

Competition Is Natural

Children become eager to show off their burgeoning skills, to see how they stack up against others, and so they begin to compete. Such comparisons can help us grow.[22] Competition is no longer helpful, however, when we're determined to win no matter what by cheating, changing the rules or basically doing whatever it takes to avoid losing.

'Competition becomes more sophisticated as we grow,' explains clinical psychologist Dr Eric Herman. 'It becomes a problem when you can't enjoy your own success. Or you become resentful of other people that are doing well.'[23] Resentment is a corrosive force that we have all witnessed. 'I'm sure there are friends of mine who like to compare lives, and even use my life to feel better about their own,' admits Fatima in an online chat around competitive friends, 'but I just don't like or dwell on those things. There is a place for healthy competition, but like anything, it can become toxic very fast.'[24]

Where This Downward Path Begins

Intense competitiveness, experts suggest, often points to early unresolved life issues such as finding ourselves in hospital with a significant illness; being apart from loved ones; or living in a volatile home environment while a small child. If not addressed, these anxious feelings can often remain deep within a child's emotional memory and impact how they are around others.[25] Parents with overly high expectations don't help either – it's essential a child is supported to learn how to lose well.

To fully embrace adulthood, we must move beyond our need for constant love and appreciation. We achieve this, in part, by learning to find ways to calm ourselves when feeling rattled and not to be so terrified of failure. Often when we're in a tight spot, an unhelpful competitive streak can emerge. Dr Herman suggests we practise being more aware of *when* our overly competitive side is triggered so we can work on curbing 'those fast, fiery reactions'.[26]

Kindness Helps

It helps to cultivate a greater capacity for kindness. 'When children feel better, they behave better. They are kinder. They are considerate. They are empathetic towards other children, because they feel deeply secure inside themselves,' notes author and childcare expert Janet Lansbury.[27] The same is true of adults. We've come to regard kindness as weakness but we fail to realise that genuine kindness is underpinned by strength. No longer subject to so much fear, we're able to be generous in our thoughts, remarks and actions.

One of the great proponents of kindness was Nelson Mandela, a man who was no stranger to suffering, enduring much during the twenty-seven long years he was incarcerated on Robben Island. 'I believe that in the end it is kindness and generous accommodation that are the real catalysts for change,' he would later reflect.[28]

A Better Way Forward

In his book *The Amateurs*, historian David Halberstam tells of how when rowers share their most memorable experiences, most oarsmen admit that it's less about their winning moments than the moments of real togetherness they've experienced while out rowing with others, when 'all eight oars [are] in the water together, the synchronization almost perfect. In moments like these, the boat seemed to lift right out of the water. Oarsmen,' Halberstam explains, 'call that the moment of *swing*.'[29]

This glimpse of total togetherness allows us to sense what's possible, when we can be genuinely inclusive, striving hard to do what we love while pursuing our life goals. If we want a fulfilled life, winning can only ever be *part* of the entirety of our lives, and those of our children. As one African proverb suggests, 'If you want to go fast, go alone. If you want to go far, go together.'

Inclusion Takes Us Forward

Regardless of whether we're in a high-stakes political or business environment, or in everyday situations, we could all benefit from a reset, by moving beyond our need to win at all costs, and aiming for something more inclusive and authentic.

What if winning were less about beating others than taking the 'road less travelled', and more about daring to place ourselves where we're genuinely meant to be?

- What might your reset look like?
- Where do you suppose you are meant to be?
- How can you fine-tune your goals?
- As you pursue your goals, how best can you journey alongside others?

15

Our Blame Culture

Whenever our child/adolescent feels boxed in, we tend to flip into fight-or-flight mode. Our immature self tries to avoid the consequences of its actions by shifting the blame onto others. We blame when we don't feel safe, when we don't know how to handle mistakes or situations that scare us, or when we're desperate to let go of the discomfort. Blame, suggests Andrea Blundell of London's Harley Therapy, is 'the fine art of making others responsible for all the difficult things that happen to us'.[1] Blame is also fuelled by a willingness to escalate the tensions around an already tricky situation, regardless of how destructive this might prove.

Never Mind about the Truth

We also blame when the childish part of us is unable to accept random events, when we can't face up to the fact that, at times, the world is an uncertain place. We reframe the truth, shaping it into something more palatable and predictable.

Sherry Hamby, a professor of psychology at Sewanee: The University of the South, says, 'It's this idea that "people deserve what happens to them". There's just a really strong need to believe that we all deserve our outcomes and consequences.'[2] Our immature self asks, 'How could something awful possibly happen to those who play by the rules?'

Life isn't that simple – appalling things can and do happen to the best of us. '[P]eople blame victims so that they can continue to feel safe themselves,' suggests Barbara Gilin, a professor of social work at Widener University, who has worked with many victims over the years.[3]

> Blaming is *avoidance*. It's easier to think that the other
> party is wrong or bad, [than] to look inside ourselves …
> Accusing others blinds you.
> Gustavo Razzetti, CEO of Fearless Culture[4]

This need to blame spills over into how societies behave. 'We believe someone must pay for our suffering,' suggests Gustavo Razzetti. 'The blame culture has created an exaggerated fear of litigation and is making organizations risk-averse and over cautious.'[5] Blame and fear create a kind of paralysis, where people are distrustful, inward-thinking and only looking out for themselves.

Blame Sparks More Blame

In *The Blame Contagion*, Nathanael Fast, assistant professor of management and organization at the USC Marshall School of Business, and Larissa Tiedens, a Stanford professor of organizational behavior, discovered that blaming someone in public rapidly escalates the tendency to blame.[6]

> Know that people with that attitude [of blame] tend to also
> be very self-serving, they'll gladly throw anyone under the
> bus to save themselves.
> Julian, *Reddit* forum[7]

Are some of us more likely to blame than others? Those who habitually blame are more likely to feel insecure, be more self-focused and lack good social skills[8] – all of which are characteristics of the child/adolescent.

The way through any difficulty, psychologist Carl E Pickhardt suggests, is to go easy on ourselves and others caught up in tricky situations. This is not about accepting the unacceptable, but rather looking at an event with a level head and not wasting energy by treating every awkward situation as a catastrophe. Finding a way to rectify an unfortunate event is far more effective than getting lost in blame.[9] That's not to say additional redress might not be needed, but a reasoned approach is more likely to succeed. These are skills that are way beyond the child/adolescent.

Armchair Critic

The childish part of us loves to be right (who doesn't?) and often takes a perverse delight in seeing things go wrong. This is a flawed way to operate, even more so now, with our voyeuristic high-tech culture, where people are happy to pass swift, often merciless judgements on others. 'Now, thanks to social media, thousands, if not millions, represent a faceless humungous audience ready to be cynical, condescending, patronising and sometimes oppressing,' reflects Azrin Mohd Noor, founder of the Sedania Group. 'Now everyone can be a critic or self-proclaimed expert.'[10]

Blame is a convenient default position for those stuck in their child/adolescent ways, allowing them to cling to their highly edited view of the world, delivering a false sense of assurance. 'I remember that I was a much better parent before I had children,' admits organisational consultant Rhonda Scharf, 'because once I had my kids, things were far more difficult to deal with than I had thought they would be. After I had kids myself, I stopped criticizing other parents.'[11]

No one likes to fail or lose control, yet with all the uncertainties and vulnerabilities our child selves experience, is it any surprise our immature self defaults to blame as a convenient way out? Blame keeps us stuck in a wearying loop of blaming and complaining, boring those close to us senseless. It also fractures relationships, as no one wants to be around those who duck and weave every time something goes wrong. Our willingness to blame can also encourage those around us to resort to cover-ups. A bad situation is often made worse, sometimes with devastating consequences.

Blame is just a lazy person's way of making sense of chaos.
Douglas Coupland, *All Families Are Psychotic*[12]

Little Is Learned

The child/adolescents' problem-solving skills are basic at best. They feel increasingly vulnerable whenever things go awry. While they may dodge a bullet when they fail to take responsibility, they might soon find themselves in a much more serious situation, lacking the skills to keep themselves and others safe.

'You'll often see kids blame others and point the finger at someone else when you hold them accountable for their behaviour,' says James Lehman, who has worked for decades with at-risk youth. 'Very often they see themselves as the victim, no matter how aggressive or abusive their behavior,' he adds. The solution, he suggests, is to teach children and adolescents good communication and negotiation skills. 'Challenge your child's thinking and hold him [or her] accountable.' They will often use anger and tantrums, storming off, but a parent has to stand firm. When a child avoids a confrontation, make sure they know that you'll revisit this issue when they return, Lehman advises.[13]

Helping Kids Problem-solve

It's essential to actively encourage children to be honest and teach them how to 'read' situations and problem-solve. No one likes an accident, but to be able to express true remorse and offer a solution for a mishap is empowering. These invaluable life skills help our kids, and the child/adolescent in us, to grow up and to be genuinely confident.

To help our children move beyond their natural tendency to blame and complain, we need to nudge them out of their insular view of the world. Involve them in community activities and volunteering, where they can learn to be comfortable around a range of people, each with their own problem-solving skills. The best time for a child or adolescent to learn these essentials is when their parents are still around but parents also need to have matured to effectively help them develop the tenacity needed.

When Blaming Becomes a Habit

TV fosters our blame culture, encouraging us to heap scorn on complete strangers. In the comfort of our lounge rooms, we've come to delight in picking through the intimate details of other people's lives. 'Reality TV shows force feed us scenes of one character blaming another,' reflects Andrea Blundell of London's Harley Therapy, 'and newspapers are awash with stories about how all of society's problems are to be blamed on politicians or terrorists, and [with the implicit suggestion that] there is nothing we can do.'[14]

This soul-crushing dynamic is most evident in sport. Over a decade ago Sir Alex Ferguson, the football manager of Manchester United, called out all the 'mocking' in the UK. 'You see it on all these TV shows, where the panellists criticise the contestants. There's a mocking industry now, and it's even generated by television programmes.' Paul Jewell of Wigan Athletic agrees. 'It's gone past criticism and passion, it's reached the point of hatred. It's sad, but that's the way football is going.'[15] We now see this dynamic in sporting codes, making the role of coaches, even those coaches working with young kids, barely tenable.

Blame is a weapon the child/adolescent uses to decimate others, which can cause harm. Where does this leave our young people, who witness this level of judgement daily on social media? How, then, can they develop a healthy belief in themselves and others?

'Young people need a safe climate in which they can explore the consequences of their choices and behavior, without judgments about success or failure – without blame, shame, or pain,' say educators Jane Nelsen, Lynn Lott, and H Stephen Glenn.[16] Without this level of understanding and guidance, they fall prey to dark emotions. 'Guilt,' family therapist Darlene Lancer reminds us, 'can be an unrelenting source of pain.'[17] Guilt and pointing the finger prevent our young from making progress – as weeks, months, even years are lost in blaming others.

The Toxic Workplace

Blame is thriving in the workplace. 'There is an underlying blame culture [happening at work]: people calling out mistakes,' Greg says in a thread on blame work cultures, 'publicly, cc'ing seniors in passive-aggressive emails to increase the visibility of mistakes, a lack of thank yous/ gratitude for work done right, and loss of trust for work done wrong. Instead of talking about how to improve things, the team talks about what someone has done wrong.'[18]

The tendency towards cover-ups and half-truths that a blame culture fosters don't help in moments that stretch us. When we're going through periods of significant change, there are likely to be teething problems and even mistakes. Given the rate of change we're currently experiencing, we all need to realise this. We don't need child/adolescents panicking and looking for someone to blame.

When we can admit to our shortcomings and give others some slack, we build confidence and encourage those around us to be more transparent. But we have to see things as they are, not how we'd like them to be. 'Maintain an accurate assessment of your successes and failures,' business leader Todd Henry suggests, 'so that you can continue growing in your efforts.'[19]

> **On a personal level, a lack of accountability can be deadly to our efforts to do brilliant work.**
> Todd Henry, CEO of Accidental Creative Consultancy[20]

Moving Beyond Blame

Smart workplaces recognise that transparency and problem-solving are critical to success, particularly in high-risk environments such as hospitals and the airline industry. They know mistakes happen that are not necessarily from poor work practices, but also that workplaces are complex environments, where human error is a reality. Here everyone's focus is on telling things as they are and promptly fixing a situation, as people's lives are at stake.

'A deep set of research shows that people who blame others for their mistakes,' says Nathaniel Fast, co-author of the *Blame Contagion* study, 'lose status, learn less, and perform worse, relative to those who own up to their mistakes.'[21] By contrast, no-blame work cultures tend to be more progressive. Here everyone's time and energy are directed into paying attention to the detail and to learning, and in helping fellow employees be more deft at correcting mistakes when something takes an unexpected turn.

Telling It How It Is

Blame can be contagious but so is a willingness to take ownership of an issue in more enlightened workplaces. 'When people see others taking responsibility for their mistakes or failures,' notes *New York Times* columnist Alina Tugend, 'they also copy that, creating a better overall work environment.'[22]

> **Inevitably, things go wrong – it's how a business takes**
> **action to improve that really matters.'**
> Annemie, *Reddit* forum[23]

'Honesty is an oil that lubricates the functioning of high reliability organisations,' Nathaniel Fast believes. 'Without honesty, organisations don't have a true overview of where they are, and therefore aren't able to make effective and informed decisions.'[24] Informed decision-making, he insists, means using the best expertise available in an organisation to guide decisions, rather than automatically deferring to those at the top. During the COVID-19 pandemic, this approach led to more favourable outcomes in those locations where health experts were empowered to direct resources.

Standing Tall

Ownership, accountability and responsibility are 'very rewarding and empowering', insist the professionals at Best Practice Consulting in the ACT. 'We get to experience the power of our choices and our actions, and we no longer "think and feel" we are helpless victims.'[25] If we do nothing to wind back the tendency to blame, we simply get more of the same. 'When this blame shifting infiltrates an organization, it can become toxic,' Todd Henry of Accidental Creative Consultancy reflects.

'It erodes collaboration and trust and causes everyone to waste energy in the attempt to avoid being left without a chair when the music stops.'[26]

What Kind of Leader Are You?

The childish part of us can use blame as a smokescreen to hide our inexperience when we've no idea what to do about a problem. When we become leaders, the child/adolescent within often feels extremely vulnerable and so is tempted to pretend to have all the answers. As a fledgling leader, if you take this approach, you'll never mature or develop a good leadership style but will resort to finger-pointing and to grabbing all the credit, whether you deserve it or not. This wastes time, resources and goodwill, and immature leaders often become paranoid because they just don't grow. Instead, they lose control, leaving behind a trail of devastation.

> **An organization that has perfected the blame game is one where hidden fear – fear of failure, of confrontation, of difficult tasks – runs rampant.**
> Mike Staver, *In Business*[27]

'A good manager will look for WHAT to blame, a bad manager will look for WHO to blame,' Azim reflects in a discussion on blame. [28]Author of *Extreme Ownership* and former US Navy SEAL Jocko Willink agrees. 'Leaders must own everything in their world. There is no one else to blame. Leaders must always operate with the understanding that they are part of something greater than themselves and their own personal interests.'[29] Blame-free workplaces funnel their energy into excellence, learning and improving their practices, which doesn't mean an absence of accountability. Regular feedback can swiftly improve the way an individual or group operates.

How Scapegoating Works

How do blamers settle on who's at fault? Some time back, French historian René Girard coined the phrase 'the scapegoat mechanism', noticing how people tend to imitate each other. Over time, this leads to competition and conflict, which can create anger and frustration. Looking for someone who'll find it hard to fight back, they settle on a scapegoat, feeling better as they unite against a common foe.

The scapegoat is never innocent but is deserving of sacrifice in the eyes of those who victimise, regardless of the truth of a situation.[30] Scapegoating may satisfy the childish part of us, but it's not a great outcome for those we choose to blame.

> **The search for a scapegoat is the easiest of all**
> **hunting expeditions.**
> Dwight D Eisenhower, former general and US president

When We Become the Scapegoat

Children learn the questionable art of scapegoating early. We can all recall schoolyard incidents we'd rather forget. Those who fail to grow up carry this willingness to victimise into adult life. Communities and nations also scapegoat, especially during vulnerable times. During the 14th century, the Black Plague was blamed on Jewish people, resulting in whole villages being destroyed, and countless people losing their lives.

Those who've witnessed Budapest's 'Shoes on the Danube Bank' installation have a sense of the unthinkable acts that blame can unleash. Dozens of pairs of carefully sculpted shoes sit by the river's edge to commemorate how, between December 1944 and January 1945, thousands of Jewish and Roma people were arrested and lined up on the edge of the Danube. Before they were shot, they were forced to remove their shoes, as footwear was in short supply. The Danube was a convenient backdrop to these atrocities, as the river then swept away the bodies of these poor souls.

Blame It on Your Parents

When things go awry, parents are often blamed. Some parenting is negligent, sometimes it can even be abusive, yet most parents do a decent job, despite their very human shortcomings. When a group of researchers wanted to know why some kids survive poor parenting relatively unharmed while others are permanently scarred, they discovered that a person's level of resilience was in direct relation to how they viewed what had happened to them during their childhood and teen years.

Those who get lost in blame – of themselves, their parents and their unfortunate experiences – are the least likely to make progress.[31] The solution is for the child/adolescent in us to make peace with past family difficulties. 'Blame then forgive,' suggests adjunct professor of psychology at the University of San Francisco Jim Taylor.[32] This is no easy task, but by trying to understand a parent and recognise their failures, we're better placed to let go of the hurt – if necessary, with professional help. This won't change how a parent behaves, but it can liberate our wounded child self from the toxicity of the past.

The Stories We Tell

So much of what imprisons the child/adolescent is in the stories we feel compelled to air. Yet if we hope to progress, the childlike part of us needs to let go of all those stories of blame, not just the sad stories from our dysfunctional childhood but those of the failed relationships and less-than-ideal workplaces that we stew over.

There is always room for personal improvement. However, if we are unwilling to accept criticism, especially constructive criticism, the child/adolescent in us will forever run the show. We'll never move beyond our gnawing sense of inadequacy and learn how to give of our best. We all need to find the courage to move beyond any child/adolescent tendencies to play the victim and to choose a more empowered way to take charge of our destiny and start to make good things happen.

What to Do with Blame

If we are on the receiving end of blame, Ann Friedman, a Los Angeles–based essayist and media entrepreneur suggests, there are four types of feedback. First, there's expert feedback, in which we listen to those with excellent advice, who can help us fine-tune what we do. Second are those who love what we do and have our best interests at heart. This feedback from experts and those who love us, Friedman insists, is to be valued. Next are our frenemies – enemies posing as friends – then the haters who seek to bring us down. Comments from them serve no useful purpose.[33]

> We live in a culture of complaint, because everyone is always looking for things to complain about. It's all tied in with the desire to blame others for misfortunes and to get some form of compensation into the bargain.
> Alexander McCall Smith, bioethicist[34]

When an exchange starts drifting towards blame, we need to change gear and engage in more mature thinking and conversation instead of allowing the fearful child in us to take over. Equally important is our willingness to stare truth in the face and learn from unfortunate situations, which is why debriefs are so valuable. They help us to understand how a situation went off track, and how best to sort it and avoid such events in the future.

In one onine forum, Connor talks of feeling lucky to work in a no-blame culture in which he and his co-workers identify errors 'as a team'. Everyone is focused on solutions, so they all feel much better about arriving at what's needed.[35] Management consultant Ben Dattner suggests it is essential that such debrief processes are conducted in a spirit of 'good-faith'.[36] This doesn't rule out one-on-one time with the person at the heart of the issue but if we are genuinely focused on finding a solution rather than blaming, we'll conduct that exchange with respect, and in confidence.

No-blame Environments

This more thoughtful approach requires emotional maturity to dial down the intensity of a situation. Blame, by contrast, offers a blunt, often ill-formed response. The child/adolescent in us loves immediacy, so in the heat of the moment we simply want the situation to go away. Life's not that straightforward. It takes additional effort to understand that there's often more than one reason why we find ourselves somewhere we'd rather not be. In understanding this, we're more likely to arrive at a more nuanced response.

In a powerful blog piece, a child and adolescent psychiatrist at John Hopkins Healthcare Hospital Baltimore, Justine Larson, shares how she tries to arrive at the truth of a child's issue. As she talks with the family, she's learned not to jump at what might at first glance seem like an obvious conclusion. 'In my work life I continue to struggle to balance a humility about what we don't know with a confidence in what we do know,' she admits. 'I struggle with keeping the tendency to blame parents in check while at the same time calling parents to task about their parenting when necessary.' Unless she takes time and care to resist blame and to dig deeper, the true reason for a child's problem may not become apparent to her.[37]

We can only achieve the level of insight Justine Larson embodies through patience and perception. This is a skill that needs to be worked on. It comes with a more mature outlook. We're then able to settle on more *complete* solutions and put thorny issues to bed. Life can be exacting, and sometimes it brings us down to earth with a crash. Instead of defaulting to our childish predilection for blame, we're better served if we can find a more nuanced way forward. Pioneering women's health expert Dr Christiane Northrup describes this as risking 'telling the truth to ourselves'.

A More Considered Response

Many life situations upset us, threatening to derail us. The best response is to move beyond blame and see what's really going on.

- In a stretching situation, take a deep breath. Note your emotions, but don't drown in them.
- Try to identify the key issues. How is everyone feeling?
- What's created this situation? How are the others involved likely to be thinking, to respond? Understanding and respect are important here.
- Was this a deliberate act of thoughtlessness? Has it happened before?
- How can you bring down the heat a little, so everyone can talk sensibly? What is a fair and reasonable response?
- Are there highly sensitive issues at play?
- Try to wait until everyone has calmed down before arriving at any solutions.
- If you're at fault, apologise. Make a meaningful gesture. Words can slip off the tongue, but gestures require thought and effort. Together, these actions help build much-needed bridges.

16

Where Are the Grown-ups?

It's difficult to be an effective parent if you haven't yet grown up. Lacking the skills to deal with life's tricky people and situations, you're probably still experiencing all the vulnerabilities a child feels, so you're not in the best place to teach your kids empathy and resilience, how to have strong boundaries and how to handle everything from boredom to bullying. You're probably uncomfortable about disciplining your kids too.

> **Despite our addiction to all things adolescent, we still expect to be treated like adults. 'Don't tell me what to do,' we say. 'Every opinion matters' and 'Treat me with respect,' we add. Of course, fools actually do not deserve respect and their opinions are, at best, a thorough waste of time and, at worst, dangerous.**
>
> John Stonestreet, 'Adolescent Culture'.[1]

When we want to be our child's friend, it's important to recognise some part of us is wanting to be a child too. If we truly care about our kids, we need to be the grown-up, to be a grounded, consistent person they can have confidence in and learn from. When we don't make this all-important transition to adulthood, we become a less than ideal role model.

When Parents Fail to Parent

Parents with a childish mindset do themselves, and their kids, few favours. Like children, they are often victims of mood swings and display far too much attitude. Increasingly, teachers are on the receiving end of immature behaviour from parents, having to deal with habitual rudeness and parents repeatedly ignoring school rules, as well as online and face-to-face verbal attacks.

Some parents resort to physical intimidation. Teacher targeted bullying and harassment (TTBH) is now rife. Some parents are simply malicious, filling their Facebook and Twitter feeds with their ire, while others are practised at pushing back hard, determined to exact special treatment for their little darlings.

When Parents Act Out

American psychologists Robert Evans and Michael Thompson put this trend down to 'an epidemic of anxiety' among parents, coupled with 'a culture of competitiveness and loneliness'. These experts see schools dealing with parents with serious personality disorders, marked by a clear lack of trust and a suspicion that teachers don't have the interests of their pupils at heart.[2]

All the feedback I've had from teachers bears this out. Apart from overestimating a child's abilities, some parents see any attempt to discipline their child as a personal insult. Instead of responding like a grown-up and working *with* the school to help a child deal with their shortcomings, any attempt at discipline can descend into all-out warfare.

What Happens to Our Kids?

Kids then take their cues from their parents, perpetuating these unhelpful traits. One study found that parents who were warm towards their children boosted their self-esteem, while those who overvalued what a child did created narcissistic tendencies.[3] Over-praising sells kids short, setting them up for a difficult time as an adult.

With life moving so fast and many parents time-poor, parents feel anxious about giving their kids the best, creating what UK sociologist Frank Furedi calls 'paranoid parenting'. In their determination to get the most out of every experience their child has, some lose perspective, but this is no excuse for treating teachers and coaches badly.

According to psychologists Evans and Thompson, bullying parents have little self-awareness, always needing someone else to blame. There's no point in rational conversations with such parents, as they are suffering from what Evans and Thompson describe as 'arrested social and emotional development'. The best way to deal with childish parents is to treat them as 'an outrageous and aggressive high school student', these experts suggest.[4]

Infantile Behaviour Up Close

Teaching is now more about 'managing expectations' and 'keeping stupid ass parents at bay', reflects music teacher Sasha in an online chat about problematic parents. At least once a month he gets complaints from parents about how he said something in class that they didn't like. 'Nothing horrible or mean, but practical things like "please remember to practice/work on your music", or "please remember to bring your music/reeds/valve oil to class", or my favourite, "please ask your parents to repair your instrument"'.[5]

'School concerts,' Tracy says in the same thread, 'now come with a whole range of issues, from parents ignoring reserved seats, to thinking nothing of leaving in the middle of a performance, once their child has finished.'[6] In this online discussion, Fiona also describes her experiences of bad parental behaviour. After handling everything from drunk parents to those who talk through performances, the school has had to rethink how it conducts these gatherings. The teachers have produced an etiquette guide for parents, and behaviour at school concerts has improved.[7]

> My best 'wtf' parent story was when a parent approached me WHILE I WAS CONDUCTING A SONG, and when I didn't respond to them they nudged me out of the way so they could take a picture.
>
> Liam, *Reddit* forum[8]

One Pew Research Center report indicates that over half the parents surveyed believed a parent can never be too involved in their child's education. Almost half the parents felt their children's successes and failures were more a reflection of how they were doing as parents than an indication of their child's strengths and weaknesses.[9]

When Kids Fly the Nest

How does this new generation of young adults cope with this level of oversight and protection once they leave home? A 2016 report from Britain's Higher Education Policy Institute noted that the usual uni student experiences of moving away from home for the first time, dealing with less structured learning and living with strangers was proving extremely challenging for many first-time uni students. This, suggests UK sociology professor Frank Furedi, is evident in students from a wide range of backgrounds, and is the result of parents treating their young people like kids.[10]

Given parents' high, possibly unrealistic expectations of their kids, it's not hard to see how this pressure might become unbearable. 'The competitive world of parenting, especially among the wealthy, connected and powerful means that parenting becomes a zero-sum game,' reflects Ramani Durvasula, a psychology professor at a California State University. 'The loaded dice and the backbreaking competitiveness of the admissions process are yielding a generation of adolescents who are plagued with disturbingly high levels of anxiety, depressive symptomatology, wavering self-esteem, and an achievement orientation that allows no room for mistakes, circumspection, or authenticity.'[11]

> **Students today are more like children than adults**
> **and need protection.**
> Eric Posner, University of Chicago[12]

Parental Interference at Work

More disconcerting is how over-the-top parenting is manifesting in the workplace. One Michigan State University employer recruitment survey revealed that four out of ten parents now research information on prospective companies for their uni student children, almost a third sent out résumés for their children, while just over a quarter of companies sampled had parents contact them to try to influence hiring decisions. Twelve per cent of parents had attempted to set up an interview for their child, while 15 per cent of parents with university-age students had rung and complained when their child wasn't hired.

Parents now also get involved in work assignments, to help their kids meet work deadlines and polish up their work. Some employees won't meet with their employer, if they're to be disciplined, without having a parent present. Mothers are more likely to attend career information days on behalf of their kids, while a growing number of dads are getting involved with salary negotiations.[13]

This is what disempowering a whole generation looks like. A 2016 OfficeTeam survey, which looked at helicopter parenting in the workplace, reported that one in three managers had experienced parental interference at work. These employers told of a variety of issues, from one mother Skyping in during her child's interview, to parents calling to see why their children weren't hired.[14]

> Twenty years ago, parents *told* their children to get a job.
> Ten years ago, parents *encouraged* their children to
> get jobs. Now, parents are attending job interviews
> alongside their children.
>
> Amy Morin, psychotherapist[15]

Many millennials also remain financially dependent on their parents. They state they'd like to be free, but almost three-quarters of this generation in the US alone currently enjoy a level of financial support from their parents.[16] This creates a condition of helplessness that keeps young people forever fragile and beholden to their parents.

In his iconic work *The Fall of Public Man*, sociologist Richard Sennett talks of how, when we burden relationships with our unspoken need for others to provide us with 'security, rest and permanence', we set ourselves and others up for failure. The childish self is more likely to assume there's something wrong with the relationship when, inevitably, it sours, failing to see that their unreasonable expectations are sabotaging an otherwise good relationship.

Increasing Pressure on Employers

The intensive investment some parents have in their kids places an additional onus on employers in the duty of care they're now expected to provide. Workplaces have to accommodate a generation more used to making demands than requests. This forces employers into having to work harder at bolstering a young employee's confidence on the one hand, while also encouraging that young person to learn from and acknowledge the greater expertise of those around them.

Workplaces are also having to teach emerging generations that listening is as important as sharing their own ideas. They also need to explain the importance of work etiquette and that appropriate dress at work is essential. With this generation averse to or fearing feedback, organisations have to work to assist them to accept feedback with an open mind and with grace.

> **We're seeing the return of the *in locus parentus* [sic]**
> **employer.**
> Neil Howe, CEO LifeCourse Associates[17]

One friend, who has worked in the theatre for a couple of decades, told recently of how stressful his job had become. As associate director, he has to give detailed feedback to performers. Recently, he's noticed a palpable fear when he approaches a young performer after a show, which means he has to spend time reassuring them before he can give them much-needed feedback.

How Employers Are Responding

This kind of input is increasingly necessary if employers want to get the job done. One 2017 CBI/Pearson workplace survey indicated that 32 per cent of employers were dissatisfied with graduate 'attitudes and behaviours' around 'self-management' and 'resilience'. A third were less than impressed with graduate literacy, and almost a third felt graduate numeracy needed improvement. There was a need seen for greater personal development alongside the academic achievements graduates bring to a workplace.[18]

When UK marketing guru Simon Sinek launched his 'Millennials in the Workplace' YouTube piece, it attracted over a million views. He spoke of how a generation 'given everything for nothing' has created a tsunami of unmet expectations at work. 'They're thrust into the real world and in the instant they find out they're not special, their mums can't get them a promotion, that you get nothing for coming in last – and by the way, you can't just have it because you want it.'[19]

Crescens George, the chief operating officer of Be Wiser Insurance Group, admits to wasting huge amounts of time on 'graduate ego massaging', which takes the shine off whatever talent a new graduate might bring to the workplace.[20] Naturally, children and adolescents need plenty of guidance, but knowing what are reasonable expectations around performance and mentoring in the workplace is now a tough call for employers. Having to use valuable time to compensate for employee gaps in behaviour and on-the-job tasks due to inadequate parenting isn't ideal.

Much-needed Resilience

How much easier life would be if our young had been exposed to situations that helped them be more resilient. Resilience needs challenges to make it strong. Iconic educator Jean Illsley Clarke goes further, stating that over-parenting is a form of child neglect.

Clarke's research has discovered that overindulging kids happens at all income levels. 'Too many things [possessions],' she reports, 'result in lack of respect for things and people. Doing things for our children that they should be doing themselves results in helplessness and lack of competence. Lack of structure results in irresponsibility. What we found in our big study was that nobody said "thank you" to their parents, but the word "resent" came up often.'[21]

Clarke and her colleagues have come up with an overindulgence checklist for parents. They suggest parents ask if a scenario they're attracted to is likely to enhance their child's life experience or if they're simply pandering to their child and taking up a disproportionate amount of the family resources in the process.

The Praising Dilemma

While parenting is a complex business, the most effective solutions can be relatively straightforward. In one Stanford University study, in which children were given a puzzle to solve, some were praised for their intelligence, the rest for their effort. All were then asked to choose between two new puzzles, one was harder than the other. Most of those who were praised for their effort chose the more difficult puzzle.

> **A child is embedded in interactions with friends, family, community. The way those other systems are functioning plays a huge role in the capacity of that child to overcome adversity.**
> Ann S Masten, University of Minnesota[22]

Later, when these same kids were given a different difficult puzzle to work on, those praised for their effort enjoyed the new test and worked hard at it, while those who'd been praised for their intelligence gave up more easily, fearing they weren't 'smart' after all. This suggests that children who are overpraised are less likely to give something a go unless they're sure of success.[23]

Well-off Kids Now at Risk

Exposing this new generation to an abundance of life skills is far more helpful than simply caving in and doing what they want in the moment. Youth from wealthy homes have been identified by experts as a newly vulnerable group. Affluenza is rapidly spreading among upper-middle-class, white-collar families, and their children are exhibiting higher substance use, depression and anxiety levels needing urgent intervention.[24]

Another study found that 'across the years, our focus groups with affluent teens have revealed several troubling trends regarding drinking'. Adolescents getting involved in binge drinking is 'distressingly common'. With easy access to large amounts of alcohol, these kids were frequently drinking to get drunk and 'party hard'.

Wealthy students not caught up in substance abuse displayed the highest 'anxious-depressed' symptoms, as well as rule-breaking behaviour. They also had 'the poorest levels of attachment to their parents. Displaying feelings of alienation, these kids were also most subject to parental criticism.'[25] All these risky teen behaviours are seen as forms of self-injury. The 'relentless pressures of upward mobility in a culture of affluence has become "The American Nightmare"', observes Tim Kasser, a psychology professor at Knox College.[26]

Privilege Doesn't Always Deliver

'Elite educations do not render a person immune from mental illness or bad marriages, nor are they guarantees of lifetime ease,' reflects Ramani Durvasula, a psychology professor at California State University. 'The real losers in all of this,' she adds, 'are the entitled parents' children … [who] will be sorting through the psychological wreckage for a long time. They will have to unlearn their parents' message.'[27]

Achievement is regarded as a good thing, but immature parents are being caught up in our performance culture. They overschedule, put pressure on their children, see them more as an investment or as a path to parental and/or social success. It's no surprise, then, that the American Psychological Association's 'Stress in America' research project revealed that one in five children worry 'a lot'.[28] One HealthAmerica study stated that 41 per cent of children aged nine to thirteen felt stressed all or most of the time, as they had too much to do, and 78 per cent wished they had more free time.[29]

Psychologist Dr Madeline Levine says that children from well-off middle-class homes are three times more likely to suffer depression and anxiety in later life, and are more vulnerable to drug abuse, self-harm and even suicide. Yet 'deep down', she adds, 'we all know that the greatest gift anyone can give to their child is a loving and trusting validation of their essentially different-from-us selves'.[30]

> **Encourage, enable but don't push is my philosophy.**
> **I do insist homework is done, but beyond that I let them**
> **decide on activities, certainly no extra tutoring,**
> **6 hours plus homework is plenty.**
> Bram, a parent responding to an article in *The Guardian*[31]

Achievement Isn't Everything

This pressure on kids to get good grades and perform well often comes at the expense of a child learning important social skills such as kindness, observes psychology professor Suniya Luthar of Arizona State University. She found that the children whose parents valued achievements over kindness were more likely to be anxious and depressed.[32]

Too many parents also exhibit a 'worrying over-identification' with their children's performance. Peter Congdon, an educational psychologist, tells of one child who was forced to take early-morning swimming lessons. 'She didn't want to be a champion swimmer, but she was doing it to please her father,' he says. What effect does this dynamic have?

In an article in *The Irish Times*, Dave Hannigan, a long-time resident of Long Island, New York, describes seeing kids give up because they no longer have a life beyond sport. '[It's] no surprise at all to those of us who have experienced firsthand the toxic culture created by martinet coaches in search of the next big thing, and demented parents trying to live vicariously through the achievements of their offspring.'[33]

Life doesn't have to be this way. 'As a primary school teacher in Dublin in the late 1960s, I would bring my school team of [Gaelic]) footballers to the 15-acres in the Phoenix Park every Wednesday to play games against other schools,' recalls Martin, responding to Dave Hannigan's article. 'NOT A PARENT IN SIGHT! And the kids had fun, it was enjoyable, and I had fun encouraging them. So, my belief is that parents should NOT be able to attend their children's sporting events.'[34]

> **Striving and perfectionism can be the loneliest emotional space to occupy.**
> Cayden, a parent responding to an article in *The Guardian* [35]

Helping Kids Join the Dots

A good parent helps their kids to move beyond self-interest. They are not afraid to talk to their children about issues, to assist them to unpack the pros and cons of a situation. Whether it's discussing the Black Lives Matter or #MeToo movements, helping an elderly neighbour or discussing homelessness after passing someone sleeping rough, parents play a key role in helping their kids better comprehend and appreciate their world.

Good parents also assist their children to find ways to get involved with their community, so that one day their kids can create, and appreciate, their own sense of community. To achieve this, they need to develop their life skills, learn how to problem-solve, be flexible and resilient, work well with others and build a solid friendship group. Parents encourage best by listening and being there when something matters to their child, letting them learn to pace themselves and encourage *their* choices.

A Better Way Forward

There are so many ways to empower kids. Start early, and make sure your kids have a childhood.

- Choose age-appropriate toys, clothes and experiences.
- As soon as they're able, encourage your child to dress themselves.
- Helping with household chores should be seen as a privilege, as it assists kids to gather practical life skills, and respect the work required to run a home.
- Children need to learn patience – to save and wait for things. A one in, one out policy helps them think about the environment, and what they really want.
- Kids also need to learn respect and how to make guests feel welcome in their home.
- Encourage thankyou letters, and small gestures of thanks.
- Ensure there's a culture of recycling, fundraising and volunteering. Take time to celebrate the joy these activities bring.

17

Toxic Happiness

We all hope for happiness, but for the child/adolescent the pursuit of happiness can easily become a full-time job. Expecting always to be happy, our child self much prefers to neatly sidestep life's big questions and challenges, then wonders why those issues never seem to go away.

Marketers play on this expectation, offering us a measure of happiness with almost every product we purchase. Too often, our immature selves seize at these promises, frequently working to the point of exhaustion, to afford the saccharine dreams on offer. Thought leader Bryant H. McGill suggests this scramble to buy happiness is a new form of slavery. 'We think we're the consumer,' he reflects, 'but we're the consumed.'[1]

> **The greatest fear that human beings experience is not death, which is inevitable, but consideration of the distinct possibility of living a worthless life.**
> Kilroy J Oldster, *Dead Toad Scrolls*[2]

Happiness versus Wellbeing

What constitutes happiness? 'The great majority of adolescents and young adults in the developed world say they are happy, healthy and satisfied with their lives, and their life expectancy continues to rise,' notes Australian researcher Richard Eckersley. Other studies, he points out, track a clear drop in wellbeing, with young people suffering growing chronic issues such as obesity, diabetes, heart disease, some cancers and mental illness.[3]

Children willingly place their happiness in the hands of others, looking to parents and others to help cheer them up whenever they feel down. While we continue to work hard to stay upbeat, we're not winning in the happiness stakes. In the UK alone there are over 70 million anti-depressant prescriptions annually, almost *double* that a decade ago. The latest US figures suggest a 64 per cent increase in the use of antidepressants in just fifteen years.

Keeping Up the Good Vibes

Our performance culture prods, if not bullies, us into presenting only our happy self to the world. 'It has become all of our jobs,' suggests teacher Stewart Dunn, 'to paint a picture of positivity for ourselves and the outside world.'[4]

'Modern Western culture is a health hazard,' Richard Eckersley insists, 'a form of "cultural fraud" promoting images and ideals of "the good life", which serve the demand for economic growth, especially through increased consumption, but do not meet [our] psychological needs or reflect [our] social realities.'[5]

> **It's definitely NOT all sunshine and bunnies
> out there, folks.**
>
> Kate Willis, *Goodreads* reviewer[6]

Some time back, *Women's Health* magazine displayed several Instagram posts, alongside the feelings their contributors had when posting.

Rachel, aged twenty-one, perched on top of her fridge full of fun and attitude. Caption: 'Was there a party, if I wasn't on top of the fridge?' – but Rachel admitted, 'I didn't want to go to this party. I felt so empty, I was shaking, because what if everyone actually hates me?'

Marilyn, forty-eight, smiling as the sun shines through the window. Caption: 'Sometimes you just have to smile, especially when you are this cute!', later confessing, 'Today is a tough one. Feeling sad, overwhelmed, and emotionally drained trying to cope with my father's death.'[7]

The disconnect between the images Rachel and Marilyn posted and their true feelings helps us see just how poignant and disturbing our childlike need to constantly project 'happy' can be. The hundreds of thousands of fake images of happiness posted daily are injurious because they fail to reflect the many threads of our lives.

How Do I Really Feel?

In promoting wall-to-wall happy faces and lives, the immature parts of us encourage others down this same poisonous track, eroding our emotional health and theirs in the process. The child/adolescent much prefers to live by avoidance and half-truths – but what does this achieve? 'When we paint over our true emotions we make it difficult to create and foster honest, open relationships,' counsels Stewart Dunn. 'We show one side to a friend, and then when we need or want them to be there for us, and they are not, we become upset or feel hurt. We expect them to see behind a closed door.'[8]

Danish psychology professor Svend Brinkmann says that insisting we're constantly happy can leave us emotionally stunted. But we need to understand that negative thoughts and feelings can be useful to help us make sense of the world. If we've little real experience of dealing with less welcome thoughts and emotions, how are we likely to fare when something truly unfortunate happens? Put simply, the world darkens when we or someone close to us remains silent, when we really need to share our concerns.[9]

Losing Touch with Reality

We can have too much of a good thing, psychologist Celine Sugay suggests, whether it's too much food or exercise, washing our hands or sleeping. 'A person who is extremely happy, and always happy,' she says, 'may not be completely in touch with what's real and what's not.'[10] We need to recognise there'll always be moments that dismay us – and dark nights of the soul. There isn't a marriage, workplace or family that doesn't face crises.

> **Many people think excitement is happiness ... But when you are excited you are not peaceful. True happiness is based on peace.**
> Thich Nhat Hanh, *The Art of Power*[11]

Selling Our Kids Short

Our kids must have a realistic view of the world. Avoidance of all unpleasantness means they end up with few tools for when life gets bumpy. In a powerful piece in *The Atlantic*, Greg Lukianoff, CEO of the Foundation for Individual Rights in Education, and social psychologist Jonathan Haidt, of New York's Stern School of Business, express their concern at the growing trend they describe as the 'flight to safety' – the removal of 'dangerous' structures in playgrounds and every possible health or safety threat, leaving our children 'coddled'. 'What are we doing to our students,' they ask, 'if we encourage them to develop extra-thin skin in the years just before they leave the cocoon of adult protection and enter the workforce?'[12]

The data doesn't look encouraging. Almost all mental health directors in one US survey stated that the number of students with *severe* psychological issues on campus is increasing. Emotional distress is also reported as 'high and rising'. As far back as 2014, the American College Health Association told of how 54 per cent of university students were suffering 'overwhelming anxiety'. Comparing these figures with students five years earlier revealed a 49 per cent increase in extreme anxiety among more recent students.[13]

Recasting Our Experience of Work

The pressure to fit into highly persuasive narratives of happiness is now creeping into the workplace. It is important to be positive and to do our best at work but there are times when some adjustments are needed so things don't veer off track. Sticking to the company script when that narrative is no longer valid doesn't help any outfit grow its potential. Happiness for its own sake encourages superficial values and interactions. There's little to be gained by promoting 'happy' over competent.

> **Corporate downsizers fire every third person,**
> **then put up inspirational posters in the halls to**
> **cover the psychic wounds.**
> Ralph Whitehead, social critic[14]

The Only Way Is Up

Over two decades ago, Ralph Whitehead noted the sudden growth in motivational products focused on the workplace. 'With the virtual disappearance of the stable corporation, guaranteed lifetime employment is becoming only a memory,' he reflected. 'Workers now have to rely on their own skills and energies, and must constantly sell themselves to their employers,' he surmised, adding, 'Changes in the economy are turning us all into salespersons.'[15]

To sell oneself well, a worker is expected to be relentlessly upbeat – someone prepared to go the extra mile, regardless of whether they have the time and resources to do their job properly, or of how well or poorly they're paid, or even of whether they're victims of wage theft. Even when the security guard arrives at your desk and demands you pack up your things, if you hope for future success, then you'd better keep on smiling.

> **This was the corporate world's great gift to the laid-off employees and overworked survivors – positive thinking.**
> Barbara Ehrenreich, *Bright-Sided:*
> *How Positive Thinking Is Undermining America*[16]

Dr Spencer Johnson's *Who Moved My Cheese?* is a motivational story of two mice who enjoy a limitless supply of cheese until one day the cheese is gone. Driven by hunger, the mice seek long and hard, until they find more cheese. The moral of the story being that when changes occur, an employee needs to chase new cheese with a steely determination.

This 'classic' has been given to countless individuals when they lose their jobs and has sold over thirty million copies. It offers such pearls as 'What you are afraid of is never as bad as what you imagine' and 'The quicker you let go of old cheese, the sooner you find new cheese'. Or, as Jeff puts it in a thread on the book, 'Laid off? Why it's just a chance to better yourself! … You just need to try harder! Put on those little mouse running shoes and run that maze!'[17]

Questionable Expectations

When responsibility is only down to workers to play the game (be accountable), there's less onus on employees to do the right thing. And once the immature parts of us insist others should change their behaviour to create the outcome we hope for, then we're all treading on very thin ice, suggests sociologist Will Davies. 'It's not long before you're in the sort of, rather more bullying dimension of workfare and the austerity agenda saying, "Well, you've got to get out of bed soon, and that way, none of these bad things would happen to you as much, and you'll stop feeling sorry for yourself".[18] This kind of positive thinking, suggests Barbara Ehrenreich, requires a great deal of discipline. And there's absolutely no excuse for failure. Any failure to meet your goals is down to you not trying hard enough or believing enough.[19]

When Things Go Wrong

Sociologist Karen Cerulo warns that optimism can blind us to the truth of a situation. If we focus purely on the positive, we may well underestimate the real negatives demanding our attention. In *Never Saw It Coming*, Cerulo examines the impact of our unwillingness to read the warning signs before Hurricane Katrina, the NASA *Challenger* disaster and the Iraq War.

'The reductionism of a lot of happiness science, or the happiness industry, when adapted by the business world, or in policy settings, is regrettable,' sociologist Will Davies insists. 'We lose the nuance, and the ambiguity, and the mysteries of human life in the process.'

With face scanning and other recognition technologies such as Affectiva and Realeyes we're now able to read how a person is feeling. Beyond Verbal technology, for example, monitors our tone of voice, and can rate how happy we are at any time. Neuroscience can get inside our heads and track what's happening. How might this access to data play out in the future? Davies asks.[20]

A Better Way Forward

Mature work cultures encourage honest feedback from all employees, an approach which encourages *everyone* to be more engaged and productive, creating a solution-oriented, more transparent workplace. The McKinsey Global Institute suggests that engaged workers are 20 to 25 per cent more effective in the workplace.[21]

Honest feedback empowers us to be the best we can be at work, genuinely invested in what's happening. Where people are comfortable giving and receiving honest feedback, trust and respect grow. Behavioural statistician Joseph Folkman assessed the ability of over 100,000 leaders to give honest feedback and found greater trust in leaders who were more transparent.[22] Truth spoken kindly and fairly liberates the best in us.

When Sickness Becomes Failure

Having to stick to a happy script can imprison us. In these more health-conscious times, being healthy brings many benefits but can also leave people feeling vulnerable, if not guilty, should they receive a serious or terminal diagnosis. We've all witnessed friends feeling like they've failed, believing they've let themselves and others down by getting sick.

> **Happiness can't be reduced to a few agreeable sensations.**
> **Rather, it is a way of being and of experiencing the world –**
> **a profound fulfilment that suffuses every moment and**
> **endures despite inevitable setbacks.**
> Matthieu Ricard, Buddhist monk[23]

Some years back, two unrelated friends, brilliant women, discovered they had serious, possibly terminal, breast cancer. Determined to create a miracle, they both refused medical intervention. While these beautiful women were unfailingly upbeat, they both lost their lives. Positive thoughts alone won't always get us over the line.

Stick to the Script

Enforced happiness can also be a form of control. 'We tend to think that tyrants rule through fear – fear of the secret police, of torture, detention, the gulag,' reflects writer Barbara Ehrenreich, 'but some of the world's most mercilessly authoritarian regimes have also demanded constant optimism and cheer from their subjects.'[24] Some regimes are fixated on people sticking to the script. When East Germany was part of the USSR, a staggering 91,000 people were employed by the secret police, the Stasi, to monitor the East German people while a further 173,000 worked as informants. That's a lot of effort to sustain a happy narrative.

This inability to deal with the truth is evident in drug company cover-ups, local government corruption, environmental disasters and the unwillingness of some institutions, most notably the Catholic Church, to deal honestly and transparently with child abuse. Sometimes it takes immense courage to stand up for what is right. But that's what being a fully fledged adult demands of us.

When Emotional Health Takes a Dive

While the child in us might prefer to live in bliss, research suggests that pretending always to be happy actually puts the pressure on. One University of California Berkeley study found that those who judged their negative emotions, rather than accepting them, ended up more stressed. Those who didn't rush to change their less comfortable emotions enjoyed better psychological health and emotional resilience overall.

University of Melbourne study co-author Professor Brock Bastian reminds us that being unhappy sometimes is 'normal and healthy'. 'When people place a great deal of pressure on themselves to feel happy, or think that others around them do [have these expectations of them], they are more likely to see their negative emotions and experiences as signals of failure.' The result? These attitudes only add to our unhappiness.[25]

It's thought that our very avoidance of uncomfortable emotions creates many psychological challenges. 'Avoiding negative emotion buys you short-term gain, at the price of long-term pain,' explains psychology professor Noam Shpancer of Otterbein University. Our emotions can be a 'source of information' – a bit like a weather forecast. All our emotions are useful and can tell us about everything from our health and work to the company we keep.

Sit on the sofa and be tired. Admit that you feel lonely.
Fiona Thomas, mental health blogger[26]

Accepting a negative emotion, Shpancer states, helps diminish 'its destructive power'. This counter-intuitive approach, he says, is akin to a swimmer caught in a rip. Losing control as they're drawn further from the beach, often swimmers panic – fighting the current, they end up drowning. The swimmer who goes *with* the current finds the current loses its force and they can then swim safely back to the shore.[27] 'True happiness – and true emotional intelligence,' suggests Steve Handel, founder of The Emotion Machine, 'requires that we see the gifts in every emotion, not just joy and pleasure, but also in temporary pain and suffering.'[28]

You Can't Buy Happiness

A recent American Time Use Survey (ATUS), which measures happiness, found that happiness grew for low-income workers when they became more financially secure by earning more than US$25,000 a year. Happiness began to tail off when annual salaries nudged past US$100,000. Those in higher income brackets also experienced the 'least sense of purpose'. Paul Dolan, a professor of behavioural science at the London School of Economics, suggests, 'If you are not struggling to make ends meet, I propose that you rein in the social narrative that encourages you to endlessly pursue more money.'[29]

Life is tricky and complicated at times but it's in engaging with others that we find meaning and fulfilment. 'The strongest predictor of happiness is not money, or external recognition through success or fame,' June Gruber, assistant professor of psychology and neuroscience at the University of Colorado, insists. 'It's having meaningful social relationships … the best way to increase your happiness is to stop worrying about being happy, and instead divert your energy to nurturing the social bonds you have with other people.'[30]

Paul Dolan agrees: 'Happiness is situated in what we do and who we spend time with. It does not reside in some story we tell ourselves about what we think should make us happy.'[31] Also, we vastly overestimate what pleasurable moments can deliver, according to Harvard psychologist Daniel Gilbert. 'Neither positive nor negative events hit us as hard, or for as long, as we anticipate,' he insists. He also found that in our frantic search for happiness, we often tend to seek out more variety than we need. 'We all think we should try a different doughnut every time we go to the shop,' he says, 'but the fact is that people are measurably happier when they have their favorite on every visit – provided the visits are sufficiently separated in time.'[32]

Working on Ourselves

We often have a good reason to feel down at times, but just trying to bury our unhappy feelings doesn't always work and we may need assistance to deal with these emotions. Talking with someone we trust can help – that's when we learn that our expectations may be too high. Perhaps we're exhausted, burnt out or feel we've let ourselves down, and we may need professional help.

Daring to go deeper can deliver huge dividends. 'I tend people's trauma for a living,' NLP practitioner Justice Bartlett explains. 'They don't come to me to pretend their pain is not there; they come to me to face it with compassion and skilful means. I have to stay open to it, and yet not get bogged down by it ... New Age spiritualism often has us thinking that by simply focusing on the positive, we can somehow heal our wounds, and the wounds of the world. This is immature and ineffective. To grow, heal and change, we need to face our discomfort.'[33]

Embracing the ups and downs of life demands courage. If we choose avoidance, we continue to struggle with our pain. Philanthropist Ashley Dawson-Damer admits, 'I had to wait ten more years before I found the doctor who would help me to unravel a complex life ... a woman, who listened, who helped me find my way through. Therapy laid bare my life, as layer upon layer was examined. So much was explained, and so much was now understood.'[34]

Beyond Happiness

Almost two decades ago, Jonathan Haidt of the Stern School of Business got college students to examine the nature of happiness. Some were shown video clips of Mother Theresa, while the control group saw an 'emotionally neutral but interesting documentary', followed by *America's Funniest Home Videos*.

The 'happy videos' inspired people to go off and do things for themselves, while the 'elevation' experienced after seeing Mother Theresa's life and works prompted those students to focus more on others. As human beings, 'we are easily and strongly moved by the altruism of others', Haidt reflects. Positive moral emotions, he suggests, are 'a new frontier', with 'vast potential' to improve our lives and our society.[35]

We can also experience this 'elevation' in nature, especially when we travel to wilderness areas. We are embraced by something far more uplifting than is found in everyday life. It's in these pristine, off-the-beaten-track locations that we sense, for even a brief moment, where we fit in the cosmos.

A Smaller, More Personal Vision

'The happy moments aren't the big Hollywood ones,' suggests British writer Tobias Jones, 'they are little glimpses of hope.'[36] True happiness is something quieter, less obvious than the bright lights the child/adolescent hankers for. Life asks our immature selves to look beyond the obvious and question if the assumptions we've made around happiness hold weight.

Austrian psychologist and survivor of the horrors of the holocaust Viktor Frankl suggests that purpose is the cornerstone of life – far more than the search for happiness.[37] To find our sense of purpose, we have to let go of our childish expectations of happiness, so we can explore the possibilities in front of us.

Witnessing the level of need in their inner-city Sydney community during the pandemic, Michelle Gomes and Maureen Lee set up a Blessings Box – a pine wardrobe found in a back lane that they turned into a street pantry with the slogan 'Take What You Need, Leave What You Can'. This helps support those struggling to feed themselves – a hungry Uber driver, someone who's lost their job, or someone who's just having a bad day and is in need of a little kindness.[38]

Inviting feedback, Gomes and Lee soon saw how much the Blessings Box meant to those needing help, and to the community, who felt proud to live in a place where people were happy to share. Women from wealthier suburbs turned up with generous donations of food; and rough sleepers, who were finally housed, looked 'happy and shiny' as they helped themselves to pasta to cook their own meal for the first time in years.[39] This shows us what's possible when we let go of our childish quest for constant happiness and embrace larger, more fulfilling possibilities.

True Happiness

Bad and sad things happen. It's part of life. We each need to thrive, but how best to achieve this?

- Try to be more mindful of the quiet joys in each moment.
- Spend time around those who make your soul sing.
- Find your *own* way of expressing a purposeful life – and share your insights with others.
- Take time to celebrate little and big milestones in meaningful ways.
- Don't dwell on all the issues around you. Follow the dictates of your heart.
- Savour all the good and beautiful moments in the day. Recognise that difficulties come, and also that they go.
- Dare to get help if you're not coping – we all have those times when we feel like we're drowning.
- Be your best self, for your own sake, and for the sake of those who love you.
- Who could benefit from your help right now?

18

Believe It and It's Yours

Never before has so much been promised to our child/adolescent selves. The almost limitless motivational literature available leads us to expect the world. 'No matter who or where you are right now,' one motivation expert assures us, 'as long as you sincerely believe in yourself, you can make it. It does not matter whether you are a doctor, a janitor, a teacher or if you are poor and in debt.'[1]

These messages appeal to our childlike self, that part of us that hopes to magically find ourselves living in a dream home, with a dream partner, wardrobe and bank balance, with little or no effort.

We might experience a lucky break, or a moment of serendipity, but that's not how we achieve all we're capable of. The road to being a good neurosurgeon, hairdresser or marine biologist demands more than wishful thinking. Training for such professions will bring challenges, often lots of study and sacrifices along the way. This is not what our child self wants to hear.

The Dangers of Make-believe

Some of our dreams will be fulfilled, bringing us much joy and satisfaction, but some dreams won't eventuate. Our timing may be out, our dreams may not fit our talents or someone brighter may just pip us at the post – which doesn't mean our dream wasn't valid, just that we might not land where we'd hoped.

Vincent van Gogh failed to sell a painting in his short, frequently tumultuous life. Should he have packed up his paints and gone home? A dream that fails to reach others may provide us with a much-needed learning curve, invaluable friendships or more resilience. Today, of course, van Gogh's paintings are priceless.

> **We're addicted to positive thinking, Oprah and *The Secret*
> has sent the whole world on a bender.**
> John Gravois, *Slate*[2]

We need to remain grounded but also be willing to give our dreams all the love, passion and hard work we can. Groundedness anchors us and gives us a firm foundation, qualities not seen in those in our emerging generation who simply want to be rich and, if possible, famous.

What's the Cost?

In his book *The High Price of Materialism*, Knox College psychology professor Tim Kasser, investigating kids wanting to be rich, found that their dreams were sparked by regular exposure to the lives of celebrities and reality TV. Some kids lived in homes where must-have items were in short supply, while others grew up in vulnerable circumstances and saw wealth as a way of creating a safe future for themselves. As dazzling as these dreams may be, is this the best we can offer our young?

Regardless of our background, the child/adolescent in us does love things that sparkle and stories of straw being spun into gold. Is the desire to be rich a worthy goal in itself, or is it more helpful to understand what's driving our need to be wealthy? Our immature self aches to belong, to have others admire us and to free ourselves from life's ups and downs.

When we understand what's driving us, we see our aspirations in a new light, and can then assist our kids to do likewise.

Not Much Substance Here

Prosperity literature is cloyingly self-focused, playing to our child/ adolescent yearnings. When we're struggling financially, our childish self is tempted by get-rich-quick schemes, hoping that a free home or apartment might just land in our lap in exchange for some serious positive thinking on our part. This incomplete thinking can only ever lead us down a rabbit hole, as we lose precious time longing for what is unlikely to eventuate. Where is the encouragement to plan and save, to work towards what we want?

During my years in book publishing, I read countless manuscripts by self-styled motivational gurus who'd left their highly paid corporate jobs to encourage others along the wealth creation track. None of them ever inspired readers to think about *why* they wanted what they did, about the true nature of happiness or of giving back. Intriguingly, all of these wealth gurus worked only with those who were already relatively well off. This was when my discomfort with prosperity narratives began.

That's Not How It Works

'Money management really isn't about math; it's emotional!' suggests one coach who describes themselves as a 'financial lifeguard', empowering people to rescue their 'financial dignity'.[3] These messages resonate with our immature selves, which are drawn to dreams of affluence and unreality. Our child self doesn't want to worry about working out a budget when it's easier to keep dreaming of a wealthy future. The difficulty with this thinking is that real life is far more complex and volatile than these simplistic formulas suggest.

A Little Perspective Helps

Even those who live modestly now have so much more than our forebears, and thus much to be grateful for. Our immature selves aren't interested in such details. We're too busy looking at what everyone else has and wanting more to see how this pattern of envy and fear of missing out plays out. Never have we had so much stuff – but where has this access to so many possessions left us?

Currently, around ten million households in the UK have no savings at all.[4] Added to this, 53 per cent of American households have no emergency savings, putting millions at risk of eviction and other dire consequences.[5] One in ten Americans admits they'd struggle to find the money for an 'unexpected $400 expense'. Others say they'd have to use a credit card, pay day loan, sell something, or borrow from a family member to settle a bill this size.[6] It's not just low-income Americans who'd struggle – a quarter of those earning $150,000 a year also admit to having no savings.[7]

What Are We Doing?

How did our child/adolescent selves come to be so vulnerable? A recent Foodbank Australia survey found that one in five kids was missing meals, with some even taking to chewing paper to try to feel full.[8] Food Secure Canada reports that 'hunger is something that we at the hospital increasingly see among the families that bring their children to us for medical attention each and every day'.[9] In France, three million children currently suffer from some form of deprivation, with a million kids turning up at school hungry every day.[10]

These vulnerable kids need us to get out of our child/adolescent silos and care. It is possible that we've been so caught up in our wealth goals that we've neglected to keep essential services, such as schools and hospitals, in good shape. What biting social issues will this likely lead to?

This impoverishment is happening while we sit in the comfort of our homes, dreaming of the next treat we'd like to indulge in. Is this what genuine fulfilment looks like, or is this yet another manifestation of the child/adolescent wanting to be doted on and showered with life's bounty?

In taking care of ourselves, it is possible we've lost sight of 'enoughness'. A friend told me recently about a family member who's constantly depressed and had spent well over $100,000 on a new kitchen. Eighteen months later she fell out of love with her kitchen, had it ripped out and spent more than twice as much on a complete makeover. Does she really think a new kitchen will help with her depression? This may seem ludicrous but many of us fall into the same trap.

> **Prosperity is a way of living and thinking, and not just having money or things.**
> Eric Butterworth, former NYC Unity minister[11]

Sharing the Good

We're told we need to be positive at all times, which for most of us means working extra hard at our positive thinking. Positivity is a good attribute, as long as it's underpinned with realism. The flip side of this is that if you have a major loss – a job, a business or long-term relationship – you're judged as not being upbeat enough and failing in the optimism stakes. How can you or I possibly fail, given the sea of motivational videos, podcasts, books, DVDs and online courses available to assist us to overcome all obstacles and create all the wealth we wish for?

God Rewards the Good

What happens when wealth is equated with godliness? 'If you're struggling with your finances,' Pastor Joel Osteen of Lakewood Church in Houston offers, 'get around blessed people, generous people, people who are well off.'[12] Networking can be helpful, but it's no substitute for hard work, focus, talent and timing. The child/adolescent much prefers an easier route, hoping that by mixing with wealthy people, their affluence will somehow rub off on them.

The more we examine abundance literature, the more intriguing and, at times, bizarre it gets. 'How can you follow the sixth-richest pastor in the world?' one member of the Lakewood congregation was asked about his pastor, who lives in a multi-million-dollar, three-storey home with a swimming pool and parking for twenty cars. Their reply was, 'We don't want to follow a loser.'[13]

Don't Burst My Bubble

As we hide away in a nest crammed full of stuff, our childish self has little interest in engaging with others outside our narrow circle. We're too busy daydreaming about what we want from life. The wider realities of what's happening in the world are extremely low on our agenda.

Socialising with New York's elite during the effervescent years of the 1920s, F Scott Fitzgerald was well placed to write about the astonishing wealth and reckless pursuit of happiness he witnessed. In his novel *The Beautiful and the Damned*, Gloria realises her dreams, finding a rich husband, only to watch him slide into alcoholism and despair. Idle and self-indulged, Gloria is indifferent to others, stating, 'I don't care about truth. I want some happiness.'

This is the child/adolescent speaking – one who doesn't want to have to think about homelessness, environmental degradation or our swiftly changing geopolitical situation, which threatens the foundations of democracies around the world. Western 'high-consumption' lifestyles, independent researcher Richard Eckersley argues, are 'hostile to health and wellbeing' and require huge resources, which damage the environment and our social health. 'Modernity does not represent the best of all possible worlds, or even the best path to it,' he states. 'Its benefits are emphasised, but its costs are underestimated.'[14]

> **Lust for possession and greed has ravaged the soul of humanity like a great cancer, metastasizing throughout society in the form of a nouveau post-human, consumer hedonism.**
> Bryant McGill, *Voice of Reason*[15]

A New Gospel

This infantile ache for bucketloads of possessions and constant excitement to magically land in our lives has spilled over into some forms of Christianity, where God and/or Jesus appear to resemble something between Father Christmas and the tooth fairy. The 'blab it and grab it' or 'health and wealth' gospel encourages people to name what they want from life, then claim it. As the mega US evangelist Kenneth Copeland puts it, 'The basic principle of the Christian life is to know that God put our sin, sickness, disease, sorrow, grief, *and poverty* [emphasis added] on Jesus at Calvary.'[16]

It's perplexing to think that Jesus died to save us all from poverty, unless we judge the poor as losers and somehow undesirable, if not damned. Granville Oral Roberts, one of the pioneers of the prosperity gospel, once stated, 'I tried poverty, and I didn't like it.'[17] Such callous comments lack respect for those less fortunate. 'The world is a dangerous place,' Albert Einstein once noted, 'not because of those who do evil, but because of those who look on and do nothing.'[18] We must catch our childish thinking. When we fail to do so, we let go of our hold on reality and can end up failing ourselves and others.

In one *YouTube* segment during the COVID-19 pandemic, Pastor George Pearson offered 'supernatural harvests', including 'supernatural debt cancellation', with 'every need supplied, even in the toughest times'.[19] The language used to describe the astonishing level of divine abundance awaiting us could make you think you've landed on another planet. As the Pulitzer prize–winning author of *Bright-Sided,* Barbara Ehrenreich, puts it, 'He fixeth my speeding tickets, he secureth me a good table in the restaurant, he leadeth me to book contracts.'[20]

Big Plans

Who'd have thought the gospels could swell one's bank account? Televangelist Gloria Copeland explains how in *God's Will Is Prosperity.* 'You give $1 for the gospel's sake, and $100 belongs to you. You give $10 and receive $1,000. Give $1,000 and receive $100,000. Give one airplane and receive the equivalence of ten airplanes ... In short, Mark 10:30 is a very good deal.'[21] This statement makes the eyes pop. It's tailormade for the child/adolescent who likes a good deal, or even better a freebie.

Pastor Creflo Dollar of Atlanta's World Changers Church International goes further, suggesting that once we've made our demands clear to God, like the genie in the bottle, God is there to serve us, and is thus *obliged* to follow our dictates. 'When we pray, believing that we have already received what we are praying for, God has no choice but to make our prayers come to pass,' Dollar insists.[22] However, even Dollar reached the limits of plausibility when he asked his congregation for a Gulfstream G650 private jet – the biggest, fastest, most luxurious and most technologically advanced available. After a severe backlash, Pastor Dollar had the good sense to let go of this request.

Position Yourself for Wealth

It's easy to become fearful when we're in a difficult space. Few would argue that a positive outlook is conducive to a life with less angst, but to equate wealth with spiritual advancement is a stretch, particularly when looking at the lives of some of the most successful televangelists. 'There is enough in the world for everyone,' suggested the old-style evangelist Frank Buchman, who founded the Moral Rearmament movement, 'but not for everyone's greed.'

And what of the countless millions struggling to make ends meet, including those in developing countries living on a dollar or less a day? Are they living in poverty because they don't believe in themselves or because they don't 'have it together'? Or are they more courageous than the rest of us as they continue to get out of bed in the morning and do everything humanly possible to care for themselves and their family with such slender resources? Is poverty, famine and disease purely a state of mind?

When the Prosperity Gospel Fails Others

Our childish obsession with over-the-top prosperity makes the child in us ever more self-obsessed. It also makes us more judgemental of those who fall short and so are undeserving of a helping hand. Houston's Pastor Joel Osteen presides over one of the largest churches in the US, with some 52,000 people attending weekly services. With a net worth around US$50 million, he is one of the brightest stars in the evangelical firmament. All was going well until Lakewood Church, a former basketball arena, failed to open to flood victims when Hurricane Harvey hit in 2017, leaving some 30,000 people homeless. While four of Houston's mosques and seventeen churches attended to the needy, Lakewood was noticeably absent in the charity stakes until, after a barrage of criticism, Lakewood helped out a few hundred residents.

We shouldn't be surprised by this as the infantile mindset doesn't like having to deal with life's messiness. When you're committed to an abundance agenda, you're not amused by those who don't make the grade. Reflecting on the Hurricane Harvey incident, Kate Bowler, an associate professor at Duke Divinity School, said, 'What observers want to see right now is that there is a language of charity embodied in American Christianity, and that generosity knows no denomination.'[23]

If God has a refrigerator your picture would be on it. If He had a computer, your face would be on the screensaver.
Pastor Joel Osteen, Lakewood Church[24]

This focus on prosperity is a world away from the first of Buddhism's Four Noble Truths, which reminds us that suffering is an intrinsic part of life and is fuelled by our long wish lists, our many desires. Or the reflections of Sufi mystic Rumi, who stated, 'You have to keep breaking your heart until it opens.'

If spirituality has any value, surely it is to feed our spirit and equip us for life's letdowns, betrayals and losses. In helping us mature, surely it encourages us to face up to and help deal with injustice towards others. As Franklin D Roosevelt once observed, 'The test of our progress is not whether we add more to the abundance of those who have much; it is whether we provide enough for those who have too little.' Growing up is about striving for wisdom, by embracing rather than avoiding life in all its fullness, including the difficult and distressing bits, and teaching our kids to do likewise.

A Better Way to Prosper

Living in a well-off country, we have the opportunity to realise many dreams. Sometimes our aspirations can end up as a long list of 'must-haves' that ultimately fail to deliver the satisfaction we hoped for.

- Think about when and where you fall into fanciful thinking. Be aware of when you are vulnerable to questionable dreams.
- What do you want most in the world? Why do you want this? Is it to impress others, or to fulfil something deep within?
- Make time to savour each achievement – sit with it, reflect on it, and see how it may inform your future.
- Head for those aspirations that make your heart dance. Know that in bringing joy and fulfilment your way, your authentic goals are more likely to inspire others.
- Be grateful to all those who enable you to do all you do – those who grow your food and make your clothes, those who ensure you have clean water, safe roads and good health care.
- Practise generosity – take pleasure in seeing others do well, and in sharing your good fortune with others, so that life always has a celebratory feel.

19

News and Infotainment

Part of growing up is taking an interest in what's going on around us. With numerous sources of local and international news on- and offline, our news climate is complex. In the latest figures, Yahoo News is America's leading source of website news, followed by Google News, *Huff Post* and CNN. The burgeoning social media platforms are also now squeezing out traditional media outlets, leaving everyone scrambling for more content.

With our shorter attention spans, it's not hard to see why 43 per cent of Americans now rely on Facebook for their news. Around two-thirds of Australians use the TV news to stay informed, while less than a third read newspapers to keep up to date.

> **You determine your own media diet, right,**
> **and a lot of it is junk food.**
> Geneva Overholser, former chair of the
> board of the Pulitzer Prize[1]

Rapid Turnaround

News sources have changed, and so has the news cycle, accelerating way beyond anything previous generations of journalists dealt with. Citizen journalists are now also part of the mix, reporting live on YouTube's *Citizen*

Tube channel, and CNN's *iReport*, making news gathering much more dynamic and able to connect directly with sources. Previously, journalists were experts in radio, TV or print, but now there's a growing expectation that a journalist will be across all these channels, as well as social media.

These changes have brought about a greater hope for the spread of democracy and freedom. As we watched the Arab Spring and other uprisings unfold in the mid-2010s, we applauded these gains, which gave a new immediacy to what was happening beyond our shores and allowed the voices of the oppressed to be heard. But the ease and speed of this process doesn't necessarily deliver the results we hope for. We are learning that the road to freedom and democracy is long and hard.

Conflict Abounds

Over the last decade we've also seen the rise of rogue players, who embrace these new media to sow division, create chaos and promote fear and confusion across the world. The child/adolescent loves high emotion and lots of drama and takes a perverse delight in conflict, with little sense of how such destructive behaviour may play out. When we're immature we're happy to observe structures being pulled down, with little thought of what might replace them.

> **In the digital space, we are encouraged to be outraged**
> **by everything – but it only distracts us from fighting the**
> **biggest problems we need to tackle.**
> Ashley 'Dotty' Charles, writer, rapper and activist[2]

Call That News?

Part of the problem lies in the volume of 'news' coverage available to us. Our current news climate exposes us to more information in a day than our forebears experienced in a lifetime. Between 2016 and 2018 alone, we generated 90 per cent of all the data that has ever existed in the world, while Google facilitates a staggering 40,000 searches a second.[3] How can our news outlets possibly pierce through this sea of facts and figures, and give us a coherent picture of our world?

This constant need to fill the news cycle 24/7 creates a continual scramble for content in newsrooms. News releases are now even more about timing. What would once have been a minor update in standard business hours now has the capacity to be big news if shared during off-peak times. With such a rapid turnover of news stories, news outlets end up rehashing old news items, refreshing the content with a new photo or quote, or using material straight from press releases. Award-winning British investigative journalist Nick Davies has aptly dubbed this 'churnalism'.[4]

With the constant flood of information, the child/adolescent has drifted away from 'serious' to less challenging news, if not clickbait that contributes little in the way of real understanding. 'At the end of the day [news organisations] are businesses looking for more views,' states Rohan Upadhyay, a contributor to *Dialogue and Discourse*. '... [N]ews media doesn't have a "liberal bias" or a "conservative bias" – it has a "viewership bias".' The main goal of the news, Upadhyay insists, is to be addictive, providing us with daily doses of sensation rather than strong facts that help point us towards good solutions.[5] Where solutions are offered, they're frequently simplistic and fail to take into account the complexity of a problem.

Emotionally Charged Content

Most news is now designed to evoke a strong emotional response, to get as large an audience as possible without a close look at the facts. Reducing news to little more than sound bites pleases the immature self, which doesn't much care for complexity and has little patience for detail.

Amid this ever-shifting sea of possibilities, the truth becomes a fragile thing. To verify content and tease out a topic takes far more time and effort than is available. In his book *Flat Earth News*, a call-out of the shortcomings of the current media landscape, Nick Davies suggests that 'if truth is the object and checking is the function [of the news], then the primary working asset of all journalists, always and everywhere, is time. Take away time and you take away truth.'[6]

> **American media pitches to the lowest common**
> **denominator of the audience ... who over-emote at shallow**
> **but emotionally-provocative sound bites.**
> E James Brennan, *Quora* forum[7]

Seriously, Is That News?

'When hard news goes soft, entertainment takes over,' suggests associate professor of communication at the University of California, San Diego, Daniel Hallin. If we take current affairs shows, we see how the visuals and studio set-up are designed to *look* like a full-on newsroom. But most of the content on offer is soft news at best. 'What all these stories have in common,' Hallin notes, 'is that they are about everyday life – and about its disruptions and exaltations (crime, illness, the hero, the celebrity, the rescue).'[8] It's not that there isn't a place for such formats, just that they don't inform us about the biting issues of the day. Our immature selves delight in these easy-to-digest snippets as they help keep us entertained.

Acclimatisation to lightweight news stories has made us 'intellectually lazy', David Shaw states. Why put in the effort to analyse different news stories when we can enjoy an hour or so of entertaining viewing each day?[9]

Thomas Patterson, a professor of government and the press at Harvard University, says this is because too few young people have a 'news habit'. They are now more concerned with building their careers than thinking about how to be a worthwhile citizen.[10]

Most people want no-problem news, goes-down-easy news, Yahoo! headlines, news that evokes feelings, even if those feelings are feelings of fear.
David Shaw, *Media Matters* columnist[11]

Easily Digestible News

A few decades ago, all the major networks presented serious news, Marc Gunther, a senior writer at *Fortune* magazine, reminds us. The calibre of their newsgathering delivered serious prestige to their network, but more competition between networks, rising costs and the ratings wars meant they struggled to retain audiences.

Shows such as *20/20* and *A Current Affair* offered plenty of drama and high emotion, which was appealing on many fronts. Without overseas news bureaus and needing relatively small production teams, these were soon delivering their networks pleasingly high ratings for a relatively low cost. 'These stories were produced and broadcast for their entertainment value, not to illuminate any significant broader issue,' Gunther reflects, adding, 'Magazine stories, in general, have a common thread. They are driven more by emotion than by ideas.'[12]

Blunt Messages

Many daily news programs followed suit, using dramatic graphics and grabs to create adrenaline-packed news segments. The advent of the

24/7 news cycle and lots of competition meant the pressure was on for networks to gain and keep audiences. In the new, lighter formats, only the basics are captured, assumptions are made and stereotypes reinforced.

With this easy-to-digest content, our childlike selves feel free to make snap, frequently ill-informed decisions. We fall into judging people at face value, writing them off as fat, lazy or stupid, or worse, and we like seeing those who are different or difficult taken down. Our partially formed self is quick to assert that those in the firing line 'had it coming to them' anyway.

'Comfortable' conclusions about people and situations that annoy or baffle us make us and them vulnerable. We grasp only the slenderest of facts and reframe the truth so it is more to our liking. Rather than engaging with the issues of the day and helping solve them, like small children we take a simplistic view or look to others for solutions.

Why do we watch what we do? 'To look at a homicide that happened seven years ago, and look at who did it – it's good entertainment ... It has no ethical or redemptive value,' states *Honest Truths*, an American report into the ethics of contemporary documentary making.[13]

Who Misses Out?

'The most disturbing and obvious consequence of this diminishing focus [on more substantial news] is the lack of understanding of and sympathy for those fleeing war, poverty and persecution in their countries of origin,' reflects Julian Petley, Professor of Screen Media and Journalism in the School of Arts at Brunel University, London. 'This is seen particularly clearly in the UK ... in the bleak hostility shown by many to the refugees crossing the Channel, a hostility which is fanned daily by much of the press. The fact that many of the Home Office and immigration officials ... have been revealed as being unable even to locate on a map the countries from which [the refugees have] come is a terrible condemnation of the state of ignorance of the wider world.'[14]

Ignorance can lead us into dark places. Looking back at the 2016 US presidential elections, former strategist and executive chairman of Breitbart News Steve Bannon stated, 'We got elected on "Drain the Swamp", "Lock Her Up", "Build a Wall".'[15] This proved to be an insanely brilliant move. Bannon is a skilled strategist, well aware that millions of people have become hooked on adrenaline and the shock value of the moment, and he exploits this trend for all it's worth.

> [I]n our media-saturated world there is no guarantee that complex facts and difficult nuances will win out in a battle with simplistic sloganising.
> Julian Petley, Brunel University[16]

The child/adolescent enjoys excitement and unpredictability, feeling angry and scared. Networks work with this dynamic. Their roller-coaster 'news' programs leave us addicted to high emotion and fearful of those who are different. 'The profit motive incentivizes news providers to addict their audience by sensationalizing the news and generating conflict to fuel the viewers' resentments,' philosopher Benjamin Cain reminds us. 'The result is more infantilization.'[17]

Keeping Everyone Honest

Good journalism is valuable in helping guard against corruption and other abuses of power. But what happens when every attempt is made to obscure the truth? On a number of occasions, former US president Donald Trump told his supporters, 'Stick with us. Don't believe the crap you see from these people [the journalists in attendance]. The fake news. What you're seeing and reading is not what's happening.'[18]

Trump was well aware of what he was doing: bring down the truth tellers and you have a free hand. As Steve Bannon put it, 'The real opposition is the media. And the way to deal with them is to flood the zone with shit.'[19] While we're all guilty of being drawn into the occasional media titillation, chasing silly, hyped-up stories has real consequences.

> **I believe in being truthful, not neutral. And I believe we**
> **must stop banalizing the truth. We have to be prepared to**
> **fight especially hard right now for truth.**
> Christiane Amanpour, chief international correspondent at CNN[20]

'When we have a president [Trump] who essentially says you shouldn't believe anything [journalists] say,' reflects Geneva Overholser, formerly on the editorial board of *The New York Times*, 'we become a people who don't know what to believe. If we become a people who don't believe anything, we become a people who distrust everyone.'[21] Adolescence is marked by confusion and distrust, but as we mature, the wider world makes more sense and we become more grounded, someone others can trust. What happens when we and/or our kids fail to make the leap?

Pressure to Produce More Content

Our current love affair with infotainment creates what filmmaker David Pearson describes as the 'industrialisation' of documentary making, a shift to a 'more leisure-centred, lifestyle-oriented way of living and of thinking.'[22] This suits the immature self, which prefers comfort and familiarity, with few real demands on it.

The child/adolescent would much rather escape to the country, watch contestants create and plate impossibly perfect meals and struggle to build their dream homes, than try to grasp current global conflicts, or discover the intricacies of other cultures. We all have the right to switch off and chill out but it's important to understand that infotainment offers little insight, especially during more stressful times.

Curiosity Matters

Political philosopher Kwame Anthony Appiah suggests we need to go beyond light entertainment as we have 'an ethical duty' to learn about others. 'I am urging that we should learn about people in other places,' he states, 'take an interest in their civilizations, their arguments, their errors, their achievements, not because that will bring us to agreement, but because it will help us to get used to one another.'[23] Often, when 'different' is served up, unless it's accompanied by a large dollop of entertainment, our immature selves get bored and switch channels, leaving essential questions and insights unanswered, and opportunities for engagement fade.

> **My brain seems to be a magnet for useless trivia and bits of**
> **nonsense. I know just enough about many topics to survive**
> **a shallow conversation, or to get myself into trouble when**
> **one gets too deep.**
> Adam, *MetaFilter* forum[24]

When Our General Knowledge Takes a Hit

In our globalised world, there's still a great deal of ignorance about much of the world, even such basic things like where nations are on the world map. One 2012 US study compared the general knowledge of 671 uni students with that of uni students from just over three decades earlier. Far fewer recent students were able to identify Paris as the capital of France; almost a third thought Baghdad was the capital of Afghanistan (instead of Iraq); and just over one out of ten placed Mount Everest in America's Appalachian Mountains (instead of the Himalayas). Latter-day students did have a much greater grasp of pop culture trivia.[25]

What's Trivia and What's Not?

Does this lack of general knowledge matter, now that we have ready access to limitless information? When my friend Helen began lecturing in media studies at university, she was delighted to have the chance to work with so many 'fresh minds'. At the end of her first lecture, Helen asked everyone to come up with what they considered to be the dozen most influential moments of the twentieth century, and was amazed to have a number of students challenge her. Was this in the curriculum? Would they be examined on this? Was this exercise a voluntary one? Even when she explained the importance of curiosity, and that the ability to analyse situations and trends is part of being a good journalist, Helen was floored to have some students repeat their questions. Here we see the child/adolescent self at play.

It's important we strive to make sense of our world. If we don't readily grasp key aspects of our shared existence, how will we ever know where consensus is to be found and where conflict is most likely to flare up?

Maturity encourages us to seek out and understand the connections between ourselves and others, and to comprehend the reasons for our growing divides. It allows us to better understand others, to be engaged enough to take an interest in their world, and to discover how and where we can reach out in meaningful ways.

Staying Informed

Have you become addicted to infotainment? Here's how to turn this around.

- Read widely, to understand differing points of view.
- Be open to changing your stance on issues, as you can't know everything about every topic.
- Appreciate that you can understand others without agreeing with their point of view.
- Avoid shock/horror coverage, in favour of news that offers considered opinions.
- Be aware of different journalists and their reporting style – are they doing a thorough job?
- Weigh up what's being covered with your own observations in daily life.
- How might these observations be useful when interacting with others?
- How can you use what you've learned to be part of positive change?

20

Fragile Truths

Truth has become a casualty of late, with an increasing number of child/ adolescents opting for feelings over facts, the mood of the moment over science, and choosing to pitch purely for profit, regardless of the environmental and social consequences. Experts suggest this is not totally surprising. 'Humans are hardwired to dismiss facts that don't fit their worldview,' states Wake Forest University's philosophy professor, Adrian Bardon.[1] So where then does truth lie? And why is truth so important?

The Truth of the Matter

The child/adolescent has a slender hold on life's truths, which can make life extremely uncomfortable when reality bites. Part of maturing is appreciating that truth helps us remedy past errors, find better ways to progress and avoid repeating the same mistakes.

Our immature self fails to comprehend such nuances, preferring to stick to whatever script it has come up with. Denial doesn't help us deal with life's inevitable challenges. Our unexamined fears skew how we react to what's happening to us and others, creating more tension, unhappiness and uncertainty than needed.

Our escalating love affair with alternative 'truths' is concerning, particularly with so many turning to social media for information. The ever more sophisticated algorithms mean the responses to issues are often incomplete, if not misleading. Did we choose to expose ourselves only to the views we're most comfortable with or is it a habit we've fallen into? This is something we each need to think about, because the impacts can be far-reaching.

> **Everything was perfectly healthy and normal**
> **here in Denial Land.**
> Jim Butcher, *Cold Days*[2]

'[Aldous] Huxley feared the truth would be drowned in a sea of irrelevance,' Neil Postman, one of America's foremost social critics, reminds us '… In *Brave New World*, [the people] are controlled by inflicting pleasure … Huxley feared that what we love will ruin us.'[3] It's disquieting to think we might end up drowning in the things the child/adolescent is most comfortable with – shopping and entertainment, our obsession with ourselves.

Why We Believe What We Believe

The immature part of us has an unwavering belief in ourselves and what we stand for. Not wanting to challenge itself or be challenged, it listens only to the information that fits our worldview, preferring stereotypes and half-truths to less welcome facts. Social scientists call this 'motivated reasoning'.

'A human being's very sense of self is intimately tied up with his or her identity group's status and beliefs,' Adrian Bardon explains. When the facts don't fit our worldview, we tend to respond 'automatically and defensively' to this competing information.[4] The child/adolescent has a deep-seated need to feel secure, to have certainty. That's why, psychologist John Jost suggests, people are driven to defend aspects of our society that are clearly unjust, if not harmful to others. It's why some stay in bad relationships, why others with few resources continue to vote for measures that promote inequality, thinking that while things mightn't be great, at least they're a known quantity.

> How 'bout a shot of truth in that denial cocktail?
> Jennifer Salaiz, *Love Expands*[5]

'We like to have positive attitudes towards the groups we belong to. We want to believe our institutions are working well,' Jost reflects, calling this process 'system justification'. The payoff for backing our version of the status quo – even when it's clearly inadequate or unfair – is that it 'fosters a sense of social belonging-ness' so we feel safer and more attached to those around us.[6] Our immature self certainly likes to have everything sorted, but by sticking to our way of looking at things regardless, we inhibit our ability to learn, to embrace a wider view.

Where's Consensus Now?

While it's fine to disagree with others, many of us are now so polarised that whole communities and nations are fragmenting around us. The child/adolescent is also very tribal, with a penchant for snap judgements, starkly categorising others as friends or enemies, winners or losers.

Tribalism can be terrifying if you're on the outer. In such settings, difference is not to be tolerated. American social psychologist Jonathan Haidt suggests our growing polarisation comes with such strong feelings that some have morphed into hatred towards those with differing points of view. Wherever difference manifests, the childish self is happy to lash out and/or pack up its toys and go home, but our communities can't operate effectively, let alone thrive, under such conditions.[7]

Add fake news to this equation and life starts to get messy. Fake news isn't new – people have massaged the truth since the beginning of time. What has changed is the scale on which false information is now disseminated. Thanks to advances in communication technologies, fake news can spread effortlessly. 'Technology has now made it so easy to create what even a few decades ago required a large investment, whether access to printing presses, studios or broadcast transmitters,' former Reuters CEO Tom Glocer reminds us.[8]

> The internet has not only democratised information beyond people's wildest imaginings but is also replacing genuine knowledge with the 'wisdom of the crowd'.
>
> Andrew Keen, *The Cult of the Amateur*[9]

Why Fake News Appeals

For fake news to work, there has to be an appetite for it. 'One of the things we know from classic anthropological work is that misinformation thrives where people have little control over environmental threats – like volcanic eruptions, unpredictable weather patterns or disease,' states Gergely Nyilasy of Melbourne University's business school. People also want security, to belong, he adds.[10] Fake news 'bubbles' are extremely appealing to the child/adolescent in us, as they offer a sense of certainty and connection, albeit a false one.

There's little doubt that most fake news has a sensational ring. It is, after all, constructed to make the jaw drop. A recent study examining 126,000 tweets forwarded by three million users found that 'truth simply cannot compete with hoax and rumor'. Fake news enjoys far more currency than verifiable reportage, Soroush Vosoughi, the lead author of this study, confirms. While it may suit us to blame bots for fake news, that doesn't fully explain what's going on when a trumped-up story is likely to reach 1500 individuals six times quicker than a story that's true. Fake news items are 70 per cent more likely to be retweeted than a factual piece.

There are, this study suggests, two key factors that set fake news apart. First, we're attracted to the novelty, the sensation such news offers. These kinds of stories tend to come at us from left field and to have an outrageous, often conspiratorial, ring. Secondly, fake news also stirs our emotions, especially our negative emotions, leaving us shocked, angry or scared. 'The thrill of novelty is too alluring,' concludes Robinson Meyer in *The Atlantic*, 'the titillation of disgust too difficult to transcend.'[11]

> **You may not like everyone, but that doesn't give you the right to be nasty to them.**
> Eddie Jaku, Auschwitz survivor[12]

Shockamania

Fake news appeals to the child/adolescent who is easily bored and distracted and loves novelty. It also has a flair for the lurid and relishes in provoking others. These endless juicy grabs help spice up our day. All attempts to deny the truth don't change the facts, but they do make it harder to sort out what is to be believed.

Increasingly Twitter, Facebook, Instagram and other platforms are giving us misinformation and disinformation, both of which are falsehoods. Those sharing misinformation genuinely believe the material they're sending out is true, while those spreading disinformation set out to *intentionally* mislead. Either way, our ability to make good decisions is undermined. Disinformation also undermines the democratic process by attempting to corral people's opinions for personal agendas. Truth is impartial; spin and disinformation are not.

> **Everyone is entitled to his own opinion,**
> **but not to his own facts.**
> Daniel Patrick Moynihan, sociologist[13]

The many highly sophisticated troll farms – organisations devoted to manipulating social media on an industrial scale – take disinformation to a new level. Deliberately and constantly flooding platforms with fake news, troll farms add to the anger and confusion people feel, making the landscape appear ever bleaker. The child/adolescent doesn't want to have to wade through much detail anyway – it does like a good stoush.

Decimated Homes and Communities

Clint Watts, a senior fellow at America's Foreign Policy Research Institute, reminds us that the overall goal of troll farms is to influence public opinion, to 'create divisive wedges', pitting people against each other, undermining democracy, with a country then looking unstable as its people no longer trust each other. In the Mueller investigation into the likely influence the Kremlin had on America's 2016 elections, Facebook reported hundreds of links to Russian accounts, while it's suggested there were around 187 million further engagements with Instagram users. These questionable posts were viewed by an estimated 146 million people – a huge reach by any standard.[14]

This same deliberate undermining of the social order is evident in France. Around a quarter of tweets on political issues were found to be 'deliberately false', spreading extreme, highly biased, if not downright conspiratorial material, and offering up this content as hard facts. The excitement such information can generate is considerable, as is the resulting fracturing of families and communities – some of which never heal.

Addicted to the Adrenaline

Too many child/adolescents have become addicted to the massive excitement of fake news, to the point that they're now constantly searching and scrolling for the next sensational bit of news. *Le Monde* decided to expose a handful of the more outrageous fake stories circulating during the 2017 French elections, including one that stated the French election result was already in, four days before the polls closed. Marine Le Pen, fake news declared, was the clear winner. Another told of how France's investigative paper *Le Canard enchaîné* had failed to report that President Emmanuel Macron had a secret offshore bank account – yet another statement that was patently untrue.[15]

In Italy, the Five Star Movement (M5S) also has a powerful finely honed social media presence, churning out pro-Russia disinformation to millions daily. In August 2015, during Europe's refugee crisis, one M5S party blog stated that America was funding the trafficking of Libyan migrants to Italy.[16]

Given that the child/adolescent revels in outrage, drama and strong emotions, is it any wonder that we are living in hate-filled times? 'Hate is a disease which may destroy your enemy, but will destroy you in the process,' warns Auschwitz survivor Eddie Jaku, who knows the landscape of hate intimately.[17]

> **That's pretty much how we get through our own lives,**
> **watching television. Smoking crap. Self-medicating.**
> **Redirecting our attention. Jacking off. Denial.**
> Chuck Palahniuk, *Choke*

Designed to Be Destructive

Fake news is rarely harmless. The end result can be unexpected, if not catastrophic. On 1 December 2016, 29-year-old Edgar Maddison Welch entered Comet Ping Pong, a pizza restaurant in Washington DC, with a Colt AR-15 rifle, a Colt .38 handgun, a shotgun and a folding knife, and fired his assault rifle. He had been outraged by a fake news piece that told of a child trafficking ring, masterminded by Hillary Clinton and her campaign team, and operating out of Comet Ping Pong.

This supposed paedophile group was said to be involved in the physical and sexual abuse of children, satanic rituals and murder. Welch had come to Comet Ping Pong to liberate the abused children.[18] Who knows what personal experiences fuelled Welch's actions? Luckily, no one at Comet Ping Pong was injured, yet the outcome could have been very different. Allowing untruths to flourish creates ecosystems of hate and division.

When the World Is No Longer Safe

Like scary bedtime stories, these dramatic tales mesmerise our child/adolescent self. They tantalise us and leave us wanting more. When there's no place for truth, life slips into chaos, as does the social fabric. We find ourselves in a dystopian landscape where cooperation and inclusion are lost and we're each left to fight for ourselves. 'Imagine a choir where there is no conductor,' Will reflects in a chat thread on blame, '[where] everyone has a different version of the song, they never practice and often are expected to sing a new song without any notification … you have a chaotic inconsistent incoherent wall of noise that nobody enjoys.'[19]

> **Expressing doubt is how we begin a journey**
> **to discover essential truths.**
> Kilroy J Oldster, *Dead Toad Scrolls*

For most of us everyday life is less dramatic, but we can so easily end up with a lazy relationship with truth where we no longer notice how much our newsfeeds are distorting the way we see the real world. 'The truth matters,' insists American writer and social commentator Roxane Gay. 'I try to remember this every day. I try to believe this every day. And it is hard.'[20]

When We Choose Fake News Over Truth

'The difficulty is that once the genie of untruths is out of the bottle, it can be hard to control, let alone contain. We are now "reaping the whirlwind",' states Charlie Sykes, a former Milwaukee radio host with MSNBC and a leading conservative in Wisconsin who's had the courage to call out the extreme hate perpetuated by the far right.[21] 'They're like the drunken bigoted uncle at Thanksgiving,' he said after his retirement. 'You don't throw them out of the house, but you assume that at some point you can turn on the game, you can change the subject and the center is going to hold. And it didn't.' Sykes fears the many mistruths unleashed will be hard to damp down. 'That doesn't mean that there weren't things to be legitimately opposed to, but the perpetual outrage machine basically needed to keep people angry all the time. It was the business model. But the problem is, it's hard to turn that off.'[22]

Fiddling with the Facts

With so many uncomfortable truths, it's tempting to come up with our own version of reality, particularly during COVID-19. 'We are all created in the image and likeness of God. That image is seen the most by our face,' Ohio state politician Nino Vitale announced on Facebook, during the pandemic. 'That's the image of God right there, and I want to see it in my brothers and sisters' – which is why, he said, he wouldn't be wearing a face mask. A day later Vitale did a swift backflip, after receiving considerable pushback.[23] As America's Center for Information Technology and Society insists, disinformation is dangerous because it hampers people's ability to pull together. Fake news, it states, is designed to disrupt a nation's life, making conflicts among its members 'more intense'.[24]

Bridging the Gap

To come back from such a divided space, it's essential we 'agree in some minimal way about what reality looks like', suggests American historian Sophia Rosenfeld. We're not going to agree every time. 'But,' she adds, 'somehow or other, we need to have acquired some very basic, shared understandings about what causes what, what's broadly desirable, what's dangerous.'[25]

The children/adolescents among us have been running rampant but it's now time to rein them in. What if we ignored road rules, if trains turned up according to the driver's own personal timetable, if hospitals abandoned safety procedures and if everyone did their own thing? In Obama's final State of the Union Address, in 2016, he warned, 'Democracy grinds to a halt without a willingness to compromise. Or when even basic facts are contested, and we listen only to those who agree with us. Our public life withers when only the most extreme voices get attention.'[26]

Time for Greater Reflection

The child/adolescent in all of us would benefit from closer scrutiny. Looking back at his younger self, social psychologist Jonathan Haidt sees his own immaturity at play. 'I was very moralistic, very self-righteous. I think I was angry throughout the '80s, or at least in a sort of a shallow, political way.'

Then Haidt found himself working with anthropologist Richard Shweder. He taught Haidt to listen closely to what others were asserting and take the opposite view to see if that held weight. This helped Haidt progress beyond the need to always have his ideas validated, to embrace a freer approach that enables him to access fresh ways of looking at an issue.

This is a useful observation as the child/adolescent most wants to feel safe, to belong, and to enjoy the happiness that flows from these uplifting qualities. More recently, Haidt has explored happiness psychology and found that striving for our goals brings us greater happiness than achieving them. And yet, he cautions, whatever progress we make, the greater our spiritual hunger. We find genuine contentment when we're connected to others, he states.

Many of us have a way to travel yet. We need to recognise when we're still in the grip of our self-absorbed child/adolescent ways. 'The lesson from so many ancient traditions, and from social psychology, is that we need to be slower to judge and quicker to forgive,' Haidt offers. 'You can't be hating and learning at the same time.'[27] American historian Sophia Rosenfeld adds, 'Truth matters as the foundation for interpersonal trust,' she insists. 'It matters because we cannot talk to one another, much less conduct a serious debate, until we share some [agreed] principles and facts about the world at large, not to mention a consensus on how to generate them.'[28]

Judith Feder, a professor of public policy at Georgetown University, suggests the case for truth in politics is less about winning than 'generating and using truth to make [good] policy, that will promote whatever values we hold dear'. Truth, she asserts, starts with a question, while propaganda begins with the desired answer in full view.

Our immature selves get impatient at the state of politics right now and we're tempted to walk away in despair. 'But,' Feder reminds us, 'politics creates "windows" of opportunity, and in those windows, research [for truth] provides the tools or the weapons to carry the day.' Being comfortable with uncertainty and willing to keep an open mind are also essential if we hope to find new solutions and create much-needed change.[29] Gandhi insisted that truth 'is the weapon of matchless potency. It is an attribute of the brave ... It is no wooden or lifeless dogma, but a living and life-giving force.'[30] Truth is doubly precious when gifted to our children.

Alternative Facts

Whenever you're feeling stuck in a point of view, remember that in the future our outlook may well be proved completely wrong, or seem primitive at best. Here are a few ways to help widen our worldview.

- When was the last time you listened deeply to an alternative view?
- What did you learn?
- How can you become a better observer and listener?
- How might this help stretch your humanity?
- Where might you experience a more profound sense of belonging?
- How best can you respect the often unspoken struggles, fears and aspirations others wrestle with?
- How can you encourage your kids down the same path?

21

Careless

Truth is not the only casualty when our child self runs the show. We need to be wary of carelessness. When we're caught up with our own needs, we lose all perspective. This is the carelessness we saw during the height of the pandemic – people partying as normal, regardless of the consequences for the more vulnerable and the countless health workers who were risking their lives and health to help others. 'I haven't worn a mask since the start of the pandemic, if a store tells me that I have to have one, I ask them how they will enforce it and offer to call the cops on myself for them,' boasts Debra in one chat thread. 'I've already had the virus. I'm not wearing a mask anymore.'[1]

Schoolies Under the Microscope

The unchecked child/adolescent throws toys around, dumps towels and clothes on the floor, and eats all the tasty morsels in the fridge. It's always someone else's job to restock the fridge and clean up the mess at home or across the planet. Carelessness becomes a habit, unless we learn a better way.

This carelessness is seen in Australia's schoolies week. Highschool students celebrate the end of their school days with mass trips away, often to Queensland's Gold Coast, for gatherings described by one paper as 'the wildest graduate celebration in Australia'.[2]

This Australian rite of passage, attracting over 50,000 young people a year, is a huge money-spinner. But what value is it to our adolescents? One study indicated that, on average, young males were drinking eighteen standard drinks a day, while the girls were consuming thirteen standard drinks a day. Overall, 87 per cent of schoolies reported 'at least one negative outcome attributed to alcohol and other drug use'.[3] A concerning 58 per cent of these adolescents reported blacking out sometime during their time away, while one in ten got involved in a fight.[4]

How Schoolies Feel

Professor Sandra Jones of the Centre for Health Initiatives and her team polled half of a group of 500 schoolies just before schoolies week. Most expected it to be a negative experience, but with no viable alternatives, they went along with it, assuming they'd consume up to ten alcoholic beverages in one sitting, drink too rapidly and 'hook up' with a partner. One in five girls expected to have multiple sexual partners on their week away. After schoolies, when the other half of this sample was polled, the group's assumptions had largely come true. A telling 70 per cent of these adolescents rated their week away as a negative experience.[5]

How can we expect young people to grow up if this is the best we can offer as a meaningful rite of passage? What kind of template is this for adult life? In his landmark work *Adam's Return*, American writer and thinker Richard Rohr reminds us that 'you can only lead your sons and daughters only as far as you yourself have gone',[6] and that 'from whom little is demanded, nothing can be expected'.[7] Genuine rites of passage, Rohr adds, assist the adolescents to *earn* the right to transition to adulthood, and be honoured for their effort. We see this, he notes, in teachers who are tough, who push us further than we thought possible.[8]

Questionable Rites of Passage

Our adolescent ache to 'go wild' speaks to our desire to experience something more meaningful in life. Unless we know where to find real purpose, we end up with more of the same. Of course, carelessness assumes there'll always be someone to clean up after us. How can we progress individually and collectively when we're stuck in this mind-numbing loop?

It's not just adolescents who get caught up in detrimental behaviour. Events managers catering to the top end of town often now have medical staff on hand at corporate dinners and cocktail parties to ensure that everyone, including those who take their drinking and/or drug-taking too far, have access to immediate, experienced medical intervention.

How different life could be for our young people, and for us all, if we had more access to meaningful rites of passage. By their very design, rites of passage can take us way out of our comfort zone and what we thought we were capable of, creating experiences that last a lifetime. Some of the best rites of passage take students to developing countries to explore and volunteer. These young adults are soon plunged into very different ways of life, having to deal with cultural and language differences and to focus on their life skills – experiences that frequently prove life-changing.

Brianna went with a school group to Solomon Islands after the 2010 tsunami, donating tools and learning supplies to one affected local school, and helping restore the surviving school buildings. 'It's great assisting those who are less fortunate,' Brianna later admitted. 'Going to the Solomons was the best thing I've ever done.'[9] Aleisha volunteered at an orphanage in Thailand. 'I've learned not to take what you have for granted,' she said. 'There are so many people out there who are worse off, and you get an amazing amount of pleasure from giving back to others less fortunate.'[10]

Our kids don't have to leave the country to undergo powerful rites of passage. The quality of these experiences is what counts – stretching our young beyond what they thought they were capable of, so they get to glimpse just how much they can achieve for themselves and others.

When Carelessness Becomes a Habit

How can we possibly help our children grow up when we're still largely kids ourselves? What of our wider responsibilities, including that to the planet? We see the impact of our carelessness in the degradation of the environment. Our ongoing use of plastic, for example, now impacts the world's great oceans and all the fish and birdlife there.

We've known for some time about the Great Pacific Garbage Patch, three times the size of France and comprising a staggering 79,000 tons of plastic waste.[11] Breaking down into smaller and smaller pieces, 'it turns our seas cloudy and deprives plankton and algae of sunlight, compromising the whole marine food chain'.[12]

Space Junk

The many advances in space exploration have also come at a heavy environmental cost. Some 9600 satellites have been launched into space since the USSR launched its *Sputnik* satellite sixty-five years ago. Of the 5500 satellites still orbiting Earth, only 2300 still work. Every day the US military puts out an average of twenty-one warnings of likely collisions between this space junk and working satellites.[13] When will the child/adolescent within each of us step up, and care enough to clean up after ourselves and be better custodians of our planet – and now space?

Takers Keepers

The immature self is by nature a taker. It hasn't yet learned the importance of sharing, let alone giving back, and for many taking has become a habit. In the US, teens aged thirteen to seventeen account for a quarter of all shoplifters, with one in five adult shoplifters having started stealing during their teens.[14]

A separate US study puts teen shoplifters as high as 38 per cent of the population.[15] 'If I'm in a store and I see something sparkly and small I just have to have it,' Natalie admits in an online thread on shoplifting. 'I'm so used to free shit. I've been doing this without getting caught for fucking years … It's not like I need a new bracelet, I just see it and know I can steal it, so I take it.'[16]

We assume shoplifting is what poor people do. However, research suggests that shoplifting is 'more common among those with higher education and income'.[17] 'From 1998 to 2002 I was a full-time shoplifter,' Sofala says in another online chat space. '… I had left school and did not work, and spent my days shoplifting, or planning my new shoplifting attempt. I was born in a relatively rich family and, really, could have bought everything I stole. For me shoplifting was a hobby, a passion, a challenge. I did it mostly because I was bored and had enough of everything.'[18]

> **Honestly, I get why people shoplift. It's tempting to see all the free shit, and it's easy. But don't act like you're some kind of champion of the people, striking against the oligarchy for their sins. The only people you're hurting at the end of the day are the ones at the bottom of the food chain.'**
> Simon, *Reddit* forum[19]

The Impulse to Shoplift

The child's desire to steal can be prompted by depression, anger, thrill-seeking, the search for peer acceptance, feeling at a loose end or for the perverse delight of getting something for nothing. Shoplifters get an adrenaline rush from beating the system. 'The more you get away with it, the more you want to do it,' one shoplifter says in *Metro Parent*. 'And it would kill you to have to pay for anything.'[20] One of the many psychological explanations for shoplifting is poor impulse control, which is something learned (or not learned) during our childhood and teenage years.

Other People Matter Too

Shoplifting is about an absence of boundaries, a lack of consideration for others and an inability to understand what it's like to run a business with endless bills to pay. Many assume that the retailer simply orders a replacement item, but to make even a small profit, they need to factor in the cost of their rent, wages, insurance, freight, heating, lighting and so on. One Rutgers University publication suggests that if someone steals a $2 item in a store with a 10 per cent profit margin, that shop needs to sell a $20 item to recoup that loss.[21]

What's Going On Here?

'The first time is so exhilarating – you can't believe that you've done it,' Melbourne teenager Bec says on the online portal *Rosie* after stealing a tub of moisturiser. 'There is no other feeling like it. It's like a big fast truck of happiness has just hit you straight smack, bang in the face! You feel like yelling and telling the whole world.' Bec's guilt about stealing was swiftly overtaken by a craving for her 'next shoplifting high', until she was caught. Looking back, she admits that 'most of the things I stole I didn't really want or didn't fit. I think I shoplifted because I was impulsive, careless, and looking for a thrill'.[22]

Shoplifting happens across all ages and income brackets, and middle-aged shoplifters – aged between thirty-five and fifty-four – are the most common offenders. 'I stole audaciously, unforgivably, and because I knew

I could get away with it. Nobody suspects somebody like me of being a thief,' Samantha says in a *Guardian* article. As a middle-aged woman with three children and a beautiful home, she was well aware she didn't fit the profile of a shoplifter, making her shoplifting a whole lot easier. Once, her haul even included a six-foot Christmas tree.

Samantha says she didn't feel any guilt – she lived for the buzz of getting something for nothing. She was apprehended on her thirty-seventh birthday, and subsequently underwent counselling. She couldn't nail why she'd chosen to shoplift, 'apart from a yearning for thrills, and the slightly arrogant sense that I deserved nice things'.[23] According to America's National Association for Shoplifting Prevention, US$13 billion is stolen every year, which equates to a staggering US$35 million a day.[24]

When Nations Steal

Stealing also happens on a larger scale, often during times of conflict and war, or when demonstrations turn sour and looting begins. The child/adolescent literally runs riot, taking whatever they choose, knowing full well there'll be few, if any, consequences. We're beginning to appreciate that beyond all the pomp and circumstance and the wealth that colonisation delivered, it was theft on a grand scale, leaving countless people with broken, impoverished lives.

It can be hard for us to get a true sense of the loss that's felt when sacred artefacts are stolen. Nairobi bureau chief Max Bearak provides a very personal account in a powerful article for *The Washington Post*. He tells of the Pokomo people, and the loss of the Ngadji, their most sacred drum, which ended up in the British Museum. The Pokomo see the Ngadji, which stands taller than any man, as a living thing, whose sound they describe as 'the roar of a lion'.

Perhaps the most shocking aspect of this story is that this precious African drum has sat in storage in the British Museum for over a hundred years. In 2016, the Pokomo king's brother was given brief access to this beloved drum. What thoughts raced through his head when he became the first to touch his people's sacred object in over a hundred years? When asked what this drum means, the present king, His Majesty Makorani-a-Mungase VII, said, 'If you combined Britain's parliamentary mace and the Queen's crown jewels, you would still not equal the amount of cultural significance the Ngadji had for us. Its loss has stripped us of our sense of who we are.'[25]

Bringing the Ancestors Home

Equally heartbreaking is the plight of Indigenous Australians, and many other First Nations peoples, who live knowing the remains of countless loved ones and sacred objects are housed in museums the world over. It's not just overseas where the remains of many of Australia's First Nations ancestors reside. 'In the 1980s, I was sent to an Australian medical school to collect a doctor for a seminar,' one Indigenous nurse says. 'Imagine my horror when I saw hundreds of bodies of Aboriginal men, women, children and babies in giant formalin bottles.'[26] The shock of such an experience is hard to fathom.

After twenty hard years of petitioning and court battles, London's Natural History Museum handed back the remains of seventeen Indigenous Tasmanians.[27] 'Every time we bring our ancestors home is a very significant thing for us,' says Jarrod Edwards of the Tasmanian Aboriginal Centre on the repatriation of a further three Indigenous Tasmanians. 'Institutions around the world have got collections of our old people, that they continue to keep in the name of science, and to us they're people, they're our ancestors, and they deserve to be laid to rest in their homeland.'[28]

Don't we all want to see our loved ones laid to rest on home soil? As a nation, Australia goes to great lengths to bring home the remains of soldiers killed in battle, regardless of where they fell and how long ago the conflict took place. Yet our society finds it hard to extend this kindness to Indigenous Australians. Why can't we white Australians be grown-up enough to face the unpleasant fact that our forebears came and, like child/adolescents, took all they did because they were intrigued and because they could?

One count suggests some 32,000 sacred objects have been taken from Australia and are now in British museums. It is hard to explain to a secular world the immense value of these objects to First Nations peoples. How would those of us with differing spiritual beliefs feel if our most sacred objects were purloined? The outpouring of grief by Christians at the 2019 Notre Dame fire in Paris gives us some idea.

These Indigenous artefacts are beyond price to those who rightfully own them. In late 2019, a group of elders from the Gangalidda Garawa Nation received twelve of their sacred ceremonial artefacts from Manchester Museum. When elder Donald Bob saw the sacred items for the first time, he spoke with great emotion, telling how he 'felt cold, because it was the person of that thing [sacred artefact], that spirit crying for his home'.[29]

Righting Old Wrongs

Museums the world over hold countless Indigenous artefacts, largely stolen from First Nations peoples. President Emmanuel Macron is leading the way to right these wrongs. 'I am from a generation of the French people for whom the crimes of European colonialism are undeniable and make up part of our history,' he announced during a visit to the West African republic of Burkina Faso. 'I cannot accept that a large part of cultural heritage from several African countries is in France ... In the next five years, I want the conditions to be created for the temporary or permanent restitution of African patrimony to Africa.'

This was followed up by a swift edict from the Élysée Palace: 'African heritage can no longer be the prisoner of European museums.'[30]

Restitution requires understanding and respecting the spiritual values of a people, the importance of their ancestors, and the preciousness of sacred objects. First Nations peoples can teach our child/adolescent culture much about a depth of respect we're often lacking. We need to fight what Richard Rohr calls the 'tragic deafness and narcissism' of our immature selves.[31] We achieve this when we learn to walk more lightly and respectfully, and so embrace a depth of meaning in our interactions with others.

When Museums Victoria was planning its *Vikings: Beyond the Legend* exhibition, they consulted with First Nations Elders and the Aboriginal Cultural Heritage Advisory Committee as to whether they should display the Viking human remains on offer. Some Indigenous members spoke of their 'distress' at the thought of countless strangers viewing the ancestors of Viking peoples long gone. 'Indigenous laws,' they explained, 'hold that the deceased will not enjoy spiritual rest, until they are returned to their ancestral home and given the last rites in accordance with tradition.' Museums Victoria made the decision not to display Viking human remains in this exhibition.[32] This is what is possible when we leave our immature selves behind.

When We Assume We Know Best

For a deeper perspective on living and dying, and on ancestry, than our childlike selves can comprehend we need to understand just how delicate our cultural ecosystems are. If we take them at face value, we cause untold harm. At the close of World War II, the British occupation of India was clearly no longer tenable. British barrister Cyril Radcliffe was charged with dividing this huge subcontinent, home to around 390 million people.

Radcliffe was a fine barrister, but the skill set needed to divide this vast amount of land was far beyond the capabilities of any one person. He would later admit that he'd used outdated maps and census reports, as the intensity of India's summer meant it was too hot to conduct a field survey in person over the north Indian territories to be carved up. He was given only a few weeks to partition this land and chair the Boundary Commissions.[33]

On the formal signing of the partition documents, 'immediately, there began one of the greatest migrations in human history', Scottish historian, broadcaster and critic William Dalrymple reminds us, 'as millions of Muslims trekked to West and East Pakistan (the latter now Bangladesh), while millions of Hindus and Sikhs headed in the opposite direction'. The bloodshed on partition sparked the deaths of what may be up to two million people. It's thought around 75,000 women alone were raped and disfigured, if not dismembered. There were countless reports of pregnant women being brutalised and killed.[34] In many locations across the planet, this tragedy continues; the fallout from partition still impacts India today.

Fronting Up

In our child/adolescent foolishness we rush to meddle in parts of the world we know little about. We impose democracy on people with no experience of it, causing untold suffering and opening the way for less than ideal regimes to step in. In these cases there is often no comeback for victims, no thought of restitution, so we never face up to our actions.

In a conversation I had with one headmistress at a major city school, she bemoaned the lack of willingness of her students to make amends when something went wrong. Her pupils, she told me, were drawn from wealthy families, and knew it was important to appear well-mannered and to apologise when they'd done something wrong. 'The difficulty is that it's very easy just to say sorry,' she reflected. 'It's important the girls also demonstrate they're truly sorry. But this is tricky, frequently parents complain.' The immature self always seeks the easy way out; the mature self has the courage to do the right thing, even though restitution may prove costly.

Carelessness Has Many Faces

Carelessness permeates our lives in all kinds of subtle ways. This is examined forensically in the classic *The Great Gatsby*. Immersed in the glamour of their almost limitless wealth, Tom and Daisy Buchanan pass their days at extravagant parties, distracting themselves with soulless affairs. Caring little for the consequences of their actions, the Buchanans treat others, including friends, with a concerning lack of regard. After Daisy has a car accident, killing someone, they allow their friend Gatsby to take the rap. Subsequently, Gatsby is murdered by the victim's grieving husband. 'They [the Buchanans] were careless people ... they smashed up things and creatures,' reflects Nick Carraway in the book's closing chapter, 'and then retreated back into their money or vast carelessness, or whatever it was that kept them together, and let other people clean up the mess they had made.'

Not everyone has a thoughtful, adult way of seeing the world, and such people leave trails of devastation in their wake. We should never forget that our choices have power – that our community's responses, and those of our nation, are shaped by the way each of us chooses to be in the world. We need to be more conscious of our childish moments of carelessness so we can guard against them, and then assist our kids to take a wiser, more inclusive path.

A More Nuanced Approach

We can only progress when we're prepared to be honest with ourselves.

- Dare to think about your own careless moments.
- Are there still situations where you need to make amends? How might you do this?
- What prompted you to go down this negative track?
- How can you avoid this pattern in the future?
- How can you assist your kids to plot a different path?

22

Our Constant Need to Escape

Today we have the chance to escape into a dazzling array of pleasures large and small – in our achievements, in limitless purchases, in opportunities to travel and in a variety of legal and illegal substances. But we can confuse these many distractions with genuine freedom, only to drift away from the very things that deliver stability, belonging and support.

Adolescence loves the chance to have a tilt at something new but our partially formed selves don't have the awareness to pick and choose wisely, to know what feeds us. We opt instead for the chance to come and go as we like; to pick up partners and jobs, then discard them when they fail to deliver; to travel when and where we choose, on our own terms.

Drowning in Trivia

Being forever on the go isn't necessarily freedom. Our childish selves like momentum, and have got into the habit of running from any form of commitment or containment. But imprisonment can sneak into our lives in subtle ways. 'What if there are no cries of anguish to be heard [should this imprisonment happen]?' asks social critic Neil Postman. 'Who is prepared to take arms against a sea of amusements? To whom do we complain, and when, and in what tone of voice, when serious discourse dissolves into giggles? What is the antidote to a culture being drained by laughter?'[1]

When the immature part of us becomes lost in trivial pursuits, with the 24/7 availability of social media, streaming services, podcasts, TV, radio and more, we can end up 'amusing ourselves to death', as Neil Postman suggests. The child/adolescent loves to be entertained, to keep the complicated and less convenient aspects of life at bay. What, then, is the 'death' Postman is hinting at here?

An Entertaining Life

The Lumière brothers (inventors of the first commercial silent film projector) premiered their work in Moscow's Hermitage Garden in the spring of 1896. With remarkable prescience, Russian writer Maxim Gorky reflected, 'The [Lumière] Cinématographe ... activates the senses on one hand, and dulls them on the other. The thirst for such strange, fantastic sensations will grow greater, and we will be increasingly unable and less willing to grasp the everyday impressions of ordinary life.'[2]

With the endless parade of lives lived on screen, captured and delivered to us with such pleasingly impossible perfection on such a grand scale, how easily our lives and dreams can pale, to the point that they seem of little or no significance.

Lost in an entertainment-induced stupor, we become ever more addicted to sensation, and no longer able or willing to distinguish between what's real and what's not. In the process, the voice of our true selves is lost. 'Americans no longer talk to each other, they entertain each other,' Neil Postman observed. 'They do not exchange ideas; they exchange images. They do not argue with propositions; they argue with good looks, celebrities and commercials.'[3] But where does this leave us?

Surrogate Lives

'People want to live through other people's lives,' Jason suggests in a thread on the Kardashians. 'If you have *anything* special about you at all. Like if you're extremely charming, rich, have [a] special job, or if you're attractive, you'll find tons of people who will watch your life 24/7, in hopes to be a "little more like you".'[4] Over three decades ago, historian Christopher Lasch warned about losing ourselves in 'a surfeit of spectacles', noting our 'willingness to be taken in by the staged illusion of reality', which leaves us with an 'indifference to the distinction between illusion and reality'.[5]

> **Being alive is scary, so we buy into these prefabricated**
> **'meanings of life' that simplify the dread of existence.**
> Nico, *Reddit* forum[6]

This appetite for illusion can be seen in the mega popularity of *Keeping Up with the Kardashians*, despite how contrived such shows are. 'Every time we renewed for another season, I would think to myself, "How can I take these fifteen minutes of fame and turn them into thirty?"' Kardashian 'momager' Kris Jenner writes in her autobiography. 'I started to look at our careers like pieces on a chessboard,' she confesses. 'Every day, I woke up and walked into my office and asked myself, "What move do you need to make today?" It was very calculated. My business decisions and strategies were very intentional, definite and planned to the nth degree.'[7]

> **The Kardashians are famous for the same reasons that**
> **people flock to Marvel movies: they exist outside of**
> **reality … It's the same reason that people play video games**
> **or role play or gossip or anything else: they just want a**
> **break from their reality, regardless of if it's good or bad.**
> Sean, *Reddit* forum[8]

With such carefully stage-managed, dramatic and glamorous lives to tune into, why bother to put so much effort into our own lives? *Keeping Up with the Kardashians* 'is basically like junk food of the mind', admits Jade in one thread on the phenomenal success of the show. 'I can zone out to it and after a stressful day, it's nice to just focus on something a little silly. I'm also fascinated with their jet setting, rich lives. And how they always look insanely put together at all times.'[9]

Hopelessly Hooked

'Here in North America, we don't just own TVs; we're a little addicted to them,' admits Sarah Bunting, blogger and co-author of *Television Without Pity*. 'We keep them close by in case we need a fix, which is why we have them in the living room and the den, and the kitchen, and the bedroom, and on the boat, and in the cottage, and in our cars, and cleverly tucked away in a hidden panel built into the hot tub.'[10]

In just a few years, we have ever-growing immediate access to our devices, which we carry with us on buses and trains and while shopping. We keep them close at mealtimes and with loved ones. Often, they're the first thing we consult on waking and the last thing we gaze at before we drop off to sleep.

In one *Hollywood Reporter* poll, 60 per cent of adults told of binge-watching TV, with a quarter of the sample admitting to ditching time with friends in order to keep viewing.[11] While one Pew Research Center report found that almost nine out of ten participants admitted to accessing their phone during a social gathering – to call someone, read or send a message, or take a photo or video. A third of those surveyed also told of getting their phone out at the same gathering when feeling bored.[12]

This infantile love affair with our devices and their overuse comes at a significant cost, keeping us anxious and dependent, separated from companions who are willing to walk alongside us through thick and thin. Our child/adolescent selves are too distracted to give big life issues any serious sustained attention.

Wonderment

In his collection *What Are People For?*, American essayist Wendell Berry talks of the growing trend of letting go of creativity in favour of novelty, which, he suggests, is dreamed up by 'minds incapable of wonder … Novelty is sparking a new kind of loneliness [because it lacks genuine wonder]'. If we want to be truly original, he insists, we need to experience the wonder of being part of something far greater than us.[13]

What does genuine wonder look and feel like? What happens when we embrace things that are solid and true? 'The world today is sick to its thin blood for lack of elemental things,' American writer Henry Beston mused, 'for fire before the hands, for water welling from the earth, for air, for the dear earth itself underfoot. In my world of beach and dunes these elemental presences lived and had their being, and under their arch there moved an incomparable pageant of nature and the year.'[14]

Beston arrived at his place of wonderment after returning from military service in France during World War I. He spent a solitary year on a windswept stretch of the Cape Cod coast in a simple home amid the dunes and became one with the elements, in awe at what he witnessed as each season brought its gifts and very real challenges. He captured this life-changing experience in his timeless classic *The Outermost House*.

Later, Beston spent a season on a small farm in Maine, which he detailed in *Northern Farm*. 'Our civilization has fallen out of touch with night,' he reflected. 'With lights, we drive the holiness and beauty of night back to the forests and the sea; the little villages, the crossroads even, will have none of it. Are modern folk, perhaps, afraid of night? Do they fear that vast serenity, the mystery of infinite space, the austerity of stars?'[15] These are big questions that demand our attention and, in so doing, set something fundamental and powerful in us ablaze. This is the gift of daring to travel further, to look deeper, to live daily with the dance we do between doubt and certainty.

Where Our Infantile Desires Lead Us

Wonder is one of the many gifts of a life lived fully as we connect to each other and to creation in all its forms. How many of us have tasted wonder firsthand? On the delicate journey from infancy to adulthood, where do the roadblocks lie? Where do our capacious appetites for consumption and growing immersion in entertainment leave us? These are questions we need to continue to revisit if we want to taste true freedom.

> **American media pitches to ... a childish level of**
> **intelligence, just mature enough to be sufficiently**
> **suggestible to purchase the wares of their sponsors.**
> E James Brennan, *Quora* forum[16]

We need also to see where the thin ice lies. Reviewing the history of the child as consumer, Daniel Thomas Cook, an associate professor of childhood studies at Rutgers University, tells of how experts came up with the concept of the 'desiring child' in the 1950s.[17] This sparked an intense and ongoing focus on our children: how to get and retain their attention; how to market to them before they can even speak, let alone read and write. Using the best tools available, from psychology, neuroscience, animation and cultural anthropology, has led to an unprecedented pressure on our young to ensure they become good little consumers.

Afraid to Grow Up

This deliberate cultivation of our children as consumers bars them from the adult world, and from access to wonderment, filling their lives with possessions instead. This view of children as consumers 'made it unnecessary even to think about the child ever going there into adult life', reflects Diana West in *The Death of the Grown-up*, adding, 'It also drew the adult so deeply into the child's world that it became hard to leave.'[18]

Many of our escapist tendencies are likely fostered in early childhood. Rather than experiencing nature, personal creativity or imaginative play, our children are encouraged instead to pick up a device and click onto an animated show whenever they want, wherever they are, or we appease them with an hour or two at the mall or the movies.

Superficial Rules

Too many of our kids are immersed in shallow stories filled with characters that are instantly available to them in clothing, bedroom accessories and toys, in drinks, sweets and cereal packaging. This relationship with their burgeoning possessions is set up to be addictive, to capture and imprison them in a one-dimensional world.

Part of becoming a grown-up is a willingness to have the courage to see life in all its beauty as well as its terrifying complexity and brevity. That's not to suggest that grown-up life isn't redolent with joy, infused with beauty and a multitude of possibilities. 'Maturity doesn't exclude playfulness or high humor. Far from it', essayist Joseph Epstein affirms. 'The mature understand that the bitterest joke of all is that the quickest way to grow old lies in the hopeless attempt to stay forever young.'[19]

Buying Our Identity

Primed to consume, the child/adolescent is very sensitive to their choices, developing what former *New York Times* columnist John Tierney describes as 'a connoisseur's passion for plasma televisions, Kelly bags, Harry Potter movies and low-riding Gap jeans'.[20] The child self is also happy to be 'told and sold', notes British broadcaster Michael Bywater, gravitating to what are deemed the 'right' clothes, cars, homes and accessories.[21]

Plagued by Restlessness

This continual escape into entertainment and consumption leaves us forever restless, moving in and out of the family home, and in and out of jobs and partnerships. Life lived in constant motion is evident when we try to explain what we've been up to. 'I was living in a share house with friends, but have just moved back home, until I can find a studio apartment,' Clare told me. 'First, though, I need a break. So I'm off to Bali for a fortnight, then I'm going to look for a new job once I'm home. Though I may head back to London, as I kind of like it there.'

A Different Relationship with Time

In the West, German philosopher Hermann Lübbe suggests, we're experiencing the 'contraction of the present', marked by 'an increase in the decay-rates of experiences we can rely on, and by the shrinking of the amount of time we regard as the "present".' Our lessening ability to hold on to life experiences for long plays into this contraction of the present.

This creates a situation in which we're either getting ahead or slipping behind, with nothing in between, reflects Hartmut Rosa, professor of sociology and social theory at Friedrich-Schiller-University.[22] In a world packed with choices, we're also under increasing pressure to embrace whatever comes our way to feed our need for momentum. With so much to choose from, how can we be sure we're making the right choice? And how long will that choice work for us? Personal satisfaction is no longer about reaching a place of peace and contentment, so much as grasping at as many opportunities as we can, while we can.

Drowning in Choice

The child/adolescent loves choice – the more the better. 'The world always seems to have more on offer than can be experienced in a single lifetime,' Hartmut Rosa notes.[23] We need to run faster and faster, just to keep pace in this fast-moving world. 'You try to act on a faster pace, faster scale – [with] fast food, speed-dating and power naps.'[24] What we're actually experiencing isn't momentum, he suggests. It's the *illusion* of momentum, as we've become 'frozen' in time, lost in a 'directionless, frantic motion that is in fact a form of inertia.'[25]

Nothing to Hold On To

In the world of immediate gratification, nothing lasts. It is harmful too, suggests simplicity blogger Leo Babauta. This need is creating debt, clutter, bad health and mindlessness. Then, as the joy fades, we find ourselves back hungering for even more. 'Doing a huge number of things doesn't mean you're getting anything meaningful done,' Babauta cautions. 'In fact, it's so hit-and-miss that it's almost like playing a game of roulette: If you do enough tasks, one of them is bound to pay off big.'[26] This approach to life is also wearying.

More people are now working actively to slow down, through meditation and mindfulness, simplicity and gratitude, and are experiencing new levels of satisfaction and peace. 'I was obsessed with being a winner,' Patti says in one thread on mindfulness. 'Since [mindfulness practices] my mind has become more clear … It's just that in whatever situation I am in it's fine, since I can trust myself.'[27] Nelson concurs in another online forum. 'The biggest thing [meditation] has given me is that most of the time I can turn off most thought pretty easily. The peace and quiet is nice, and it helps me think better when I actually need to.'[28]

It's no coincidence that Japanese storage expert Marie Kondo is so popular, and named by *Time* magazine as one of the top 100 Most Influential People in 2015, or that Kondo's Netflix program is now aired in many locations across the globe. 'In the past century, we've swung from "buying brings happiness" to "curating and purging certain bought items brings happiness", professor of sociology at Whitman College Michelle Janning suggests.[29] Could this be the beginning of a more adult approach to our consumer culture?

False Promises

It's tempting to view our spending power and the huge array of goods available to us as a pinnacle of human achievement, given so many across the world have so little. In a *Quartz* interview, New York psychologist April Lane Benson, who specialises in shopping addiction, suggests, 'Shopping is a way that we search for ourselves and our place in the world. A lot of people conflate the search for self with the search for stuff.'[30]

One East German study compared consumer patterns before and after the reunification of Germany. It found that before reunification, goods were scarce, so East Germans spent a great deal of time sourcing items, which they then treated with care. Possessions were mended or, if beyond repair, they were often kept, in the hope their parts might be useful in the future.

On reunification, the East Germans were bedazzled by the amount of choice after so long without, but soon found the sheer number of items available overwhelming and of lower quality than what they'd been used to. Many were unhappy, hating the waste and the unwillingness to repair goods. Study participants were also dismayed at the competition creeping into relationships, creating what they called an 'elbow society', which they saw as eroding community.[31]

The Ultimate Escape

The pandemic aside, travel is another form of escape. With cheap fares and our increasingly globalised world, travel destinations have opened up like never before. Escape is a common theme in travel ads, where we're invited to 'discover your inner explorer', 'go wild', 'live fully' and 'find yourself'. For those needing to be pampered, there are packages 'in luxury's reach', with 'amazing luxury' or 'luxury without limits' on offer. We can sample 'award-winning' wines, food and experiences and disappear in tours large and small that are 'hand-picked', 'tailor-made', or 'breaking new ground'.

> **I would argue that the current trend in travelling seems to be less about experience really, but more about showing off/keeping up with the Joneses.**
> Inez, *Reddit* forum[32]

Tantalising reveals await with the chance to see 'hidden wonders' and have 'unparalleled' experiences that leave our heads exploding with possibilities, as we wrestle with the choice of 'where to next?'. Is it possible that our approach to travel has simply become yet another rabbit hole? 'The problem [with conspicuous travel] is that we are just trading one form of consumerism for another,' says Zadie, reflecting online about our obsession with travel. 'I think there needs to be more focus on travel that has value outside of boosting your Instagram follower count.'[33]

What Did You Learn?

What happens when we arrive at our much-anticipated location? Do we engage with the differing cultures and people there? Are we simply ticking off another item on our bucket list, secretly delighted at being treated to a level of luxury not experienced at home, or do we want to buy even more stuff at ridiculously low prices? While away, we happily capture hundreds of photos of ourselves moving through exotic locations as if we've just landed in some kind of theme park, and seeing the people there as little more than colourful props.

As I travel in developing countries, I'm often dismayed at the way some Westerners treat local people as servants, or as stupid because they can't make themselves understood. We forget we are guests in their country, that English is possibly only one of a number of languages they speak. The persistent bargain-hunting, squabbling over one or two dollars, shows no thought to how long it may have taken to make an object or how far someone may have travelled to bring this item to market. What of those who while away their time in luxurious bars and spas, returning home with a tan and bag full of treasures, but with little appreciation of the history, beliefs and culture, the daily struggles of local people, their sometimes quiet despair?

Child/adolescents will take as much as they can with little thought of reciprocity or respect. For those who make the leap, the gifts are immense. As Stefan reflects in a thread about travel, going somewhere new is 'about learning that you are not the centre of the world, and you may be wrong about some of your values, some of your viewpoints, some of your ideas of how humanity is. It's about understanding that your view on other cultures is as incomplete as the media coverage about the places you visit.'[34] This is a powerful way to step off the child/adolescent treadmill. It offers us, and our kids, the chance to embrace a more satisfying path.

Are we ready to make the leap?

Why We Do What We Do

What if next time you're tempted to disappear down a rabbit hole, you pause to ask yourself:

- What's really going on here? Why is life lacklustre right now?
- Is it simply because I'm a little tired or down?
- How would life look if it were uncluttered by wall-to-wall entertainment, and a constant need to consume?
- Is it time to open your drawers and cupboards, and get rid of what you don't need? To pass items on to those who could benefit from your kindness?
- What if you were to travel differently? Why not start with lesser-known parts of your town and city? What surprises await you here?
- What insights and opportunities can you pass on to your kids? What wealth of experiences can you expose them to?

23

What Does Grown Up Look Like?

Grown-ups can be hard to locate some days. Being surrounded by people wanting to remain forever young, with an absence of good role models and with marketers constantly and cleverly denigrating all gatekeepers does not encourage us to become fully functioning adults. At every turn we're encouraged to go with the flow, maintain our child/adolescent status, follow the crowd. When we remain steeped in our childish ways, we lack assurance; even the basics of life seem stressful, if not baffling.

It's interesting to appreciate how concerningly at sea some of our emerging generation feel when faced with routine aspects of daily life. 'What surprises me the most is still how *expensive* life really is,' reflects Miriam in one thread about adult life. 'Now that I know, I keep finding myself wondering how the hell my parents made it through the rough times ... I remember when I was younger how stressful it was to them, to try to keep things together and they still gave me a really good education, I have no idea how.'[1] Participating in this same thread, Nigel agrees: 'It's kinda nuts how we're [now] responsible for getting stuff done. Like to get your car registration renewed or buying/maintaining a pantry of groceries. Making a decent dinner, even. That's all on me now. No one will remind me if I don't remind myself.'[2]

When we lack the requisite life tools, even the simplest tasks can overwhelm us, leaving us little room to relax, or to experience the quiet joy that comes when we're on top of things. 'When we grow up into being an adult, often we are pressured to be "realistic". But at what cost?' Charlie demands in another online forum. 'Reality is cruel, cold, disappointing, very limiting, mundane/boring, stupid, pointless/ meaningless (often times), and depressing … especially for some of us who have fully realized it and wake up to the harsh truth.'[3]

It's hard for our young to mature if we don't show them solid ways to chart their progress and take pleasure in the strides they make. Psychologist Jeffrey Arnett defines adulthood as that point where we're able to make our own decisions, be responsible for ourselves and be financially independent.[4] We begin to take our place alongside other grown-ups, to embrace the many privileges and occasional, but inevitable, inconveniences of being on the front line.

Safe to Be Around

There's something solid and reassuring about a fully fledged adult. Operating beyond the need to constantly compete, genuine grown-ups enjoy being around others, regardless of their status. These are the people we can trust with our secrets, with our deepest anxieties. We never need question whether or not these people have our best interests at heart.

The true value of being around an adult is that they're not afraid to tell us the truth. When mature people listen, they listen deeply and kindly, without needing to be the centre of every conversation. They are willing and able to take the time to look more closely and compassionately at what's going on in a situation, before drawing their conclusions.

Solitude Helps

One of the many signs of a grown-up is being able to enjoy our own company – to be comfortable in solitude. This gives our adult selves time to reflect and replenish, to slow the cycle of always rushing around or seeking constantly to please. When you're comfortable with your own company, you've time to get to know your strengths and shortcomings, which then allows time for new possibilities to emerge.

> [When we lack solitude] we're drawn to identity-markers and to groups that help us define ourselves. In the simplest terms, this means using others to fill out our identities, rather than relying on something internal, something that comes from within.
>
> Matthew Bowker, *A Dangerous Place to Be*[5]

A Multi-layered Approach

As we settle into our adult selves, we sense there's more to life than is immediately apparent. We start to explore the layers and textures around us, and to see that it's in the *detail* that a rich and satisfying life is crafted. During the early days of the pandemic, Washington-based columnist Amelia Lester captured this nuanced process well: 'I have been really noticing the restorative power of sunlight: the calming quality of a solitary walk; and the absolutely vital service performed in supermarkets and many other workers keeping the lights on.'[6]

When we take time to ponder the detail, to sit with it and explore it, our observations and musings deepen. Becoming an adult is a type of alchemy in which we seek, wherever possible, to leave people and circumstances better than we found them. We won't always succeed but striving for the greater good feeds the spirit, as does a willingness to embrace new possibilities with thought and care so that life becomes an ongoing process of unfolding.

There will still be days when we ache to crawl back under the doona but we've learned there's little value in hiding away. Grown-ups continue to learn and grow through observation and reflection to be clearer about what's required. Whenever we face a difficult or complex task, we know to think about what's needed, forsaking what's easiest. We push beyond all feelings of inadequacy, confusion or despair, and work on our resilience, at times surprising ourselves and others with how well we dealt with certain situations and how we found a way through.

Stay Curious

The mature mind also maintains a lively curiosity about life. It takes time to stay up to date with what's happening in the world, to read fiction, to watch films and documentaries, not purely for entertainment but for a sense of how life is for others. The payoff is that we get to take in the world through a wider, wiser lens.

What the mature among us strive for is less about being right than about understanding and embracing life and finding powerful ways to learn from the people and situations that come our way. It's a willingness to keep on learning and discovering, to grow, which emerges, in part, from a preparedness to be proved wrong.

Doubt Has Value

While the child/adolescent tends to run from doubt and uncertainty, the adult realises total certainty in life is rare. We don't always have the answers, but we do have the wisdom to realise this and, where possible, to do something about it. Grown-ups have learned to distrust those who offer short cuts and lives of uninterrupted abundance and ease.

Adults know that blind certainty can sometimes be extremely destructive, as witnessed during the Nazi and other devastating regimes. 'It's important to doubt yourself, because it gives you the ability to reflect on making sure what you're doing is right. If you don't doubt yourself, you're not human,' insisted former New South Wales government minister Andrew Constance after almost losing his Malua Bay home during Australia's 2019 bushfire season.[7]

It Can't Always Be About You

There's also a sacrificial element to being an adult. This is rarely spoken about, which is a pity, as it's something we can all benefit from. Our needs can't, and shouldn't, always come first. There are times where we're asked to contribute to possibilities we'll never personally profit from. When we neglect such opportunities to reach out, our chances of creating a solid, more empowered future that we and others can benefit from is limited. 'Those who know themselves and maximize their strengths are the ones who go where they want to go,' suggests writer Nicholas Cole. 'Those who don't know themselves, and avoid the hard work of looking inward, live life by default.'[8]

> A life of dangerous adventures might seem worth it now,
> when you are young and seemingly invincible,
> but one day, you will have children, and you will
> not want that life for them.
> ML Wang, *The Sword of Kaigen*

Embrace the Wisdom of Age

What if, instead of running from ageing, we learned to sit with it, to respect those who are wise, who have walked farther than us. In India there's *padasparshan*, the beautiful custom of touching an elder's feet. This powerful gesture of greeting honours the wisdom and experience of those who've travelled further than we have. I've benefited greatly from close friendships with those who are significantly older. Their wise, grounded presence has reassured and inspired me over the years.

We witness the power of such connections in Captain Tom Moore's remarkable fundraising effort during the pandemic. Who would have thought this UK war veteran, at age 99, would inspire millions by walking the lengths of his garden to raise funds to support health workers caring for coronavirus patients? Not even sure he'd raise £1000, Captain Tom set off on his challenge anyway, never imagining he'd inspire others to donate over £30 million. In all the chaos, loss and confusion of COVID, Captain Tom responded as an adult, pointing us all forward, offering us hope with his insistence that 'tomorrow will be a good day'.

Pushing Past Our Agenda

As an adult, our focus shifts. We're more attuned to wider outcomes, beyond our own needs. We know that what we do impacts others and that our rights exist *only* so far as they don't impinge on, or harm, the rights of others. Many of us still need to get this point.

> **You must negotiate your own desires with the desires of those around you. Actions have consequences.'**
> Mark Manson, 'How to Grow the Fuck Up'[9]

At the height of the pandemic, an American friend was in despair about a colleague – a professor with COVID-19 – who continued to teach and to infect his students. When challenged, he was adamant that it was his right to teach regardless. As he was a senior member of staff, no one felt able to continue to challenge him. He was clearly capable intellectually, but was an emotional infant. Here again we see what happens when the child/adolescent is running the show.

Choosing to Make the Leap

Becoming an adult has its moments – doubly so for those who are ill-prepared. 'I have grown up in a relatively poor family. Not wanting me to face the reality of our situation, my parents spoiled me with whatever they could (even if it was not comparable to what rich kids had); Lippi says in an online chat canvassing the struggles a pampered childhood creates. 'I felt like such a complete idiot in college, because I grew up with no social skills/street smarts/self-esteem and I "let" either my parents or older sister do everything … If you could make a list of words of what I am now, I am this: apprehensive, coddled, deficient, impressionable, inept, lacking, neurotic, reluctant, timid, weak. After years of realization, I have learned I need to become a more confident adult, so I can go back to college/find a job independently.'[10]

One of the many attributes of maturity is patience. Learning to be still isn't easy but it's exhausting to be caught in the loop of continual shopping and entertainment, till we've well and truly maxed out our credit cards, amusing ourselves day and night. Lacking faith in ourselves and our choices, we tend to seize at every experience offered us, for our fear of being judged irrelevant, of being left behind. As life passes in a blur, we're hardly able to remember what we did last week, let alone several months back. As we gain a measure of wisdom, we discover there's so much more to be gained by waiting and reflecting, and ensuring that something we're attracted to is in fact what we want.

Expand Your Skillset

If we're hoping for an easy life as an adult, we've probably come to the wrong planet. Instead of spending our lives dodging discomfort, we're far better advised to invest the time needed to acquire the requisite life skills to help us through adversity. 'Being an adult is not about being comfortable doing things, it is about doing uncomfortable things,' Sunil reminds us when contemplating over-indulged childhoods online. 'The only way you learn that is to experience pain and discomfort, and to survive them ... Instead [of wishing for an easier path], wish for broader shoulders to carry your burdens.'[11]

> **Adulthood is vastly superior to teen years, provided that**
> **you actually grow up, of course.**
> Petra, *Reddit* forum[12]

A Little Failure Doesn't Hurt

Gracious in defeat, the adult self is not cowed by a little failure now and then, well aware that mistakes can be made, and more focused on solutions than on blame. It's important to own our mistakes and grieve them, but also never to give up on life, however steep the road ahead.

Bad and difficult things happen. People get sick, have accidents and die. Adults learn to sit with pain, their own and that of others, aware that there are times when we simply have to surrender to the moment. My teenage nephew Matt was out cycling in the correct lane when a ute collected him. I'm forever grateful to the truck driver who arrived at the scene and held Matt as he was dying. In that truck driver we see the adult self at work in all its power and selflessness, its blessed willingness to do the right thing.

Amid its many challenges, grown-up life offers a multitude of powerful gifts. We learn this by giving our adult self a good workout. Only then can we learn to stand tall through thick and thin, and help show the generations after us the way.

Stepping Up

Becoming an adult isn't an overnight process, but it's well worth the journey. Why not contemplate these questions and see where they take you?

- Are you a safe person to be around, or do you use the shortcomings of others to gain personal traction? How fulfilling is this?
- Could your listening skills be refined? How do you feel when you do listen deeply?
- Is it time for more solitude? Embrace a little time alone and see where it takes you.
- Certainty is comfortable, but it can also imprison. Which of your attitudes and responses could benefit from greater flexibility?
- Why not entertain the possibility that you may be wrong, or that you may need to fine-tune your views?
- What can you bring to the world that you mightn't personally benefit from?
- How can you make these insights real for your kids?

24

The Small Question of Death

While our child/adolescent selves may flirt with the idea of eternal youth, if we're serious about growing up, we need to face the fact of our mortality, and explore how much our understanding of death can offer us. 'Death is very likely the single best invention of Life,' Steve Jobs once suggested, adding, 'It's Life's change agent.'[1]

When we accept this, we're able to live with greater perspective. In medieval times, as in Buddhism, contemplation of death was seen as essential to having any hope of living a rich life. The constant presence of death, amid life, was captured in great and loving detail in pen and ink, wood and stone. These *memento mori* were salient reminders that our time here is precious – when we embrace the fragility of life, we're no longer imprisoned by our fear of death.

> **It's not the length of life, but the depth of life.**
> Ralph Waldo Emerson, poet, philosopher and essayist[2]

Who Are You Really?

In shamanic spiritual practices, meeting death experientially, and in dream and/or related states, is regarded as a basic building block for growth. This leads to what anthropologist Jonathan Horwitz says is the crucial question: 'Who am I when everything I own and love, when my life and achievements are gone, when my body is no more?'

Horwitz adds, 'I have taken to reminding myself, and other people, that I might die at any moment … Another way to [be] open to death is to be aware of death around you, from the changing of the seasons to deaths of those around you, and to be together with people who are actively dying.'[3]

Death Close Up

Many wonderful images of death help the child/adolescent in us to delve into life's deeper questions. Georgia O'Keeffe's iconic painting *Cow's Skull with Calico Roses*, painted in sepulchral white, depicts a cow's skull, bleached by the sun in America's southwestern desert. A white calico rose, often found on Mexican graves, blossoms from the skull's eye socket and jaw. O'Keeffe painted this poignant and striking work after witnessing the ravages of drought up close.

> **Death is not the greatest loss in life. The loss is what dies inside us while we live.**
> Norman Cousins, writer, professor and peace advocate[4]

Death has a way of waking us up. While visiting friends in New York one night, Washington-based journalist Matthew Knott was strolling across the roof of an apartment block when he stepped into an air shaft, falling five storeys. He miraculously didn't die. 'To come so close to death does not provide a shortcut to wisdom or contentment. It doesn't answer all your questions, or eliminate your weaknesses,' he said after his lengthy recuperation. 'The meaning comes in what I do from this point on. I have been given a second chance at life – and it's up to me to make the most of it.'[5]

Making Peace with Loss

'Faced with the awareness of death, how can an individual live a constructive life?' asks psychologist Robert Firestone. 'The answer is that we can face up to our feelings and fears, and live without sacrificing our integrity, or resorting to deadening painkillers, dishonest manipulations, and a myriad of other individual and institutional defenses.'[6]

None of us wants to lose those we love, to deal with the pain of their absence or with the knowledge that one day we too will take this road. Yet 'grief is the price we pay for love', psychiatrist and grief expert Colin Murray Parkes reminds us.[7] This is something the adult learns to make peace with.

Few of us get to experience death much firsthand these days. Not so my great-grandmother. She and a friend would wash and lay out friends and neighbours who died, as an act of love. We, however, have little sense what the moment of death is like. We often wait until we stare death in the face before we explore it, then wonder why we feel so lost.

What to Expect

'Is death as frightening as we assume?' is one of the questions the child/adolescent most wants to ask. University of North Carolina psychologists conducted two intriguing studies. First, they compared the way the terminally ill talked of their last months with how people who were well talked about death when asked to imagine the experience. Those still enjoying good health tended to use the words 'fear', 'terror' and 'anxiety', while the terminally ill spoke more of 'happiness' and 'love'.

In a second experiment, the final words of death row inmates were compared with what everyday people thought these inmates would say before execution. Again the words the inmates used were more positive than expected.[8] 'In our imagination, dying is lonely and meaningless, but the final blog posts of terminally ill patients and the last words of death row inmates are filled with love, social connection, and meaning,' states psychologist Kurt Gray, who was part of these studies.[9]

> **Death, when it approaches, ought not to take one by surprise. It should be part of the full expectancy of life.**
> Muriel Spark, novelist, essayist and poet[10]

What a world away these experiences of death are from our current celebration of Halloween, for example, with its ghoulish images and constant re-runs of old horror movies, which keep the child/adolescent in us imprisoned in a morbid fear of death. For those lucky enough to experience Varanasi, the Indian city older than Babylon, where Hindus hope to die, they have the privilege of respectfully viewing the funeral ghats with cremations in progress. So much about life comes into sharp focus in such profound moments.

Explore the Nuances

I was lucky to grow up in a culture that talked regularly of death, and of those who'd died. I was, in a sense, shown the way. When I was three or four, I'd go with my grandmother and aunt to the cemetery, to help tidy the graves and clean the headstones of family members. While we worked, they would tell me stories of these family members – their strengths and shortcomings, their quirks. I'd never met any of them but I felt I knew them. And, to this day, I love old graveyards.

In spite of these experiences, I had a great deal more to learn. When my friend Jim was in a hospice dying of AIDS, I was terrified of visiting him. I wanted desperately to be with Jim but was filled with the anxiety of not knowing what to do, of saying or doing the wrong thing, of not being able to cope. As the days passed and I got to observe

Jim's journey close up, I loved being with him. In that intimate space, all that remained was Jim's essence – that part of him I'd always loved from the moment we met. In observing the beauty of Jim's essential self, everything I was worried about dropped away. All that was left was our love for each other. I'm so grateful to Jim for teaching me so much about dying.

Keep Things Practical

The adult in us knows death isn't something to fear but to be reckoned with. To help the child/adolescent in us to deal with death, we need to find small, *practical* ways to assist those we love who are dying. For instance, if they experience rapid weight loss, they'll need new, comfortable clothes, and something to keep their feet warm.

These small details help the child in us navigate the pain of our impending loss. They help us to grow, by focusing on what is required. Providing a little more comfort for a loved one is immensely healing. It may come in the form of a gentle foot massage, or simply holding their hand or, where appropriate, getting into bed with them so they can enjoy our warmth and presence close up.

Don't Leave the Kids Out

Death also provides powerful lessons for our children when we draw them into this life-changing process. 'The word "mystery" can be a helpful one to use with even young children, when explaining the questions that arise in life which we are unable to answer,' suggests hospice nurse Andrea Warnick.[11] Encourage questions, she adds. Decorate the dying person's room with the children. Get the kids to gently apply moisturiser, where needed. Let them do their homework or other quiet activities while you're all together and thank them for being brave enough to ask questions.

'It is a true honour and privilege to be with a person as their life on Earth ends,' says Shelley, a nurse. 'Be brave and have the courage to say what you need to, say goodbye. Cry, laugh, be silent, pray, respect cultural beliefs. The most important thing is being there.'[12] So much of adult life is about turning up and doing what needs to be done. We tend to see such tasks as irksome, not realising just how much meaning and wisdom they can deliver – how they nudge us towards a greater acceptance of ourselves and an ability to connect with others – qualities we strive hard for, but so often seek in all the wrong places.

When We Experience Death Up Close

'The Buddha himself described death as the "the greatest of all teachers",' states Ken Holmes, who joined the first Tibetan Buddhist monastery in the West.[13] Our child/adolescent selves have become used to focusing almost completely on ourselves. Yet life and death, if we dare to embrace them, offer us so much more. 'For life and death are one,' poet and author Khalil Gibran reminds us, 'even as the river and the sea are one.'[14]

> **Small pleasures loom large [when dying]. As with anything**
> **in short supply, their value rises with their rarity.**
> Peter Barton, *Not Fade Away*

In *The Top Five Regrets of the Dying*, Bronnie Ware says some common regrets include: 'I wish I'd had the courage to live a life true to myself, not the life others expected of me', 'I wish I had stayed in touch with my friends' and 'I wish that I had let myself be happier'.

In his bestselling book *Not Fade Away*, which documents his journey towards imminent death, Peter Barton tells us, 'The experience of seeing death up close had made my life better. I found I was calmer, less easily distressed by unessential things. My life grew sparser and richer. There were fewer things I cared about, but those I valued seemed more precious than ever. I had a more vivid appreciation of health and time; among human virtues I now gave a higher rank to kindness.'[15]

'The wild prefaced us, and it will outlive us,' British writer and thinker Robert Macfarlane reminds us. 'Human cultures will pass, given time, of which there is sufficiency. The ivy will snake and unrig our flats and terraces, as it scattered the Roman villas. The sand will drift into our business parks, as it drifted into the brochs of the Iron Age. Our roads will lapse into the land.'[16] When we can be fully cognisant of our mortality, and the impermanence of everything around us, life has far more clarity.

'The impermanence of life can be unsettling,' admits global fashion icon Tom Ford in a *Vogue* piece. However, he reminds us, it can also help us appreciate the quiet glory of those things we tend to take for granted. 'Beauty gives me great joy, but it also gives me great sadness. When I see the rose, and I smell the rose, all I can think of is that the rose is going to wither and be dead. But that's one of the things that endows it with its beauty. If it were permanent, you wouldn't even notice it.'[17] These insights are beyond precious, whispering of the potency, poignancy and possibilities available to us when we can fully embrace life, and death, and assist our kids to do so.

Learning to Be More Comfortable Around Death

At some stage we all face our fears around death. You might like to begin your journey towards greater understanding by visiting a graveyard by yourself, or with your kids, and noting your experiences and observations there.

- In seeking to understand a little more of the mystery of death, where might you explore it in art and elsewhere?
- If a family member or someone you love is proving irksome (not abusive), how might you react were they to have a few months to live? How might this insight help you plot the way forward?
- Who do you need to forgive, and whose forgiveness do you need to seek?
- Why not practise gratitude at the end of each day – for all the people and experiences you've had?
- Are there little rituals you can add to your calendar – a shared coffee, a catch-up over a movie, a walk in the park – with the friends you most appreciate while they are still in your life?
- What can you do to help your kids appreciate these nuances?

25

Where to from Here?

Each of us needs to grow up, not just for our own sake but for the planet and all who inhabit her. We can no longer look to others to sort the many issues before us. It's time for us to dare to do those things that are difficult so we can be part of the change we ache for. That's the only way we can move on from all the issues that haunt or dismay us. This is not the time to retreat into our silos, however appealing this may be. 'The greatest danger to our future,' primatologist Jane Goodall warns, 'is apathy.'[1]

Part of evolving is in recognising those parts of us that are yet to grow up. 'We don't have psychological problems, we have problems of living,' suggests Austrian psychiatrist Thomas Szasz, 'and often what I'm doing as a psychotherapist is helping people have a life that will work.'[2]

> **Try not to become a man of success.**
> **Rather become a man of value.**
> Albert Einstein, theoretical physicist

Addicted to shopping, streaming, junk news and consuming whatever sensationalised fodder comes our way keeps us fearful, suggestible and forever lost in a state of incompleteness, of neediness. Now is an excellent time to check in on your aspirations, which may well reveal they were never your dreams in the first place. 'We need to manage the fear of missing out, by choosing to care about choice for things that really matter,' suggests Jim Bright, professor of career education and development at Australian Catholic University.[3]

'When a population becomes distracted by trivia,' social critic Neil Postman warned, 'when cultural life is redefined as a perpetual round of entertainments, when serious public conversation becomes a form of baby-talk, when, in short, a people become an audience, and their public business a vaudeville act, then a nation finds itself at risk; culture-death is a clear possibility.'[4]

Too many of us are stranded in our own version of Neverland. For all the high energy and giddy exuberance of a youthful landscape and pursuits, this can't ever be our peak life experience – to suggest otherwise sells you and our emerging generations short. It's time to reclaim our hijacked childhoods and those of our kids, to be better gatekeepers. It's time to call out entitlement wherever we see it so we can nip this destructive behaviour in the bud.

One of the many powerful messages in stories of enchantment is the importance of removing the stars from our eyes. Instead of hankering after the often plastic, highly packaged lifestyles offered us, let's forge our own way, lest we become what Indian philosopher and teacher Krishnamurti called 'second-hand human beings', living the lives others demand of us and never discovering what's 'original' and 'true' within us.

Let's embrace adult life in all its beauty and terror. Let's provide our kids with more opportunities to develop resilience and hone their innate skills, so they can step into adulthood far better prepared. First, we must let go of our vampire ways. Instead of seeking to suck all the energy out of every situation we're in, let's work on being *genuinely* alive to life and those around us. Let's infuse our days with more transparency so we're better able to appraise our weaknesses and work on them, rather than trying to paper over the cracks with our Insta images and tirelessly witty texts.

Rather than running from discomfort, let's learn how to embrace these moments with wisdom and strength, so we can continue to evolve. It's not the challenges of our post-pandemic world we need fear so much as our inability to face the future with courage, and to light the way for the generations that come after us. 'We are all facing adversity and change and we need to show significant resilience as a result,' insists Anna Meares, no stranger to suffering or loss, who, at thirty-two, became Australia's most decorated Olympic cyclist.[5]

Right now, we need a lot more from those in political life and in leadership roles. Community and connection, strong families and friendships, healthy workplaces, and the very foundations of democracy are built on engagement. We need our leaders to help grow our communities, workplaces and nation, to *lead* the way and to urge us to be strong by encouraging us to stand tall and give of our best, not just for ourselves but for each other. We need to build trust by refusing to entertain grandiosity in all its forms and by being clear about what constitutes a good win.

In return, our response to political agendas needs to be about more than chasing what personally works for us. We need intelligent yet accessible ways to embrace the complexities of our times. As adults, we must be prepared to help build a future we may not personally benefit from. It's essential that we take an ongoing interest in the moral dilemmas of our time and apply ourselves to helping come up with workable, well-thought-out solutions.

The aftermath of the pandemic and the host of other challenges we face may prove an immense gift, helping us and our kids to grow up, to live fuller lives that have room for others, to welcome and celebrate new approaches and diverse ideas. If we allow it, our life challenges can assist us to embrace attitudes and habits that can deliver genuine meaning and worth.

If we are to have any hope of stepping up and making our presence here on Earth count, we can't allow others to do all the hard lifting and decision-making for us.

This means daring to stare the facts, however unpleasant, in the face. This means becoming someone we and others can rely on, and even be inspired by. To achieve this, we need to hold a bigger vision for ourselves and the world, to let go of the blaming and complaining and turn our attention to finding inspired solutions to the issues we face, the kind of solutions that previous generations could scarcely dream of.

Appreciation

This has been a wonderful journey. I've learned a great deal. I'm so grateful to everyone who has lent their voices and expertise to these pages, enriching them in numerous ways.

Thanks to Martin Hughes and Keiran Rogers for the passion and commitment they bring to their authors. I'm appreciative, too, for the warmth and wisdom of my publisher, Kelly Doust. Thanks, too, to Trisha Garner for such a perfect book cover, to my editors Russell Thomson and Ruby Ashby-Orr for their deft work and attention to detail, and to managing editor Kevin O'Brien. Thanks to publicity manager Laura McNicol Smith and my tireless publicist Simone Redman-Jones for their great work, and to Susie Kennewell for attending so effortlessly to everything that needed to be done.

Thanks, too, to my precious writer friends Walter Mason and Rosamund Burton, who continue to walk with me through the ups and downs of each writing journey. Much gratitude also to all those who've worked tirelessly on my earlier books, helping me reach this point in time. Limitless thanks to my soul sisters for your ongoing love and belief, for never failing me.

None of this would be possible without darling Derek. We've journeyed far. Thank you for your constancy. You are the wind beneath my wings. Most of all, humblest thanks to the Great Spirit, who inspires me to continue to explore new horizons, and to find new ways to question and celebrate this mystery we call life.

Resources

Australia

Collective Shout: for parents and teachers concerned about the sexploitation of children and teens – www.collectiveshout.org

Kindness on Purpose: a school empathy-based program to help reduce bullying and increase emotional literacy and learning – www.kindnessonpurpose.com

The Panic Button Book for Kids: an interactive guide for parents to share with kids aged seven to eleven to find relief from anxiety (by Tammi Kirkness, Murdoch Books)

The Rite Journey: offers parenting plans and year-long courses for teens, helping them transition to self-aware, responsible, respectful, resilient adults – https://theritejourney.com

The Rites of Passage Institute: transformative rites of passage to strengthen a teen's sense of self and equip them with critical life skills, potential and vision – https://ritesofpassageinstitute.org

Top Blokes Foundation: helps boys and young men to increase their resilience, empathy, and respect for self and others – www.topblokes.org.au

New Zealand

Be Collective: an online hub for finding volunteer activities in your local area – www.becollective.com

Big Brothers Big Sisters: the world's largest group of volunteer mentors, working to empower a new generation – www.bigbrothersbigsisters.org.nz

Big Buddy: matches kind men with fatherless boys aged seven to fourteen, providing a strong male presence, guidance and the fun of shared activities – www.bigbuddy.org.nz

Grandparents Raising Grandchildren: supports grandparents and great-grandparents caring for grandchildren and great-grandchildren across European, Maori, Pacific and Asian communities – www.grg.org.nz

Kids Helpline: confidential counselling for parents needing help with tricky family issues – https://kidshelpline.com.au

References

Introduction

1 Simon Gottschalk, 'Essay: The Infantilisation of Western Culture', *Sight*, 17 August 2018, www.sightmagazine.cm.au

2 Steve Kux, '10 Harsh Truths about Being an Adult', *Lifehack*, www.lifehack.org

3 Joseph Epstein, 'The Perpetual Adolescent', *The Weekly Standard*, 15 March 2004, www.washingtonexaminer.com

4 Gaby Hinsliff, 'How Self-Love Got Out of Control', *The Guardian*, 7 October 2018, www.theguardian.com

5 Michael Ventura, 'The Age of Endarkenment', in Louise Carus Mahdi, Nancy Geyer Christopher and Michael Meade (eds), *Crossroads: The Quest for Contemporary Rites of Passage*, Open Court, Chicago, 1996, p. 52

Chapter 1: In Need of More Grit?

1 Liz Dangar, 'The Noughties: Conflicts and Contradictions', *B&T Weekly*, 15 June 2001, p. 12

2 Joseph Epstein, 'The Perpetual Adolescent', *The Weekly Standard*, 15 March 2004, www.washingtonexaminer.com

3 Ruth Ostrow, 'Forever Young: Immature Personality Disorder', *The Australian*, 19 May 2017, www.theaustralian.com.au

4 John Stonestreet, 'Adolescent Culture', *All About World View*, www.allaboutworldview.org

5 Andrew Calcutt, *Arrested Development: Pop Culture and the Erosion of Adulthood*, Bloomsbury, London, 2016, p. 7

6 Diana West, *The Death of the Grown-Up: How America's Arrested Development is Bringing Down Western Civilization*, St Martin's Press, New York, 2008, p. 33

7 Jacopo Bernardini, 'The Infantilization of the Postmodern Adult and the Figure of Kidult', *Postmodern Openings*, Volume 5, Issue 2, June 2014, pp. 39–55

Chapter 2: Forever Young

1 Robert J Samuelson, 'Adventures in Agelessness', *Newsweek*, 3 November 2003, www.newsweek.com

2 Andrew Calcutt, *Arrested Development: Pop Culture and the Erosion of Adulthood*, Bloomsbury, 1998, p. 6

3 Robin Marantz Henig, 'What Is It About 20-Somethings?', *The New York Times Magazine*, 18 August 2010, www.newyorktimes.com

4   Jacopo Bernardini, The Infantilization of the Postmodern Adult and the Figure of Kidult, Postmodern Openings, Volume 5, Issue 2, June 2014, 39–55.

5   Jacopo Bernardini, 'The Infantilization of the Postmodern Adult and the Figure of Kidult', *Postmodern Openings*, Volume 5, Issue 2, June 2014, pp. 39–55

6   Micki McGee, *Self-Help Inc.: The Makeover Culture in American Life*, Oxford University Press, Oxford, 2005

7   Andrew Calcutt, *Arrested Development: Pop Culture and the Erosion of Adulthood*, Bloomsbury, London, 2016, p. 7

8   Ross Posnock, *Philip Roth's Rude Truth: The Art of Immaturity*, University of Princeton Press, Princeton, 2006, p. 156

9   Global Cosmetic Surgery and Procedure Market Forecast 2020–2028, InkWood Research, inkwoodresearch.com

10   Benjamin Jang and Dhaval R Bhavsar, 'The Prevalence of Psychiatric Disorders Among Elective Plastic Surgery Patients', *ePlasty*, March 2019, 19:e6, PMC6432998

11   Melvin A Kimble (ed.), *Viktor Frankl's Contribution to Spirituality and Ageing*, Routledge, Abingdon, Oxfordshire, 2014, p. 61

12   Robert Firestone, 'Six Aspects of Being an Adult: Living Life as an Authentic Adult', *Psychology Today*, 24 June 2013

13   Coin Bertram, 'How Michael Jackson's Stardom Affected Him as an Adult', *Biography*, 26 February 2019, www.biography.com

Chapter 3: Peter Pan and His Lost Boys

1   University of Granada, 'Over-Protecting Parents Can Lead Children to Develop "Peter Pan Syndrome"', *Science Daily*, 3 May 2007, www.sciencedaily.com

2   Melissa Benn, 'Inner-City Scholar', *The Guardian*, 3 February 2001, www.theguardian.com

3   u/wanderer333, 'Wanting to Be "Rescued"', *Reddit*, 28 February 2018, www.reddit.com

4   Anonymous, responding to u/wanderer333, 'Wanting to Be "Rescued"', *Reddit*, 28 February 2018, www.reddit.com

5   Sabine Wolff, 'Culture of Entitlement a Road to Nowhere', *ABC News*, 1 Dec 2011, www.abc.net.au

6   thewayofxen, responding to u/wanderer333, 'Wanting to Be "Rescued"', *Reddit*, 1 March 2018, www.reddit.com

7   Benjamin Cain, 'American Infantilization and the Age of Reason', *Medium*, 26 November 2019, www.medium.com

8   John Kim, '8 Ways To Be An Adult', *Psychology Today*, 13 February 2017, www.psychologytoday.com

9   Carl Pickhardt, 'Social Cruelty: Why Early Adolescents Treat Each Other Mean', *Psychology Today*, 3 January 2010, www.psychologytoday.com

10   Michael Ventura, 'The Age of Endarkenment', in Louise Carus Mahdi, Nancy Geyer Christopher and Michael Meade, *Crossroads: The Quest for Contemporary Rites of Passage*, Open Court, Chicago, 1996, p. 52

11   Benjamin B Barber, *Con$umed: How the Markets Corrupt Children, Infantilize Adults, and Swallow Citizens Whole*, W.W. Norton & Co., New York, 2007

12   'New Study: 55% of YA Books Bought by Adults', *Publishers Weekly*, 13 September 2012,

www.publishersweekly.com

13   Ruth Graham, 'Against YA', *Slate*, 5 June 2014, https://slate.com

14   Bill Maher, 'Adulting', *Real Time with Bill Maher Blog*, 17 November 2018, www.real-time-with-bill-maher-blog.com

15   AO Scott, 'The Death of Adulthood in American Culture', *The New York Times Magazine*, 11 September 2014, www.nytimes.com

16   Gilbert Adair, 'The Mouse that Ate Western Civilisation', *The Independent*, 14 October 1998, www.independent.co.uk

Chapter 4: We Don't Know What We Don't Know

1   Micki McGee, *Self-Help Inc.: The Makeover Culture in American Life*, Oxford University Press, Oxford, 2005

2   Benjamin Cain, 'Childishness as the Root of Human Brutality', *Medium*, 14 March 2020, www.medium.com

3   AO Scott, 'The Death of Adulthood in American Culture', *The New York Times Magazine*, 11 September 2014, www.nytimes.com

4   Benjamin Cain, 'Childishness as the Root of Human Brutality', *Medium*, 14 March 2020, www.medium.com

5   Ruth Ostrow, 'Forever Young: Immature Personality Disorder', *The Australian*, 19 May 2017, www.theaustralian.com.au

6   David Brooks, 'The Death of Idealism', *The New York Times*, 30 September 2016, www.nytimes.com

7   Trevor Warden, 'Are You Reinforcing a Culture of Entitlement?', *Focus*, November 2015, https://focus.kornferry.com

8   Michael Hogan in conversation with Ed Cumming, 'Have Our Cultural Tastes Become Too Childish?', *The Guardian*, 24 May 2015, www.theguardian.com

9   Bret Stetka, 'Extended Adolescence: When 25 Is the New 18', *Scientific American*, 19 September 2017, www.scientificamerican.com

10   Audrey Hamilton talking with Suniya Luthar, 'The Mental Price of Affluence', *Speaking of Psychology*, Episode 18, American Psychological Association, www.apa.org

11   Kathleen Ferguson, 'Sydney's Shore School Threatens to Expel Students Over "Appalling" Muck-up Day Scavenger Hunt', *ABC News*, 23 September 2020, www.abc.net.au

12   Alexis Carey, 'Shore School Muck-up Day: Full List of School's Challenges Revealed', *News.com.au*, 24 September 2020, www.news.com.au

13   Fergus Hunter, '"This is Not Who We Are": Shore Blames Small Group of Boys for Muck-up Day Rampage Plans', *The Sydney Morning Herald*, 23 September 2020, www.smh.com.au

14   AW Geiger and Leslie Davis, 'A Growing Number of American Teenagers – Particularly Girls – Are Facing Depression', *Pew Research Center*, 12 July 2019, www.pewrcsearch.org

15   TechnDruid, 'Is Western Society Becoming More Coddled and Infantilized?', *MMO Champion*, 22 June 2019, www.mmo-champion.com

16   Eric Johnson, 'Full Q&A: NYU's Jonathan Haidt Explains the Problem with Gen Z', *Vox*, 11 January 2019, www.vox.com

17   TechnDruid, 'Is Western Society Becoming More Coddled and Infantilized?', *MMO Champion*, 22 June 2019, www.mmo-champion.com

18   Frank Furedi, 'Why Millennials Are So Fragile', 2 February 2017, www.frankfuredi.com

19   Richard Sennett, *The Fall of Public Man*, Cambridge University Press, Cambridge, 1977, p. 5

20   Michael Ventura, 'The Age of Endarkenment', in Louise Carus Mahdi, Nancy Geyer Christopher and Michael Meade (eds), *Crossroads: The Quest for Contemporary Rites of Passage*, Open Court, Chicago, 1996, p. 53

21   Liz Dangar, 'The Noughties: Conflicts and Contradictions', *B&T Weekly*, 15 June 2001, p. 12

22   Karen Eddington, *The Under Pressure Project*, www.kareneddington.com

23   Robert Firestone, 'Societal Defences Against Death Anxiety', *PsychAlive*, www.psychaliveorg

24   noctambulism responding to u/alaxsxaqseek 'Are Teenage Years The Best?' *Reddit* 14 May 2015, www.reddit.com

Chapter 5: Our Need to Be Noticed

1   Erica Goode, 'Deflating Self-Esteem's Role in Society's Ills', *The New York Times*, 1 October 2002, www.nytimes.com

2   Henri C Santos, Michael EW Varnum and Igor Grossmann, 'Global Increases in Individualism', *Psychological Science*, July 2017, Volume 28, Issue 9, pp. 1229–38, doi: 10.1177/0956797617700622

3   Leon F Seltzer, '9 Enlightening Quotes on Narcissists – and Why', *Psychology Today*, 15 April 2014, www.psychologytoday.com

4   Wayne Dyer, *Excuses Begone: How to Change Lifelong, Self-Defeating Thinking Habits*, Hay House, New York, 2009, p. 149

5   Malcolm Cowley, 'E.E. Cummings: Poet and Painter 1894–1962', *Notable American Unitarians*, web.archive.org/web/20060902151619/http://www.harvardsquarelibrary.org/unitarians/cummings.html

6   Katja Jezkova Isaksen and Stuart Roper, 'The Commodification of Self-esteem: Branding and British Teenagers', *Psychology and Marketing*, 2012, Volume 29, Issue 3, pp. 117–35, doi: 10.1002/mar.20509

7   u/anxioustogreatness, '4 Steps to Becoming an Authentic Person', *Reddit*, 26 March 2015, www.reddit.com

8   Linda Heaphy, 'Hungry Ghosts: Their History and Origin', *Kashgar*, www.kashgar.com.au

9   George T Conway III, 'Unfit for Office, Donald Trump's Narcissism Makes It Impossible for Him to Carry Out the Duties of the Presidency in the Way the Constitution Requires', *The Atlantic*, 3 October 2019, www.theatlantic.com

10   Edward A Dreyfus, 'The Need To Feel Special, Psychologically Speaking', 3 September 2010, www.edwarddreyfusbooks.com

11   Tyger AC, 'Homage to David Bohm – Metaphysics is an Expression of a World View', Dharma X, *Medium*, 25 April 2020, www.medium.com

12   Kim Pearce, 'The Last Word: Nothing's Possible', *Peppermint Magazine*, Autumn 2014, Issue 33

13   Dr Jennifer Crocker, 'Seeking Self Esteem Has Physical and Mental Costs', *Michigan News*, 7 September 2002, www.news.umich.edu

14   Bridget Webber, 'Stop Waiting for Someone to Make You Feel Special', *Medium*, 4 August

2018, www.medium.com

15 Joseph Heller, *Something Happened*, Alfred A. Knopf, New York, 1974, p. 72

16 Christopher Lasch, *The Culture of Narcissism: American Life in an Age of Diminishing Expectations*, W.W. Norton & Co., New York, 1991, p. 242

17 Erica Goode, 'Deflating Self-Esteem's Role in Society's Ills', *The New York Times*, 1 October 2002, www.nytimes.com

18 Dr Jennifer Crocker, 'Seeking Self Esteem Has Physical and Mental Costs', *Michigan News*, 7 September 2002, www.news.umich.edu

19 Erich Fromm, *The Heart of Man: Its Genius for Good and Evil*, Lantern Books, Brooklyn, 2011, p. 86

20 Emerson Csorba, 'The Problem with Millennials? They're Way Too Hard on Themselves', *Harvard Business Review*, 2 May 2016, www.hbr.org

21 Anthony Moore, 'How to Unlearn Your Constant Need to Be Liked and Chosen', *Medium*, 5 January 2018, www.medium.com

22 Ibid.

23 Michael Ventura, 'The Age of Endarkenment', in Louise Carus Mahdi, Nancy Geyer Christopher and Michael Meade (eds), *Crossroads: The Quest for Contemporary Rites of Passage*, Open Court, Chicago, 1996, p. 52

24 Martijn Schirp, 'Turning The Problem Around: Mental Health in a Sick Society', *High Existence*, www.highexistence.com

Chapter 6: What Happened to Childhood?

1 'Body Image (Children and Teens)', *Family Doctor*, www.familydoctor.org

2 'Social Anxiety in Children', *Raising Children*, www.raisingchildren.net.au

3 Maggie Hamilton, *What's Happening to Our Girls?*, Penguin Books, Melbourne, 2009, p. 21

4 Jessica Mills, 'My Mother Wears Combat Boots: A Parenting Guide for the Rest of Us', A.K. Press, Chiko, California, 2007, p. 283

5 Nancy Etcoff, *Survival of the Prettiest: The Science of Beauty*, Anchor Books, Random House, New York, 2000

6 Jiang Jiang, Yan Zhang, Yannan Ke, Skyler T Hawk and Hui Qiu, 'Can't Buy Me Friendship? Peer Rejection and Adolescent Materialism: Implicit Self-esteem as a Mediator', *Journal of Experimental Social Psychology*, May 2015, Volume 58, pp. 48–55, doi: 10.1016/j.jesp.2015.01.001

7 C.R. Consumer Reports, 'Selling America's Kids: Commercial Pressures on Kids of the 90's (Part 2)', *Advocacy*, 1 January 1998, www.advocacy.consumerreports.org

8 Helga Dittmar, Rod Bond, Megan Hurst and Tim Kasser, 'The Relationship between Materialism and Personal Well-being: A Meta-analysis', *Journal of Personality and Social Psychology*, 2014, Volume 107, Issue 5, pp. 879–924, doi: 10.1037/a0037409

9 Christopher Lasch, *The Culture of Narcissism: American Life in an Age of Diminishing Expectations*, W.W. Norton & Company, New York, 1991, p. 180

10 Joel Stein, 'Millennials: The Me, Me, Me Generation', *Time*, 21 May 2013, www.time.com

11 Choppstikk, responding to u/vicky436, 'When Did You Realize You're Not Special?', *Reddit*, 2019, www.reddit.com

12 Hermann Hesse, 'Of Destiny', in *If the War Goes On: Reflections on War and Politics*,

Allen & Unwin/Canongate, London, 2019

13   Amy Quick Parrish, 'Advice to High School Graduates: You Are Not Special', *The Atlantic*, 7 May 2014, www.theatlantic.com

14   Fionn Rogan, 'Why My Generation Must Fight to Secure Our Adulthood', *The Irish Times*, 16 August 2016, www.irishtimes.com

15   Thomas Merton, *Conjectures of a Guilty Bystander*, Crown Publishing Group, New York, 2009, p. 72

16   StripedElephant, responding to u/vicky436, 'When Did You Realize You're Not Special?', *Reddit*, 2019, www.reddit.com

17   Thich Nhat Hanh, *Being Peace*, Penguin, New York, 2011, p. 50

18   Hannah L Schacter and Gayla Margolin, 'When It Feels Good To Give: Depressive Symptoms, Daily Prosocial Behavior, and Adolescent Mood', *Emotion*, 2019, Volume 19, Issue 5, pp. 923–27, doi.org/10.1037/emo0000494

19   Lan Nguyen Chaplin, Deborah Roedder John, Aric Rindfleisch and Jeffrey J Froh, 'The Impact of Gratitude on Adolescent Materialism and Generosity', *The Journal of Positive Psychology*, 4 July 2019, Volume 14, Issue 4, pp. 502–11, doi.10.1080/17439760. 2018.1497688

20   Christopher Bergland, 'Is Encouraging Gratitude an Antidote for Materialism?', *Psychology Today*, 22 November 2018, www.psychologytoday.com

Chapter 7: Special Snowflakes

1   Jean M Twenge and Tim Kasser, 'Generational Changes in Materialism and Work Centrality, 1976–2007: Associations with Temporal Changes in Societal Insecurity and Materialistic Role Modeling', *Personality and Social Psychology Bulletin*, July 2013, Volume 39, Issue 7, pp. 883–97, https://doi.org/10.1177/0146167213484586

2   'Culture of Entitlement Not Limited to Youth', *Financial Post*, 3 November 2014, www. business.financialpost.com

3   Elizabeth Grice, 'We Have Educated Our Youth into Debt', *The Telegraph*, 26 August 2014, www.telegraph.co.uk

4   'Vulnerable Young Australians Drowning in Debt', *Centre for Volunteering*, 18 October 2017, www.volunteering.com.au

5   Derek Parker, 'Australia's Big Appetite for Consumer Debt', *In the Black*, 1 June 2018, www.intheblack.com

6   Ibid.

7   u/turtleshrugged, '25 and I Feel Like I Will NEVER Get Out of Debt', *Reddit*, 19 March 2019, www.reddit.com

8   u/isuperfuckedmyself, 'I'm 31, 45K in Debt with No Clue on How to Pay Them Off, and Have Nada in Savings. Super Freaking Out Now that I Want to Plan My Future, Any Help Would Be Greatly Appreciated!', *Reddit*, 25 December 2018, www.reddit.com

9   u/pineappletie312, '$7,000 in Credit Card Debt. Feeling Hopeless & Depressed', *Reddit*, 11 August 2020, www.reddit.com

10   Dr Rodolfo Leyva, 'Materialistic Media Makes Us Less Sympathetic to the Poor', *London School of Economics*, 1 August 2018, www.lse.ac.uk

11   Craig Lounsbrough, *The Vale of Soul-Making*, 15 November 2018, www. thevaleofsoulmaking.wordpress.com

12   Anne Manne, 'The Age of Entitlement: How Wealth Breeds Narcissism', *The Guardian*, 8
      July 2014, www.theguardian.com
13   Jana Kasperkevic, 'Restaurant Workers Stay Hungry as the Food Industry Feasts on
      Profit', *The Guardian*, 26 July 2014, www.theguardian.com
14   Jeannette Settembre, 'An Alarming Number of Children in America Can't Afford Food',
      Market Watch, 2 May 2019, www.marketwatch.com
15   Iain Wilkinson, 'Food Poverty: Agony of Hunger the Norm for Many Children in the
      UK', *The Conversation*, 30 April 2019, www.theconversation.com
16   Ibid.
17   Caroline Hancock, Silvana Bettiol and Lesley Smith, 'Socioeconomic Variation in
      Height: Analysis of National Child Measurement Programme Data for England', *Archive
      of Disease in Childhood*, 11 January 2016, Volume 101, Issue 5, 2016, pp. 413–14, doi:
      10.1136/archdischild-2015-309360
18   Leon F Seltzer, '9 Enlightening Quotes on Narcissists – and Why', *Psychology Today*, 15
      April 2014, www.psychologytoday.com
19   u/JohnJerryson, 'TIFU My Whole Life. My Regrets as a 46 Year Old, and Advice to
      Others at a Crossroad', *Reddit*, 2015, www.reddit.com
20   Agnes de Mille, *Martha: The Life and Work of Martha Graham*, Reed, New York, 1991,
      p. 264

Chapter 8: The Child/Adolescent Up Close

1   Russell W Belk, 'Possessions and the Extended Self', *Journal of Consumer Research*,
      Volume 15, Issue 2, September 1988, pp. 139–68, doi.org/10.1086/209154
2   Linda Blair, 'Millennials: Are They All About "Me"?', *Stuff*, 13 April 2018, www.stuff.co.nz
3   Committee on Communications, 'Children and Adolescents and Advertising', *Pediatrics*,
      December 2006, Volume 118, Number 6, pp. 2563–69, doi.org/10.1542/peds.2006-2698
4   Joeri Van Den Bergh and Mattias Behrer, *How Cool Brands Stay Hot: Branding to
      Generation Y*, Kogan Page, London, 2016, p. 48
5   Tim Kasser, 'Cultural Values and the Well-Being of Future Generations: A Cross-national
      Study', *Journal of Cross-Cultural Psychology*, February 2011, Volume 42, Issue 2, pp.
      206–16, doi.org/10.1177/0022022110396865
6   Tim Kasser, *The High Price of Materialism*, MIT Press, Cambridge, Massachusetts, 2002,
      p. 103
7   *2018 Grandparents Today National Survey: General Population Report*, AARP Research,
      www.aarpresearch.org doi.org/10.26419/res.00289.001
8   Jozef M Nuttin Jr., 'Affective Consequences of Mere Ownership: The Name Letter Effect
      in Twelve European Languages', *European Journal of Social Psychology*, 1987, Volume 17,
      Issue 4, pp. 381–402, doi.org/10.1002/ejsp.2420170402
9   John J Watson, 'The Relationship of Materialism to Spending Tendencies, Saving,
      and Debt', *Journal of Economic Psychology*, December 2003, Volume 24, pp. 723–39,
      doi.10.1016/j.joep.2003.06.001
10   Nicki A Dowling, Tim Corney and Lauren Hoiles, 'Financial Management Practices and
      Money Attitudes as Determinants of Financial Problems and Dissatisfaction in Young
      Male Australian Workers', *Journal of Financial Counseling and Planning*, January 2009,
      Volume 20, Issue 2, pp. 5–13

11   Lukas R Dean, Jason S Carroll and Chongming Yang, 'Materialism, Perceived Financial Problems, and Marital Satisfaction', *Family and Consumer Sciences Research Journal*, March 2007, Volume 35, Issue 3, pp. 260–81, doi.org/10.1177/1077727X06296625

12   Jean Illsley Clarke, Connie Dawson and David J Bredehoft, *How Much Is Too Much? Raising Likeable, Responsible, Respectful Children – From Toddlers to Teens in an Age of Overindulgence*, Da Capo Press, New York, 2014, p. 10

13   DJ Bredehoft, SA Mennicke, AM Potter and JI Clarke, 'Perceptions Attributed by Adults to Parental Overindulgence during Childhood', *Journal of Family and Consumer Sciences Education*, 1998, Volume 16, Issue 2, pp. 3–17

Chapter 9: Living in La La Land

1   Susan A Miller, Ellen Booth Church and Carla Poole, 'Ages and Stages: How Children Use Magical Thinking', *Scholastic*, www.scholastic.com

2   'CNN, Tweens Aim for Fame Above All Else', *The Chart*, 6 August 2011, www.thechart. blogs.cnn.com

3   Yalda T Uhls and Patricia Greenfield, 'The Rise of Fame: An Historical Content Study', *Journal of Psychology Research on Cyberspace*, 2011, Volume 5, Issue 1, Article 1, https:// cyberpsychology.eu/article/view/4243/3289

4   John Maltby, Liz Day, David Giles, Raphael Gillett, Marianne Quick, Honey Langcaster-James and P Alex Linley, 'Implicit Theories of a Desire for Fame', *British Journal of Psychology*, 2008, Volume 99, pp. 279–92, doi.org.10.1348/000712607X226935

5   Carl C. Gaither and Alma E. Cavazos-Gaither, *Gaither's Dictionary of Scientific Quotations*, Springer, New York, 2008, 204

6   John Maltby, James Houran and Lynn McCutcheon, 'A Clinical Interpretation of Attitudes and Behaviors Associated with Celebrity Worship', *The Journal of Nervous and Mental Disease*, January 2003, Volume 191, Issue 1, pp. 25–29, doi. org/10.1097/00005053–200301000– 00005

7   Philip Cushman, 'Why the Self Is Empty: Towards a Historically Situated Psychology', *American Psychologist*, May 1990, Volume 45, Issue 5, pp. 599–611, doi. org/10.1037/0003–066X.45.5.599

8   Robin Marantz Henig, 'What Is It About 20-Somethings?' *The New York Times*, 18 August 2010, www.nytimes.com

9   Ihatesaabs, responding to u/rawcookiedough, '[Serious] When Did You Realize You Weren't Special?', *Reddit*, 2016, www.reddit.com

10   '#rpTen Speaker Richard Sennett: Making Is Thinking and Vice Versa', *re:publica*, 20 January 2016, www.re-publica.com

11   u/throwaway19991968, 'I Always Want to Be the Best or Special and When I Don't I Shut Down', *Reddit*, March 2018, www.reddit.com

Chapter 10: Great Expectations

1   '#rpTen Speaker Richard Sennett: Making Is Thinking and Vice Versa', *re:publica*, 20 January 2016, www.re-publica.com

2   'Sociologist Zygmunt Bauman, Known for His Work on Modern Identity and the Holocaust, Dies at 91', *The Los Angeles Times*, 9 January 2017, www.latimes.com

3   Mokokoma Mokhonoana, *P for Pessimism: A Collection of Funny yet Profound*

References

Aphorisms: A Collection of Funny yet Profound Aphorisms, Sekoala Publishing, 2021, Mahwelereng, South Africa, 39

4   Carl E Pickhardt, 'Adolescence and Emotion', *Psychology Today*, 19 July 2010, www.psychologytoday.com

5   Khalil Gibran, *The Prophet and Other Tales*, Simon & Schuster, New York, 2019

6   Maria Semple, *Where'd You Go, Bernadette*, Hachette, New York, 2002

7   Mike Taylor, 'Hardship Early Release Super – Good Policy or Ticking Time Bomb?' *Super Review*, 26 June 2020, https://superreview.moneymanagement.com.au

8   Matt Wade, 'Super Bender: Retirement Nest-Egg Withdrawals Used to Boost Spending on Non-Essentials', *The Sydney Morning Herald*, 1 June 2020, www.smh.com.au

9   George Loewenstein and Jon Elster, *Choice Over Time*, Russell Sage Foundation, New York, 1992

10   Willa Cather, *Death Comes for the Archbishop*, Alfred A. Knopf, New York, 1927

11   Ihatesaabs responding to u/rawcookiedough, '[Serious] When Did You Realize You Weren't Special?' *Reddit*, 2016, www.reddit.com

12   Dahl, Roald, *My Year*, Jonathan Cape, London, 1993

13   Joseph Jaworski, *Synchronicity: The Inner Path to Leadership*, Berrett-Koehler Publications, San Francisco, 1996, pp. 100–01

14   Rick Nauert, 'Sense of Entitlement May Lead to Vicious Cycle of Distress', *Psych Central*, 8 August 2018, www.psychcentral.com

15   Frank Furedi, 'Why Millennials Are So Fragile', 2 February 2017, www.frankfuredi.com

16   Sally S Dickerson and Margaret E Kemeny, 'Acute Stressors and Cortisol Responses: A Theoretical Integration and Synthesis of Laboratory Research', *Psychological Bulletin*, 2004, Volume 130, Issue 3, pp. 355–91, https://doi.org/10.1037/0033–2909.130.3.355

17   Tony Schwartz, 'The Only Thing that Really Matters', *Harvard Business Review*, 1 June 2011, www.hbr.org

18   Agnès Falco, Cédric Albinet, Anne-Claire Rattat, Isabelle Paul and Eve Fabre, 'Being the Chosen One: Social Inclusion Modulates Decisions in the Ultimatum Game. An ERP Study', *Social Cognitive and Affective Neuroscience*, Volume 14, Issue 2, February 2019, pp. 141–49, https://doi.org/10.1093/scan/nsy118

19   u/throwaway19991968, 'I Always Want to Be the Best or Special and When I Don't I Shut Down', *Reddit*, March 2018, www.reddit.com

20   pastthecastlewalls, responding to u/vicky436, 'When Did You Realize You're Not Special?', *Reddit*, 2019, www.reddit.com

21   Dan Crawford, responding to 'Is It Selfish to Want to Feel Special?', *Quora*, 13 February 2018, www.quora.com

22   Adan Ghous, response to 'Do Most People Born with the Feeling that They Are the Chosen One to Success, Only to Lead a Mediocre Life Later?', *Quora*, 5 November 2017, www.quora.com

23   do_you_smoke_paul, responding to u/rawcookiedough, '[Serious] When Did You Realize You Weren't Special?', *Reddit*, 2016, www.reddit.com

24   vivvav, responding to u/rawcookiedough, '[Serious] When Did You Realize You Weren't Special?', *Reddit*, 2016, www.reddit.com

25   Lolnoon1459, responding to u/rawcookiedough, '[Serious] When Did You Realize You Weren't Special?', *Reddit*, 2016, www.reddit.com

Chapter 11: When Work Isn't Working

1   Jennie Roberson, 'How Do You Manage Overindulgence in the Workplace', *A.S.P.E.*, 24 September 2013, www.aspetraining.com

2   Amy Shannon, 'The Rise of the Entitlement Mentality', *Your Partner in HR*, 8 September 2017, www.yourpartnerinhr.com

3   George Agak, 'Why a Sense of Entitlement is Detrimental to Your Career', *Thrive Global*, 7 March 2018, www.thriveglobal.com

4   Amy Shannon, 'The Rise of the Entitlement Mentality', *Your Partner in HR*, 8 September 2017, www.yourpartnerinhr.com

5   Cindy Wahler, 'Why Entitlement Is the Number One Leadership Derailer', *Forbes*, 7 January 2019, www.forbes.com

6   Christopher Lasch, *The Culture of Narcissism: American Life in an Age of Diminishing Expectations*, W.W. Norton & Co., New York, 1991, p. 239

7   RA Wicklund and PM Gollwitzer, *Symbolic Self Completion*, Lawrence Erlbaum & Associates, Hillsdale, New Jersey, 1982

8   Otmar L Braun and Robert A Wicklund, 'Psychological Antecedents of Conspicuous Consumption', *Journal of Economic Psychology*, 1989, Volume 10, Issue 2, pp. 161–87, doi. org/10.1016/0167–4870(89)90018–4

9   'Absenteeism in the Workplace: Addressing the Culture of Entitlement', *HR Assured*, 24 June 2019, www.hrassured.com.au

10   Bianca Hall, 'The Great Aussie Sickie Falls Out of Favour: But Entitlement Culture Remains', *The Sydney Morning Herald*, 5 November 2015, www.smh.com.au

11   Ibid.

12   Emma Seppälä and Kim Cameron, 'Proof that Positive Work Cultures Are More Productive', *Harvard Business Review*, 1 December 2015, www.hbr.org

13   'Attention, Employers: Millennials Have Made Their Demands', *The Atlantic*, n.d., www. theatlantic.com

14   Vivian Giang, '71% of Millennials Want Their Co-Workers to Be a "Second Family"', *Business Insider Australia*, 16 June 2013, www.businessinsider.com.au

15   'The Millennial Moment: Why Everyone Is Paying Attention', *Elevate*, www. elevatenetwork.com

16   Richard Sennett, *The Corrosion of Character: The Personal Consequences of Work in the New Capitalism*, W.W. Norton & Co., New York, 1997, p. 87

17   Michael Gaul, 'The Millennial Churn: What It Means for Employers', *Proforma*, 26 April 2018, www.proformascreening.com

18   Richard Sennett, *The Corrosion of Character: The Personal Consequences of Work in the New Capitalism*, W.W. Norton & Co., New York, 1997, p. 87

19   Mark McClain, 'How Corporate Culture Can Make (or Break) Your Organization', *Forbes*, 6 November 2017, www.forbes.com

20   Kate Felhaber, 'Why a Bank Robber Thought Covering Himself in Lemon Juice Would Help Him Get Away', *Quartz*, 19 May 2017, www.qz.com

21   'IMF Survey: Sharp Rise in Unemployment from Global Recession', *IMF News*, 20 September 2010, www.imf.org

22   Jennie Roberson, 'How Do You Manage Overindulgence in the Workplace', *A.S.P.E.*, 24 September 2013, www.aspetraining.com

23   Amy Shannon, 'The Rise of the Entitlement Mentality', *Your Partner in HR*, 8 September 2017, www.yourpartnerinhr.com

24   David De Cremer, Daan van Knippenberg, Marius van Dijke and Arjan ER Bos, 'Self-Sacrificial Leadership and Follower Self-Esteem: When Collective Identification Matters', *Group Dynamics: Theory, Research, and Practice*, September 2006, Volume 10, Issue 3, pp. 233–45, doi:10.1037/1089–2699.10.3.233

Chapter 12: Grandiose Plans

1   55redditor55, responding to u/Gentleman-Tech, 'My Kardashian Problem', *Reddit*, November 2019, www.reddit.com

2   Rachel Adler, 'The Kardashian Effect: Makeup Guru Sir John on How the Reality Stars Influence Beauty Trends', *SC*, 2015, www.stylecaster.com

3   Jennifer Gannon, 'This Is the Kardashians' World – We're Just Following It', *The Irish Times*, 16 December 2017, www.irishtimes.com

4   u/redmambo_no6, 'People Who Keep Up with the Kardashians ... WHY?', *Reddit*, April 2018, www.reddit.com

5   Miriam Cosic, 'High Anxiety', *Good Weekend*, 29 March, 2019, www/smh.com.au

6   Jennifer Nini, '33 Thought-Provoking Quotes about Ethical, Sustainable and Fast Fashion', *Eco Warrior Princess*, 17 October 2018, www.ecowarriorprincess.net

7   Anna Hecht, '60% of Americans Underestimate the Cost of a Wedding', *Make It*, 9 September 2019, www.cnbc.com

8   'How Much Couples Spend on Weddings in 2018', *Wedded Wonderland*, www.weddedwonderland.com

9   Liz Susong, 'Bridecentrism, Bridezillas, and "The Best Day of Your Life"', *Catalyst*, www.catalystwedco.com

10 Melissa Heagney, 'Half of All Married Couples Regret Spending as Much as They Did on Their Wedding, Bank Survey Finds', *Domain*, 21 June 2019, www.domain.com.au

11 u/PeekAt Chu, 'Do You Regret Having an Expensive Wedding?', *Reddit*, 20 September 2016, www.reddit.com

12 Ibid.

13 Kelsey Borrensen, '9 Things Couples Regret Spending So Much Money on for Their Weddings', *Huffpost*, 8 January 2020, www.huffingtonpost.com.au

14 larrysharon, responding to u/Takemywordforit1997, 'What Are Grandiose Fantasies Like?', *Reddit*, 9 December 2018 www.reddit.com

15 'US Man Aims Bow and Arrow at Utah Protesters Demonstrating Against George Floyd's Custody Death', *ABC News*, 31 May 2020, www.abc.net.au

16 Amelia Lester, 'Exceptional No Longer', *Good Weekend*, 24 July 2020, www.smh.com.au

17 Jason Hickel, 'How Britain Stole $45 Trillion from India', *Al Jazeera*, 19 December 2018, www.aljezeera.com

18 Will Dahlgreen, 'The British Empire Is "Something to Be Proud of"', *YouGov*, 26 July 2014, yougov.co.uk

19 Johann Hari, 'Not His Finest Hour: The Dark Side of Winston Churchill', *The Independent*, 27 October 2010, www.independent.co.uk

20 Guy Arnold, *Africa: A Modern History*, Atlantic, London, 2017, chapter 1

21 Ngũgĩ wa Thiong'o, *Wizard of the Crow*, Harvill Secker, London, 2006

22 Peter Wolson, 'The Politics of Narcissism', *Global Policy Forum*, 15 February 2004, www.globalpolicy.org

23 Frank Summers, 'The National Propensity for Violence: A Psychoanalytic Approach', in Adrienne Harris and Steven Botticelli (eds), *First Do No Harm: The Paradoxical Encounters of Psychoanalysis, Warmaking, and Resistance*, Routledge, New York, 2010, p. 170

24 Wade Davis, *The Wayfinders: Why Ancient Wisdom Matters in the Modern World*, Anansi, Toronto, 2009, 195

25 Long Now Foundation, 'The Wayfinders: Why Ancient Wisdom Matters in the Modern World | Wade Davis', *YouTube*, 18 June 2020

26 Ibid.

27 Ibid.

28 Ibid.

Chapter 13: Win at All Costs

1 PBS News Hour, 'John McCain Addresses the Senate after Returning from Cancer Diagnosis', *YouTube*, 25 July 2017, https://youtu.be/Cw4RqZAKa5A

2 Albert Einstein, David E. Rowe and Robert Schulmann. Einstein on Politics: His Private Thoughts and Public Stands, Princeton University, New Jersey, 2013, 227

3 Michael Bradley, 'We Can't Handle the Idea That Sport Is Just Sport', *The Drum*, 21 January 2016, www.abc.net.au

4 Travis Tygart, 'Is the Win-at-All-Costs Culture Ruining Sports?', *Huffpost*, 7 April 2017, www.huffpost.com

5 Albert F Spencer, 'Ethics, Faith and Sport', *Journal of Interdisciplinary Studies*, September 2000, Volume 12, Issue 1/2, pp. 143–58

6 Daniel J Madigan, Joachim Stoeber and Louis Passfield, 'Perfectionism and Attitudes Towards Doping in Junior Athletes', *Journal of Sports Sciences*, 2015, Volume 34, Issue 8, p. 700, doi: 10.1080/02640414.2015.1068441

7 Nick J Watson and John White, '"Winning at All Costs" in Modern Sport: Reflections on Pride and Humility in the Writings of C.S. Lewis', in Jim Parry, Simon Robinson, Nick Watson and Mark Nesti (eds), *Sport and Spirituality: An Introduction*, Routledge, Abingdon, 2007, pp. 61–79

8 Michael Grimshaw, 'I Can't Believe My Eyes: The Religious Aesthetics of Sport as Postmodern Salvific Moments', *Journal of Implicit Religion and Spirituality*, November 2000, Volume 3, Issue 2, pp. 87–99, dx.doi.org/10.1558/imre.v3i2.87

9 Gabi Eissa, Rebecca Wyland, Scott W Lester and Ritu Gupta, 'Winning at All Costs: An Exploration of Bottom-Line Mentality, Machiavellianism, and Organisational Citizenship Behaviour', *Human Resource Management Journal*, July 2019, Volume 29, Issue 3, doi:10.1111/1748–8583.12241

10 Lesli Doares, 'How Competition Will End Your Marriage: A Fearless Marriage Quote', *Foundations Coaching*, 14 November 2011, www.foundationscoachingnc.com

Chapter 14: Driven to Short Cuts

1 Tracey Bretag and Rowena Harper, 'Contract Cheating in Australian Universities: Implications for Assessment, Integrity and Review of Quality and Standards', Strategic

Priority Project, 9SP16–5283, www.hes.edu.au

2   Philip M Newton, 'How Common Is Contract Cheating in Higher Education and Is It Increasing? A Systematic Review', *Frontiers in Higher Education*, 30 August 2018, https://doi.org/10.3389/feduc.2018.00067

3   Ibid.

4   Rebecca Awdry and Philip M Newton, 'Staff Views on Commercial Contract Cheating in Higher Education: A Survey Study in Australia and the UK', *Higher Education*, 14 February 2019, Volume 78, pp. 593–610, https://doi.org/10.1007/s10734-019-00360-0

5   Sanjay Das, '5 Things My Failures in Life Have Taught Me', *S.D. Global*, 2 February 2019, www.sdglobaltech.com

6   '10 White Collar Crimes that Made Headlines', *Criminal Justice USA*, 5 June 2011, www.criminaljusticeusa.com

7   Joseph Epstein, 'The Perpetual Adolescent', *The Weekly Standard*, 15 March 2004, www.washingtonexaminer.com

8   Hazem Zohny, Thomas Douglas and Julian Savulescu, 'Biomarkers for the Rich and Dangerous: Why We Ought to Extend Bioprediction and Bioprevention to White Collar Crime', *Criminal Law and Philosophy*, September 2019, Volume 13, Issue 3, pp. 479–97, doi: 10.1007/s11572-018-9477-6

9   Alan Taylor, 'Bhopal: The World's Worst Industrial Disaster, 30 Years Later', *The Atlantic*, 2 December 2014, www.theatlantic.com

10 James Frost, 'Westpac Admits 23m Anti-Money Laundering Breaches', *The Australian Financial Review*, 15 May 2020, www.afr.com

11 'JPMorgan Chase Faces a Fine of $920m for Market Manipulation', *The Economist*, 3 October 2020, www.economist.com

12 Petter Gottschalk and Lars Gunnesdal, *White-Collar Crime in the Shadow Economy: Lack of Detection, Investigation and Conviction Compared to Social Security Fraud*, Palgrave Macmillan, 2018, Cham, p. 121, http://dx.doi.org/10.1007/978-3-319-75292-1

13 Jim Gee, *Annual Fraud Indicator 2017: UK Foots the 190 Billion Annual Fraud Bill*, Crowe UK, 13 November 2017, www.crowe.com/uk

14 'Trillion Dollar Scandal', *One*, 3 September 2014, www.one.org

15 Adi, 'The Costs of a "Win at All Costs" Culture', *The Horizons Tracker*, 14 November 2019, www.adigaskell.org

16 u/throwaway_76nnn, 'Overly Competitive Co-workers', *Reddit*, 2015, www.reddit.com

17 Cheeze_It, responding to u/throwaway_76nnn 'Overly Competitive Co-workers', *Reddit*, 2015, www.reddit.com

18 Simon Longstaff, 'The Financials Stack Up for Investing in Ethical Infrastructure', *The Australian Financial Review*, 26 October 2020, www.afr.com

19 Mark Wager, 'Winning at All Costs – Is It Worth It?', *Australasian Leadership Institute*, 17 February 2014, www.australasianleadershipinstitute.com

20 Lance Carter, 'Amy Poehler's Harvard College Graduation Speech: "Find a Group or People Who Challenge and inspire You"', *Daily Actor*, 27 May 2011, www.dailyactor.com

21 Jane McCarroll, 'What Winning Means to Me: It Doesn't Just Mean Coming First', *New Zealand Management*, September 2017, www.management.co.nz

22 Karen Horsch, 'Kids Who Just Gotta Win', *Parents*, www.parents.com

23 Shelby Stewart, 'Teaching Control to Your Overly Competitive Child', *Metro Parent*,

1 January 2020, www.metroparent.com

24 cellists_wet_dream, responding to u/jiffypizza, 'Have You Ever Felt Competitive with Your Friends, or Had to Deal with Friends Who Felt Competitive with You?', *Reddit*, 15 July 2015, www.reddit.com

25 Hand In Hand Parenting, 'How to Help Super-Competitive Kids Relax Without the Struggle', *Motherly*, wwww.mother.ly

26 Shelby Stewart, 'Teaching Control to Your Overly Competitive Child', *Metro Parent*, 1 January 2020, www.metroparent.com

27 Janet Lansbury, 'How to Handle Boastful, Competitive Behavior', www.janetlansbury. com

28 Lorne Ubis, 'Change Agents in the Spirit of Mandela', www.highlights.lornerubis.com

29 Joseph Jaworski, *Synchronicity: The Inner Path to Leadership*, Berrett-Koehler Publications, San Francisco, 1996, p. 97

Chapter 15: Our Blame Culture

1 Andrea Blundell, 'Why We Put the Blame on Others – and the Real Cost We Pay', *Harley Therapy*, 10 September 2015, www.harleytherapy.co.uk

2 Kayleigh Roberts, 'The Psychology of Victim-Blaming', *The Atlantic*, 5 October 2016, www.theatlantic.com

3 Ibid.

4 Gustavo Razzetti, 'How to Stop Playing the Blame Game', *The Liberationist*, www. liberationist.org

5 Ibid.

6 University of Southern California, 'Shifting Blame Is Socially Contagious', *Science Daily*, 22 November 2009, www.sciencedaily.com

7 amanfromthere, commenting on 'A Culture of Blame', *Reddit*, 7 September 2018, www. reddit.com

8 Wake Forest University, 'What You Say about Others Says a Lot about You, Research Shows', *Science Daily*, August 3, 2010, www.sciencedaily.com

9 Carl Pickhardt, 'Social Cruelty – Why Early Adolescents Treat Each Other Mean', *Psychology Today*, 3 January 2010, www.psychologytoday.com

10 Azrin Mohd Noor, 'MySay: The Threat of Armchair Critics', *The Edge*, 1 November 2019, www.theedgemarkets.com

11 Rhonda Scharf, 'Are You an Armchair Critic?', *HuffPost*, 26 August 2018, www. huffingtonpost.ca

12 Douglas Coupland, *All Families Are Psychotic*, Bloomsbury, New York, 2008, p. 120

13 James Lehman, 'Child Outbursts: Why Kids Blame, Make Excuses and Fight When You Challenge Their Behaviour', *Empowering Parents*, www.empoweringparents.com

14 Andrea Blundell, 'Why We Put Blame on Others – and the Real Cost We Pay', *Harley Therapy*, 10 September 2015, www.harlettherapy.co.uk

15 Louise Taylor, 'Dancing on Ice to Blame for McClaren Woe, says Ferguson', *The Guardian*, 31 March 2007, www.theguardian.com

16 H Stephen Glenn, Jane Nelsen and Lynn Lott, *Positive Discipline in the Classroom: Developing Mutual Respect, Co-operation and Responsibility in Your Classroom*, Penguin Random House, Canada, 1993

17   Darlene Lancer, *Freedom from Guilt and Blame: Finding Self-Forgiveness*, Smashwords Inc, 2015

18   u/kwaliflower 'How to Get Rid of a Blame Culture in the Workplace, *Reddit*, 9 December 2019, www.reddit.com

19   Darlene Lancer, Freedom from Guilt and Blame: Finding Self-Forgiveness, Smashwords Inc, 2015

20   Todd Henry, 'Toxic: Dealing with a Culture of Blame', *Accidental Creative*, www.accidentalcreative.com

21   Nathanael J Fast, 'How to Stop the Blame Game', *Harvard Business Review*, 13 May 2010, www.hbr.org

22   Eilene Zimmerman, 'The Problem with Pointing Fingers', *The New York Times*, 12 March 2011, www.nytimes.com

23   noshorts_, commenting on 'A Culture of Blame', *Reddit*, 7 September 2018, www.reddit.com

24   Nathanael J Fast, 'How to Stop the Blame Game', *Harvard Business Review*, 13 May 2010, www.hbr.org

25   'Eliminating a Culture of Blame', *Best Practice Consulting*, www.bestpracticeconsulting.com.au

26   Todd Henry, 'Toxic: Dealing with a Culture of Blame', *Accidental Creative*, www.accidentalcreative.com

27   Mike Staver, 'The Strength of No Blame Game Leadership', *In Business*, January 2013, www.inbusinessphx.com

28   blaktronium commenting on 'A Culture of Blame', *Reddit*, 7 September 2018, www.reddit.com

29   Jocko Willink and Leif Babin, *Extreme Ownership: How Navy Seals Lead and Win*, St Martin's Press, New York, 2015, p. 77

30   Gabriel Andrade, 'Rene Girard: The Scapegoat Mechanism', *Internet Encyclopaedia of Philosophy*, www.iep.utm.edu

31   Peter Kinderman, Matthias Schwannauer, Eleanor Pontin and Sara Tai, 'Psychological Processes Mediate the Impact of Familial Risk, Social Circumstances and Life Events on Mental Health', *PLOS ONE*, 16 October 2013, Volume 8, Issue 10, e76564, doi.org/10.1371/journal.pone.0076564

32   Jim Taylor, 'Personal Growth: Blame Your Parents for Your Problems', *Psychology Today*, 2 April 2012, www.psychologytoday.com

33   Ann Friedman, 'The Disapproval Matrix', www.annfriedman.com

34   Alexander McCall Smith, *The World According to Bertie*, Little Brown, London, 2007

35   BreakFixBill commenting on 'A Culture of Blame', Reddit, 7 September 2018, www.reddit.com

36   BreakFixBill commenting on 'A Culture of Blame', Reddit, 7 September 2018, www.reddit.com

37   Justine Larson, 'Blaming Parents: What I've Learned and Unlearned as a Child Psychiatrist', *Scientific American*, 15 April 2011, www.blog.scientificamerican.com

Chapter 16: Where Are the Grown-ups?

1   John Stonestreet, 'Adolescent Culture', *All About World View*, www.allaboutworldview.org

2   Robert Evans and Michael G Thompson, 'The Rude, Demanding Parents Who Bully Schools', *Dallas News*, 17 June 2016, www.dallasnews.com

3   Eddie Brummelman et al., 'Origins of Narcissism in Children', *Proceedings of the National Academy of Sciences of the United States of America*, 24 March 2015, Volume 112, Issue 12, pp. 3659–62, https://doi.org/10.1073/pnas.1420870112

4   Robert Evans and Michael G Thompson, 'The Rude, Demanding Parents Who Bully Schools', *Dallas News*, 17 June 2016, www.dallasnews.com

5   naranjitayyo, responding to byu/punkass_book_jockey8, 'Entitled Parents Behavior at a Public School Performance', *Reddit*, February 2019, www.reddit.com

6   byu/punkass_book_jockey8, 'Entitled Parents Behavior at a Public School Performance', *Reddit*, February 2019, www.reddit.com

7   rbancowgirl42, responding to byu/punkass_book_jockey8, 'Entitled Parents Behavior at a Public School Performance', *Reddit*, February 2019, www.reddit.com

8   Beethovensbuddy, responding to byu/punkass_book_jockey8, 'Entitled Parents Behavior at a Public School Performance', *Reddit*, February 2019, www.reddit.com

9   'Parenting in America', *Pew Research Center*, 17 December 2015, www.pewsocialtrends.org

10   Frank Furedi, 'Why Millennials Are So Fragile', 2 February 2017, www.frankfuredi.com

11   Ramani Durvasula, 'The Delusion of Meritocracy and the Culture of Enlightenment', *Psychology Today*, 21 March 2019, www.psychologytoday.com

12   Frank Furedi, 'Why Millennials Are So Fragile', 2 February 2017, www.frankfuredi.com

13   Phil Gardner, 'Parental Involvement in the College Recruiting Process: To What Extent?', Collegiate Employment Research Institute, Michigan State University, Research Brief 2 2007, https://files.eric.ed.gov/fulltext/ED509853.pdf

14   'Mom to Employer: "Do You Mind if I Sit in on My Son's Interview?', *Robert Half*, 16 August 2016, www.rh-us.mediaroom.com

15   Amy Morin, 'Parents, Please Don't Attend Your Adult Child's Interview', *Forbes*, 29 August 2017, www.forbes.com

16   'The Millennial Moment: Why Everyone Is Paying Attention', *Elevate*, www.elevatenetwork.com

17   Todd Henneman, 'Talkin' about Their Generations: The Workforce of the '50s and Today', *Workforce*, 15 March 2012, www.workforce.com

18   Sarah Harris, 'Bosses Say Graduates Can't Cope with Office Life', *The Daily Mail*, 10 July 2017, www.dailymail.co.uk

19   Simon Sinek, 'Millennials in the Workplace', *YouTube*, 28 December 2016, https://youtu.be/5MC2X-LRbkE

20   Tanith Carey, 'What's the Problem with Millennials in the Workplace?', *The Telegraph*, 10 July 2017, www.telegraph.co.uk

21   Erica Pearson, 'Here's How to Tell Whether You're Overindulging Your Kids', *Moneyish*, 16 April 2018, www.marketwatch.com

22   Ann S Masten, 'Maximizing Children's Resilience', *American Psychological Association*, September 2018, www.apa.org

23   Amelia Santaniello, 'The Praise Puzzle: How to Motivate Kids to be Successful', *CBS Minnesota*, 15 November 2012, www.minnesota.cbslocal.com

24   HS Koplewicz, A Gurian and K Williams, 'The Era of Affluence and Its Discontents',

Journal of the American Academy of Child and Adolescent Psychiatry, 2009, Volume 48, Issue 11, pp. 1053–55, doi: 10.1097/ CHI.0b013e3181b8be5c

25   TM Yates, AJ Tracy and SS Luthar, 'Nonsuicidal Self-Injury among "Privileged" Youth: Longitudinal and Cross-sectional Approaches to Development Processes', *Journal of Consulting and Clinical Psychology*, 2008, Volume 76, Issue 1, pp. 52–62, doi: 10.1037/0022–006X.76.1.52

26   Tim Kasser, *The High Price of Materialism*, MIT Press, Cambridge, Massachusetts, 2002

27   Ramani Durvasula, 'The Delusion of Meritocracy and the Culture of Enlightenment', *Psychology Today*, 21 March 2019, www.psychologytoday.com

28   Christopher Munsey, 'The Kids Aren't All Right', *American Psychological Association*, January 2010, www.apa.org

29   Dangers of Over-Scheduling Your Child', *Health eNews*, www.ahchealthenews.com

30   Christopher Munsey, 'The Kids Aren't All Right', *American Psychological Association*, January 2010, www.apa.org

31   ajchm, responding to Emine Saner, 'How Pushy Should Parents Be?', *The Guardian*, 6 August 2016, www.the guardian.com

32   Audrey Hamilton in conversation with Professor Suniya Luthar, 'The Mental Price of Affluence', *Speaking of Psychology*, Episode 18, www.apa.org

33   Dave Hannigan, 'Pushy Parents Still Ruining Sport for Kids in Pursuit of Glory', *The Irish Times*, 11 September 2019, wwww.irishtimes.com

34   Martin F, responding to Dave Hannigan, 'Pushy Parents Still Ruining Sport for Kids in Pursuit of Glory', *The Irish Times*, 11 September 2019, wwww.irishtimes.com

35   Next Exit, responding to Emine Saner, 'How Pushy Should Parents Be?', *The Guardian*, 6 August 2016, www.the guardian.com

Chapter 17: Toxic Happiness

1   Bryant McGill, The Voice of Reason: Speaking to the Great and Good Spirit of Revolution of Mind, Lyon Publishing, Mapleton, Iowa, 2012

2   Kilroy J Oldster, *Dead Toad Scrolls*, Booklocker, 2015

3   Richard Eckersley, 'Is Modern Western Culture a Health Hazard?', *International Journal of Epidemiology*, April 2006, Volume 35, Issue 2, pp. 252–58

4   Stewart Dunn, 'The Terror of Toxic Positivity', *Medium*, 14 February 2019, www.medium.com

5   Richard Eckersley, 'Is Modern Western Culture a Health Hazard?', *International Journal of Epidemiology*, April 2006, Volume 35, Issue 2, pp. 252–258

6   Kate Willis, Review of Karen A Cerulo, *Never Saw It Coming*, University of Chicago Press, Chicago, 2006, www.goodreads.com

7   Carrie Arnold, '8 Women on How They REALLY Felt When They Took These Smiling Instagram Pics', *Women's Health*, 19 April 2017, www.womenshealthmag.com

8   Stewart Dunn, 'The Terror of Toxic Positivity', *Medium*, 14 February 2019, www.medium.com

9   Rachel Hosie, 'Why Trying to Be Happy All the Time Could Be Dangerous', *The Independent*, 9 March 2017, www.theindependent.co.uk

10   Celine Sugay, 'The Dark Side of Happiness: Can We Have Too Much of a Good Thing?', *Positive Psychology*, 10 July 2019, www.positivepsychology.com

11 Thich Nhat Hanh, *The Art of Power*, HarperOne, San Francisco, 2009

12 Greg Lukianoff and Jonathan Haidt, 'The Coddling of the American Mind', *The Atlantic*, September 2015, atlantic.com

13 Ibid.

14 William A Davis Boston, 'Motivation for Sale, People Are Looking for Inspiration Over the Counter', *The Buffalo News*, 10 August 1994, www.buffalonews.com

15 Ibid.

16 Barbara Ehrenreich, *Bright-Sided: How Positive Thinking Is Undermining America*, Picador, New York, 2010, p. 116

17 human_beans responding to u/alreadytakenusername 'TIL that the book 'Who Moved My Cheese' became a '90s Bestseller', *Reddit*, 2013, www.reddit.com

18 David Edmonds, 'William Davies on the Happiness Industry', *Social Science Space*, 28 September 2015, www.socialsciencespace

19 Barbara Ehrenreich, *Bright-Sided: How Positive Thinking Is Undermining America*, Picador, New York, 2010, p. 8

20 David Edmonds, 'William Davies on the Happiness Industry', *Social Science Space*, 28 September 2015, www.socialsciencespace

21 'The Importance of a "Feedback Culture", and How You Can Build It in the Workplace', *TruQu*, www.truqu.com

22 Joseph Folkman, 'What Is Honest Feedback?', *Forbes*, 29 November 2019, www.forbes. com

23 Matthieu Ricard, 'This Is Your Life – Show Up for it Mindfully', in Sarah van Gelder and the staff of YES! Magazine (eds), *Sustainable Happiness: Live Simply, Live Well, Make a Difference*, Penguin Random House, New York, 2015, pp. 55–60

24 Barbara Ehrenreich, *Bright-Sided: How Positive Thinking Is Undermining America*, Picador, New York, 2010, p. 201

25 Jamie Ducharme, 'Trying to Be Happy Is Making You Miserable. Here's Why', *Time*, 10 August 2018, www.time.com

26 Fiona Thomas, 'Is Toxic Positivity Ruining Your Mental Health?', *Metro*, 20 March 2019, www.metro.co.uk

27 Noam Shpancer, 'Emotional Acceptance: Why Feeling Bad is Good', *Psychology Today*, 8 September 2010, www.psychologytoday.com

28 Steve Handel, 'Toxic Happiness: The Downsides of Too Much Joy', *The Emotion Machine*, 21 May 2011, www.theemotionmachine.com

29 Paul Dolan, 'The Money, Job, Marriage Myth: Are You Happy Yet?', *The Guardian*, 6 January 2019, www.theguardian.com

30 'Happiness Has a Dark Side', *Association for Psychological Science*, 16 May 2011, www. psychologicalscience.org   Paul Dolan, 'The Money, Job, Marriage Myth: Are You Happy Yet?' *The Guardian*, 6 January 2019, www.theguardian.com

31 Paul Dolan, 'The Money, Job, Marriage Myth: Are You Happy Yet?', *The Guardian*, 6 January 2019, www.theguardian.com

32 Claudia Dreyfus, 'The Smiling Professor', *The New York Times*, 22 April 2008, www. nytimes.com

33 Justice Bartlett, '"Positive Vibes Only" Is Toxic: The Danger of New Age Spiritualism', *Elephant Journal*, 21 January 2020, www.elephantjournal.com

34 Ashley Dawson-Damer, *A Particular Woman*, Ventura Press, Sydney, 2020, pp. 251–52
35 J Haidt, 'Elevation and the Positive Psychology of Morality', in CLM Keyes and J Haidt, (eds), *Flourishing: Positive Psychology and the Life Well-Lived*, American Psychological Association, Washington DC, 2003, pp. 275–89
36 Tobias Jones, 'Humanity Can Astonish You', *Red Magazine*, May 2016, p. 72
37 Olivia Remes, 'Smiling Depression: It's Possible to Be Depressed While Appearing Happy – Here's Why That's Particularly Dangerous', *The Conversation*, 19 February 2019, www.theconversation.com
38 'Take What You Need, Leave What You Can', *UTS*, 3 April 2020, www.uts.edu.au
39 Panel moderated by Verity Firth, 'Life After Lockdown: Kindness in Lockdown', City of Sydney, 17 June 2020, www.whatson.cityofsydney.com.au

Chapter 18: Believe It and It's Yours

1   Team the Wisdom Post and Sophia in Success, 'Top 10 Success Principles to Learn from Rhonda Byrne', *The Wisdom Post*, www.thewisdompost.com
2   John Gravois, Review of Karen A Cerulo, *Never Saw It Coming*, University of Chicago Press, Chicago, 2006
3   Christine Luken, '4 Lies Money Gurus Tell You', *The Financial Lifeguard*, www.christineluken.com
4   James Melville, 'The Coronavirus Crisis, "Debt and No Savings Will Leave Millions Vulnerable"', *The Byline Times*, 16 March 2020, www.bylinetimes.com
5   Catherine S Harvey, 'Unlocking the Potential of Emergency Savings Accounts', *AARP Public Policy Institute*, October 2019, www.aarp.com
6   'Report on the Economic Well-Being of U.S. Households in 2018 – May 2019', *The Federal Reserve*, www.federalreserve,gov
7   Catherine S Harvey, 'Unlocking the Potential of Emergency Savings Accounts', *AARP Public Policy Institute*, October 2019, www.aarp.com
8   Jessica Longbottom, 'Australian Children Going Hungry, Report Finds, with One in Five Kids Missing Meals', *ABC News*, 15 April 2018, www.abc.com.au
9   'Too Many Canadian Kids Are Going Hungry', *Food Secure Canada*, www.foodsecurecanada.org
10 Colin Randall, 'Soul-Searching in France as Poverty Leaves One Million Children Hungry', *The National*, 11 May 2019, www.thenational.ae
11 Eric Butterworth, *Spiritual Economics: The Prosperity Process*, Unity Books, Unity Village, Missouri, 2001
12 Edward Luce, 'A Preacher for Trump's America: Joel Osteen and the Prosperity Gospel', *Financial Times*, 18 April 2019, www.ft.com
13 Ibid.
14 Richard Eckersley 'Is the West Really the Best? Modernisation and the Psychosocial Dynamics of Human Progress and Development', *Oxford Development Studies*, April 2016, Volume 44, Issue 3, pp. 349–65
15 Bryant McGill, the *Voice of Reason: Speaking to the Great and Good Spirit of Revolution of Mind*, Lyon Publishing, Mapleton, Iowa, 2012
16 David W Jones, '5 Critical Errors of the Prosperity Gospel', *Intersect*, 16 October 2019, www.intersect.org

17   Edward Luce, 'A Preacher for Trump's America: Joel Osteen and the Prosperity Gospel', *Financial Times*, 18 April 2019, www.ft.com

18   Rafael Morgan Ríos, 'The Tenth Anniversary of the OECD Anti-Bribery Convention – Its Impact and Its Achievements', *OECD*, Rome, 21 November 2007, HYPERLINK "http://www.oecd.org" www.oecd.org

19   Pastor George Pearson talking with Gloria Copeland, 'Isaac's Supernatural Harvest', *Kenneth Copeland Ministries*, 9 June 2020, www.kcm.org

20   Barbara Ehrenreich, *Bright-Sided: How Positive Thinking Is Undermining America*, Picador, New York, 2010, p. 133

21   Glyn J Ackerley, *Importing Faith: The Effect American 'Word of Faith' Culture on Contemporary English Evangelical Revivalism*, Pickwick Publications, Oregon, 2015, p. 197

22   David W Jones and Russell S Woodbridge, *Health, Wealth, and Happiness: Has the Prosperity Gospel Overshadowed the Gospel of Christ*, Kregel Publications, Grand Rapids, Michigan, 2010, p. 57

23   Laura Turner, 'The Joel Osteen Fiasco Says a Lot about American Christianity', *BuzzFeed News*, 30 August 2017, www.buzzfeed.com

24   Edward Luce, 'A Preacher for Trump's America: Joel Osteen and the Prosperity Gospel', *Financial Times*, 18 April 2019, www.ft.com

Chapter 19: News and Infotainment

1   Geneva Overholser in conversation with Charles Overby, 'A Crisis in Journalism and Democracy', 14 March 2020, www.genevaoverholser.com

2   Ashley 'Dotty' Charles, 'How to Actually Make Change in the World of Online Outrage', *Refinery 29*, 19 July 2020, www.refinery29.com

3   Bernard Marr, 'How Much Data Do We Create Every Day? The Mind-Blowing Stats Everyone Should Read', *Forbes*, 21 May 2018, www.forbes.com

4   Nick Davies, *Flat Earth News: An Award-Winning Reporter Exposes Falsehood, Distortion and Propaganda in the Global Media*, Vintage, London, 2008, p. 63

5   Rohan Upadhyay, 'The Real Reason News is Sensationalized – and How You Can Tell', *Medium*, 21 August 2019, www.medium.com

6   Nick Davies, *Flat Earth News: An Award-Winning Reporter Exposes Falsehood, Distortion and Propaganda in the Global Media*, Vintage, London, 2008, p. 63

7   E James Brennan, 'Why Is American Society Infantilized So Much?', *Quora*, 7 June 2018, www.quora.com

8   Daniel Hallin, 'Whatever Happened to the News?', *Center for Media Literacy*, www.medialit.org

9   David Shaw, 'News as Entertainment Is Sadly Becoming the Norm', *The Los Angeles Times*, 11 July 2004, www.latimes.com

10   Ibid.

11   Ibid.

12   Marc Gunther, 'The Transformation of Network News: How Profitability Has Moved Networks out of Hard News', *Nieman Reports*, 15 June 1999, www.niemanreports.org

13   Pat Aufderheide, Peter Jaszi and Mridu Chandra, *Honest Truths: Documentary Filmmakers on Ethical Challenges in Their Work*, Center for Media and Social Impact,

September 2009, p. 3

14 Email exchange, 25 August 2020

15 Bannon to Michael Lewis: @davidjoachim, *Twitter*, 10 February 2018, https://twitter.
    com/davidjoachim/status/962038522226987008?lang=en

16 Julian Petley, 'The BBC Should Stop Placating Bullies and Apply These Simple Fixes',
    Open Democracy, 7 February 2020, www.opendemocracy.net

17 Benjamin Cain, 'American Infantilization and the Age of Reason', *Medium*, 26 November
    2019, www.medium.com

18 Rob Tornoe, 'Trump to Veterans: Don't Believe What You're Reading or Seeing', *The
    Philadelphia Inquirer*, 24 July 2018, www.inquirer.com

19 Bannon to Michael Lewis: @davidjoachim, *Twitter*, 10 February 2018, https://twitter.
    com/davidjoachim/status/962038522226987008?lang=en

20 'Christiane Amanpour Drops Truth Bomb on Trump Era Press: I Believe in Being
    Truthful, Not Neutral', *Daily Kos*, 27 November 2016, www.dailykos.com

21 Geneva Overholser in conversation with Charles Overby, 'A Crisis in Journalism and
    Democracy', 14 March 2020, www.genevaoverholser.com

22 David Naden, Francesca Pomili and Michael Grigsby, 'Documentary Is Dead – Long
    Live Documentaries', *Vertigo*, Volume 2, Issue 7, Autumn–Winter 2004

23 Kwame Anthony Appiah, *Cosmopolitanism: Ethics in a World of Strangers*, Norton, New
    York, 2006, p. 68

24 Rokusan, 'Are Polymathy and General Knowledge in Decline?', *MetaFilter*, 28 September
    2009, www.metafilter.com

25 Sarah K Tauber, John Dunlosky, Katherine A Rawson, Matthew G Rhodes and Danielle
    Siztman, 'General Knowledge Norms: Updated and Expanded from the Nelson and
    Narens (1980) Norms', *Behavior Research Methods*, January 2013, Volume 45, Issue 4, doi.
    org/10.3758/s13428–012–0307–9

Chapter 20: Fragile Truths

1   Adrian Bardon, 'Humans Are Hardwired to Dismiss Facts that Don't Fit Their
    Worldview', *The Conversation*, 1 February 2020, www.theconversation.com

2   Jim Butcher, *Cold Days*, Penguin Random House, New York, 2012

3   Neil Postman, *Amusing Ourselves to Death: Public Discourse in the Age of Show Business*,
    Penguin, New York, 2005, pp. xix–xx

4   Adrian Bardon, 'Humans Are Hardwired to Dismiss Facts that Don't Fit Their
    Worldview', *The Conversation*, 1 February 2020, www.theconversation.com

5   Jennifer Salaiz, *Love Expands*, www.loveexpands.com

6   John T Jost, *The Theory of System Justification*, Harvard University Press, Cambridge,
    Massachusetts, 2020

7   Peter Wehner, 'Jonathan Haidt Is Trying to Heal America's Divisions' *The Atlantic*, 24
    May 2020, https://www.theatlantic.com

8   'The Impact of Fake News', *Linklaters*, www.linklaters.com

9   Andrew Keen, *The Cult of the Amateur*, Currency, New York, 2007, p. 35

10 Gergely Nyilasy, 'Fake News in the Age of COVID-19', *Pursuit*, 10 April 2020, www.
    pursuit.unimelb.edu.au

11 Robinson Meyer, 'The Grim Conclusions of the Largest-Ever Study of Fake News', *The

Atlantic, 8 March 2018, www.theatlantic.com

12 Helen Pitt, 'Pursuit of Happiness', The Sydney Morning Herald, 1–2 August 2020

13 Steven R Weisman, 'An American Original', Vanity Fair, October 2010, www.vanityfair.com

14 Mike Sneider, 'Robert Mueller Investigation: What Is a Russian Troll Farm?', USA Today, 16 February 2018, www.usatoday.com

15 Chloe Farand, 'French Social Media Awash with Fake News Stories from Sources "Exposed to Russian Influence" Ahead of Presidential Election', The Independent, 22 April 2017, www.independent.co.uk

16 Alberto Nardelli and Craig Silverman, 'Italy's Most Popular Political Party Is Leading Europe in Fake News and Kremlin Propaganda', BuzzFeed, 30 November 2016, www.buzzfeed.com

17 Helen Pitt, 'Pursuit of Happiness', The Sydney Morning Herald, 1–2 August 2020

18 Michael Sebastian and Gabrielle Bruney, 'Years After Being Debunked, Interest in Pizzagate Is Rising', Esquire, 24 July 2020, www.esquire.com

19 Mike-Plan2IT commenting on 'A Culture of Blame', Reddit, 7 September 2018, www.reddit.com

20 Roxane Gay, 'Truth Matters: In a Year of Untruths', Medium, 8 December 2017, www.medium.com

21 Mark Z Barabak, 'How a Top Conservative Radio Host Took on Trump, Lost His Audience and Faith, but Gained a New Perspective', The Los Angeles Times, 30 January 2017, www.latimes.com

22 Steve Paulson in conversation with Charlie Sykes, 'How the Right Lost Its Mind and Charlie Sykes Lost His Faith in The GOP', 4 November 2017, www.ttbook.org

23 Elisha Fieldstadt, 'Ohio Lawmaker Refuses to Wear Mask Because He Says It Dishonors God', NBC News, 7 May 2020, www.nbcnews.com

24 'The Danger of Fake News in Inflaming or Suppressing Social Conflict', Center for Information Technology and Society, www.cits.ucsb.edu

25 Sophia Rosenfeld, 'Why Truth Matters for Democracy', ABC Religion and Ethics, 23 October 2019, www.abc.net.au

26 Ron Elving, 'Obama Closes His Run of Speeches to Congress with Appeal for Broad Reform', NPR, 30 January 2016, www.npr.org

27 Peter Wehner, 'Jonathan Haidt Is Trying to Heal America's Divisions', The Atlantic, 24 May 2020, www.theatlantic.com

28 Sophia Rosenfeld, 'Why Truth Matters for Democracy', ABC Religion and Ethics, 23 October 2019, www.abc.net.au

29 Judith Feder, 'Why Truth Matters: Research versus Propaganda in the Policy Debate', Health Services Research, June 2003, Volume 38, Issue 3, pp. 783–87, doi: 10.1111/1475-6773.00146

30 Mohandas Gandhi (edited by Homer A Jack), The Wit and Wisdom of Gandhi, Dover Publications, New York, 2012

Chapter 21: Careless

1 Debra ref = nectarween16 responding to u/Chaotic_Rain, 'Don't Shame People For Not Wearing Masks When They've Been Sold Out for Months', Reddit, 20 June 2020, www.reddit.com

2   Aidan Wondracz, 'Schoolies Come Clean on Their Outrageous Antics as They Keep Shocking Onlookers on the Gold Coast', *Daily Mail Australia*, 24 November 2018, www.dailymail.co.uk

3   Dan I Lubman, Nic Droste, Amy Pennay, Shannon Hyder and Peter Miller, 'High Rates of Alcohol Consumption and Related Harm at Schoolies Week: A Portal Study', *Australian and New Zealand Journal of Public Health*, 2014, Volume 38, pp. 536–41

4   Amy Pennay, 'Sex, Drugs and Alcohol: What Really Goes on at Schoolies', *SBS News*, 28 November 2013, www.sbs.com.au

5   News, 'Schoolies Week No Fun for Most: UOW Researchers', *The Illawarra Mercury*, 14 November 2011, www.illawarramercury.com.au

6   Richard Rohr, *Adam's Return: The Five Promises of Male Initiation*, Crossroads, Michigan, 2004, p. 13

7   Ibid., p. 86

8   Ibid., p. 83

9   Maggie Hamilton, *Secret Girls' Business*, Penguin Random House, Sydney, 2012, p. 53

10   Ibid., p. 23

11   '"Great Pacific Garbage Patch" Is Massive Floating Island of Plastic, Now 3 Times the Size of France', *ABC News*, 24 March 2018, www.abcnews.go.com

12   'Great Pacific Garbage Patch', *National Geographic*, www.nationalgeographic.org

13   Alexandra Witze, 'The Quest to Conquer Earth's Space Junk Problem', *Nature*, 5 September 2018, www.nature.com

14   'Rite of Passage or Cry for Help? Why Teens Shoplift', *Web MD*, www.webmd.com

15   Judith C Forney and Christy A Crutsinger, 'Juvenile Delinquents' Perceptions of Shoplifting Motives: The Influence of Socialization, Age and Gender', *Journal of Family and Consumer Sciences*, Volume 93, Issue 1, pp. 31–36

16   u/bdsbnsisisnsn, 'I'm Done with Shoplifting', *Reddit*, 1 August 2019, www.reddit.com

17   Carlos Blanco, Jon Grant, Nancy Petry and H Blair Simpson, 'Prevalence and Correlates of Shoplifting in the United States: Results from the National Epidemiologic Survey on Alcohol and Related Conditions (NESARC)', *American Journal of Psychiatry*, 2008, Volume 165, Issue 7, pp. 905–13, doi: 10.1176/appi.ajp.2008.07101660

18   u/tornadoes, 'IAMA Master Shoplifter. AMA', *Reddit*, 29 December 2009, www.reddit.com

19   u/Leveros, 'People Who Think Shoplifting Is Okay Because They're "Only" Stealing from Big Corporations', *Reddit*, 20 November 2017, www.reddit.com

20   Samantha Morton, 'The Deal Why Kids Steal', *Metro Parent*, 8 April 2019, www.metroparent.com

21   'Shoplifting: How Much Does It Cost Your Community?', *L.Y. Lawyers*, 23 November 2017, www.lylawyers.com.au

22   Anonymous, 'Confession: I Was a Teenage Shoplifter', *Rosie*, 10 December 2015, www.rosie.org.au

23   Samantha Booker, 'Confessions of a Middle-Class Shoplifter: Stealing for Kicks, Even Down to Gifts for Her Children. How One Woman's Obsession Ended in a Police Cell', The *Daily Mail Australia*, 2 March 2011, www.dailymail.co.uk

24   Samantha Morton, 'The Deal Why Kids Steal', *Metro Parent*, 8 April 2019, www.metroparent.com

25   Max Bearak, 'Kenya's Pokomo People Ask the British to Return What Was Stolen: Their Source of Power', *The Washington Post*, 9 August 2019, www.washingtonpost.com

26   'Horrors of the Past', *Koori Mail*, 28 March 2007, Issue 397, p. 24

27   Maev Kennedy, 'Aboriginal Remains Return to Tasmania after 20-year Fight', *The Guardian*, 13 May 2007, www.theguardian.com

28   Felicity Ogilvie and Carla Howarth, 'Aboriginal Remains Return to Tasmania from ANU Collection, with a Call to Change the Law', *ABC News*, 6 December 2016, www.abc.net.au

29   'Manchester Museum Returns "Stolen" Sacred Aboriginal Artefacts', *BBC News*, 21 November 2019, www.bbc.com

30   Tristram Hunt, 'Should Museums Return Their Colonial Artefacts?', *The Guardian*, 29 June 2019, www.theguardian.com

31   Richard Rohr, *Adam's Return: The Five Promises of Male Initiation*, Crossroads, Michigan, 2004, p. 36

32   'Why Has Museums Victoria Decided Not to Display Human Remains in Vikings: Beyond the Legend?', *Museums Victoria*, www.museumsvictoria.com.au

33   Manan Kapoor, 'A Sloppy Surgery: How Cyril Radcliffe Carved the Indian Subcontinent', *The Telegraph*, www.telegraphindia.com

34   William Dalrymple, 'The Great Divide: The Violent Legacy of Indian Partition', *The New Yorker*, 22 June 2015, www.newyorker.com

Chapter 22: Our Constant Need to Escape

1   Neil Postman, *Amusing Ourselves to Death: Public Discourse in the Age of Show Business*, Penguin, New York, 2006, p. 156

2   David Naden, Francesca Pomili and Michael Grigsby, 'Documentary Is Dead – Long Live Documentaries', *Vertigo*, Volume 2, Issue 7, Autumn–Winter 2004

3   Neil Postman, *Amusing Ourselves to Death: Public Discourse in the Age of Show Business*, Penguin, New York, 2006, pp. 92–93

4   diff2, responding to u/Gentleman-Tech, 'My Kardashian Problem', *Reddit*, November 2019, www.reddit.com

5   Christopher Lasch, *The Culture of Narcissism: American Life in an Age of Diminishing Expectations*, W.W. Norton & Co., New York, 1991, pp. 86–87

6   55redditor55, responding to u/Gentleman-Tech, 'My Kardashian Problem', *Reddit*, November 2019, www.reddit.com

7   Kris Jenner, *Kris Jenner … and All Things Kardashian*, Gallery Books/Karen Hunter Publishing, Simon & Schuster, New York, 2011, p. 277

8   TonyArkitect, responding to u/Gentleman-Tech, 'My Kardashian Problem', *Reddit*, November 2019, www.reddit.com

9   Anonymous, responding to u/redmambo_no6, 'People Who Keep Up with the Kardashians … WHY?', *Reddit*, April 2018, www.reddit.com

10   Tara Ariano and Sarah T Bunting, 'Television without Pity: 752 Things We Love to Hate (and Hate to Love) about TV', *Excerpt*, Summer Books 2007, *NPR*, 4 June 2007, www.npr.com

11   Sam Sabin, 'Most Young Adults Have an Appetite for Binge-Watching Shows', *Morning Consult*, 6 November 2018, www.morningconsult.com

References

12   Lee Rainie and Kathryn Zickuhr, 'Americans' Views on Mobile Etiquette', *Pew Research Center*, 26 August 2015, www.pewresearch.org

13   Wendell Berry, 'What Are People For?' *Daily Good*, 18 July 2016, www.dailygood.org

14   Henry Beston, *The Outermost House: A Year of Life on the Great Beach of Cape Cod*, Owl Books, Henry Holt & Company, New York, 1992, p. 10

15   Henry Beston (edited by Elizabeth Jane Coatsworth), *The Best of Beston: A Selection from the Natural World of Henry Beston from Cape Cod to St. Lawrence*, Nonpareil Books, Boston, 2000, p. 28

16   E James Brennan, 'Why Is American Society Infantilized So Much?', *Quora*, 7 June 2018, www.quora.com

17   David Thomas Cook, 'Knowing the Child Consumer: Historical and Conceptual Insights on Qualitative Children's Consumer Research', *Young Consumers*, August 2009, Volume 10, Issue 4, pp. 269–82, doi.org/10.1108/17473610911007111

18   Diana West, *The Death of the Grown-Up: How America's Arrested Development is Bringing Down Western Civilization*, St Martin's Press, New York, 2008, p. 33

19   Joseph Epstein, 'The Perpetual Adolescent', *The Weekly Standard*, 15 March 2004, www.washingtonexaminer.com

20   John Tierney, 'Adultescent', *The New York Times*, 26 December 2004, www.nytimes.com

21   Michael Bywater, *Big Babies: Or Why Can't We Just Grow Up?*, Granta, Cambridge, 2006

22   Hartmut Rosa, 'Social Acceleration: Ethical and Political Consequences of a Desynchronized High-speed Society', *Constellations*, 2003, Volume 10, Issue 1, pp. 3–33, doi.org/10.1111/1467–8675.00309

23   Ibid.

24   Hartmut Rosa, 'Why Are We Stuck behind the Social Acceleration?', *YouTube*, 11 March 2015, https://youtu.be/7uG9OFGId3A

25   Hartmut Rosa, 'Social Acceleration: Ethical and Political Consequences of a Desynchronized High-speed Society', *Constellations*, 2003, Volume 10, Issue 1, pp. 3–33, doi.org/10.1111/1467–8675.00309

26   Leo Babauta, *The Power of Less: The Fine Art of Limiting Yourself to the Essential ... in Business and in Life*, Hay House, New York, 2008, p. 4

27   u/Shogun123, 'My Personal Experience with Meditation and Mindfulness after 6 Months', *Reddit*, 16 June 2017, www.reddit.com

28   getimoliver, 'Can I Hear a Few Personal Stories about How Meditation Has Affected Your Life?', *Reddit*, 11 October 2015, www.reddit.com

29   Michelle Janning, 'Deep Stuff: A Sociologist Sorts Through the Marie Kondo Phenomenon', *Humanities Washington*, 15 March 2019, www.humanities.org

30   Marc Bain and Quartz, 'The Neurological Pleasures of Fast Fashion', *The Atlantic*, 25 March 2015, www.theatlantic.com

31   Pia A Albinsson, Marco Wolf and Dennis A Kopf, 'Anti-consumption in East Germany: Consumer Resistance to Hyperconsumption', *Journal of Consumer Behaviour*, November 2010, Volume 9, Issue 6, pp. 412–25, doi/10.1002/cb.333

32   auchjemand, responding to u/ibopm, 'A Rant about the Modern Obsession with Travelling', *Reddit*, 12 October 2016, www.reddit.com

33   u/ibopm, 'A Rant about the Modern Obsession with Travelling', *Reddit*, 12 October 2016, www.reddit.com

34   hanswurstautomat, responding to u/ibopm, 'A Rant about the Modern Obsession with Travelling', *Reddit*, 12 October 2016, www.reddit.com

Chapter 23: What Does Grown Up Look Like?

1   ImDefinitelyClueless, responding to u/obvioustroway, '"Grown-Ups" of Reddit, What Is One Thing About Adult Life That Still Surprises You to This Day?', *Reddit*, 23 January 2016, www.reddit.com

2   Dragoncafe, responding to u/obvioustroway, '"Grown-Ups" of Reddit, What Is One Thing About Adult Life That Still Surprises You to This Day?', *Reddit*, 23 January 2016, www.reddit.com

3   byu/nikiwonoto, 'To Grow Up and Being an Adult (Adulthood) Is Overrated and Depressing', *Reddit*, 7 February 2020, www.reddit.com

4   (Jeffrey Arnett) Christopher Munsey, 'Emerging adults: The in-between age', *Monitor* Staff, June 2006, Vol 37, 7, 68, www.apa.org

5   Brent Crane, 'The Virtues of Isolation', *The Atlantic*, 30 March 2017, www.theatlantic.com

6   Amelia Lester, 'Light in the Storm', *Good Weekend*, 11 April 2020, www.smh.com.au

7   Benjamin Law in conversation with Andrew Constance, 'Dicey Topics', *Good Weekend*, 24 April 2020, www.smh.com.au

8   Nicholas Cole, '20 Things Most People Learn too Late in Life', *Medium*, October 2017, www.medium.com

9   Mark Manson, 'How to Grow the Fuck Up: A Guide to Humans', Mark Manson, www.markmanson.net

10   u/JushtFinisht, 'I've Been Babied and Sheltered Almost My Entire Life. How Do I Grow into an Adult?', *Reddit*, 27 December 2015, www.reddit.com

11   chattymcgee, responding to u/JushtFinisht, 'I've Been Babied and Sheltered Almost My Entire Life. How Do I Grow into an Adult?', *Reddit*, 27 December 2015, www.reddit.com

12   econoquist, responding to u/alaxsxaqseek, 'Are Teenage Years the Best?', *Reddit*, 14 May 2015, www.reddit.com

Chapter 24: The Small Question of Death

1   Steve Jobs, *Motivating Thoughts of Steve Jobs*, Prabhat Prakashan, New Delhi, 2017

2   George Willis Cooke, *Ralph Waldo Emerson: His Life, Writings, and Philosophy*, J R Osgood Publisher, Michigan, 1881, 353

3   Karen Kelly interviews Jonathan Horwitz, 'Shamanism, Death and Life', *Scandinavian Center for Shamanic Studies*, 2006, www.shamanism.dk

4   Jeffrey Berman, Death in the Classroom: Writing About Love and Loss, State University of New York Press, 2009, 215

5   Matthew Knott, 'Fall Guy', *Good Weekend*, 24 October 2020, www.smh.com.au

6   Robert Firestone, 'Societal Defences Against Death Anxiety', *PsychAlive*, www.psychaliveorg

7   Colin Murray Parkes and Holly G. Prigerson, *Bereavement: Studies of Grief in Adult Life*, Routledge, Abingdon-on-Thames, 2009, 1972

8   Amy Norton, 'Dying May Not Be as Awful an Experience as You Think', *Medical Xpress*, 7 July 2017, www.medicalxpress.com

9   Kellie Scott, 'Your Stories of Being There When Someone Died', *ABC Life*, 27 August

2019, www.abc.net.au

10   Paul Theroux, *On the Plain of Snakes: A Mexican Journey*, Penguin, London, 2020, p. 254

11   Andrea Warnick, 'Children at the Bedside of a Dying Family Member or Friend', *Canadian Virtual Hospice*, May 2019, virtualhospice.com

12   Kellie Scott, 'Your Stories of Being There When Someone Died', *ABC Everyday*, 23 August 2018, www.abc.net.au

13   Ken Holmes, 'Buddhism and Death', Kagyu Samye Ling, www.samyeling.org

14   Khalil Gibran, *The Little Book of Love*, Oneworld Publications, London, 2017.

15   Laurence Shames and Peter Barton, *Not Fade Away: A Short Life Well Lived*, 2003, Rodale, Emmaus, Pennsylvania, p. 62

16   Robert Macfarlane, *The Wild Places*, Penguin, London, 2007, pp. 316–17

17   Rob Haskell, 'A Man for All Seasons: Inside the World of Tom Ford', *Vogue*, 15 August 2019, vogue.com

Chapter 25: Where to From Here?

1   Greg Callaghan, 'Actions Speak Louder ...' *Good Weekend*, 20 June 2019, www.smh.com.au

2   Miriam Cosic, 'High Anxiety', *Good Weekend*, 29 March 2019, www.smh.com.au

3   Jim Bright, 'Frozen in the Glare of Endless Options', *The Sydney Morning Herald*, 23–24 November 2019, www.smh.com.au

4   Neil Postman, *Amusing Ourselves to Death: Public Discourse in the Age of Show Business*, Penguin, New York, 2006, pp. 155–56

5   Karyn J Wilson, Erin Semmler, and Melissa Maykin, 'Retired Cycling Champion Anna Meares Opens Up About Her New Book', *ABC Capricornia*, 28 April 2020, www.abc.net.au

Bibliography

Barber, Benjamin B., *Con$umed: How the Markets Corrupt Children, Infantilize Adults, and Swallow Citizens Whole*, Norton & Co., New York, 2007

Beston, Henry, *The Outermost House: A Year of Life on the Great Beach of Cape Cod*, Owl Books, Henry Holt & Company, New York, 1992

Calcutt, Andrew, *Arrested Development: Pop Culture and the Erosion of Adulthood*, Bloomsbury, 1998

Cerulo, Karen A., *Never Saw It Coming: Cultural Challenges to Envisioning the Worst*, University of Chicago Press, Chicago, 2006

Clarke, Jean Illsley, Dawson, Connie, and Bredehoft, David J., *How Much Is Too Much? Raising Likeable, Responsible, Respectful Children – From Toddlers to Teens in an Age of Overindulgence*, Da Capo Press, New York, 2014

Davies, Nick, *Flat Earth News: An Award-Winning Reporter Exposes Falsehood, Distortion and Propaganda in the Global Media*, Vintage, London, 2008

Ehrenreich, Barbara, *Bright-Sided: How Positive Thinking Is Undermining America*, Picador, New York, 2010

Etcoff, Nancy, *Survival of the Prettiest: The Science of Beauty*, Anchor Books, Random House, New York, 2000

Hanh, Thich Nhat, *Being Peace*, Penguin, New York, 2011

Kakutani, Michiko, *The Death of Truth*, William Collins, Harper Collins, London, 2018

Kasser, Tim, *The High Price of Materialism*, MIT Press, Cambridge Massachusetts, 2002

Bibliography

Lasch, Christopher, *The Culture of Narcissism: American Life in an Age of Diminishing Expectations*, W.W. Norton & Company, New York, 1991

Macfarlane, Robert, *The Wild Places*, Penguin, London, 2007

McGee, Micki, *Self-Help Inc.: The Makeover Culture in American Life*, Oxford University Press, Oxford, 2005

Postman, Neil, *Amusing Ourselves to Death: Public Discourse in the Age of Show Business*, Penguin, New York, 2006

Rohr, Richard, *Adam's Return: The Five Promises of Male Initiation*, Crossroads, Michigan, 2004

Sennett, Richard, *The Corrosion of Character: The Personal Consequences of Work in The New Capitalism*, W.W. Norton & Co., New York, 1997

——, *The Fall of Public Man*, Cambridge University Press, Cambridge, 1977

Van Den Bergh, Joeri, and Behrer, Mattias, *How Cool Brands Stay Hot: Branding to Generation Y*, Kogan Page, London, 2016

Ventura, Michael, 'The Age of Endarkment 1993', edited by Louise Carus Mahdi, Nancy Geyer Christopher, Michael Meade, *Crossroads: The Quest for Contemporary Rites of Passage*, Open Court, Chicago, 1996

West, Diana, *The Death of the Grown-Up: How America's Arrested Development is Bringing Down Western Civilisation*, St Martin's Press, New York, 2008